AF559905

MICRO FINANCING OF RURAL WOMEN THROUGH SELF-HELP GROUPS

By

Dr. K. Kanniammal
Associate Professor
Department of Commerce
Avinashilingam Institute for Home Science and Higher Education for Women
Coimbatore - 641 043
Tamil Nadu
(INDIA)

DISCOVERY PUBLISHING HOUSE PVT. LTD.
NEW DELHI-110 002

Published by:
Tilak Wasan
DISCOVERY PUBLISHING HOUSE PVT. LTD.
4383/4B, Ansari Road, Darya Ganj
New Delhi - 110 002 (India)
Phone : +91-11-23279245, 43596064-65
Fax : +91-11-23253475
E-mail : discoverypublishinghouse@gmail.com
sales@discoverypublishinggroup.com

website : www.discoverypublishinggroup.com

***First Edition:* 2015**

ISBN: 978-93-5056-716-6

Micro Financing of Rural Women through Self-Help Groups

© Author

All rights reserved. No part of this publication should be reproduced, stored in a retrieval system, or transmitted in any form or by any means: electronic, mechanical, photocopying, recording or otherwise, without the prior written permission of the author and the publisher.

This book has been published in good faith that the material provided by authors is original. Every effort is made to ensure accuracy of material, but the publisher and printer will not be held responsible for any inadvertent error(s). In case of any dispute, all legal matters are to be settled under Delhi jurisdiction only.

Printed at:
Infinity Imaging Systems
Delhi

PREFACE

India has one of the largest networks of bank branches in the world, but the hundreds of millions of poor people in the country are largely out of it. Banks were nationalized three and a half decades ago with the hope and promise that their products and services would reach the poor. Despite the phenomenal increase in the physical outreach of the formal credit institutions in the past several decades, the rural poor continue to depend on informal sources of credit. Institutions have also faced difficulties in dealing effectively with a large number of small borrowers, whose credit needs are small and frequent and their ability to offer collaterals is limited. Besides, cumbersome procedures and risk perceptions of the banks have left a gap in serving the credit needs of the rural poor.

Micro finance interventions are globally well recognised as an effective tool for poverty alleviation and for improving the socio-economic conditions of the poor. The impact of the micro finance programme through SHGs has been effective in making a positive social change to all the members, irrespective of the direct borrowers of the micro credit. Women are an integral part of a country's economy and their contribution to national development is crucial. Women's active involvement in economic activities will lead to their socio-economic upliftment. Micro finance through women Self-Help Groups is a paradigm shift towards the development of women through an increase in income and employment generation, leading to poverty alleviation. In India, organization of Self-Help Groups, especially for micro finance and micro enterprise development programme, constituted a widely accepted development strategy for poverty reduction and empowerment of women. The National Bank for Agriculture and Rural Development (NABARD) has pioneered the concept and implemented the SHG-Bank Linkage Programme in 1992 and has been successfully exercising it since then; and the SHGs have now become a predominant component of the Indian financial system. Women SHGs have shown remarkable growth during the last two decades in India and are fast emerging agencies for the socio-economic development of the rural areas.

Out of necessity and enterprise, those locked out of the banking world now found the way of micro finance as a heavenly programme. Millions of poor and illiterate women in India are today using small loans to rewrite their present and future, by using common reserve to propel their entrepreneurship and group business activities. Micro finance is a profitable proposition for the commercial banks and is a sustainable measure to reduce poverty levels.

This book is an outcome of the research programme on the impact of Micro finance through the Self-Help Groups – Bank Linkage Programme on Rural women in Coimbatore district of Tamil Nadu. As such, this book has important policy implications to the government, banks and micro finance institutions, NGOs, SHGs and the educational institutions.

Author

ACKNOWLEDGEMENT

I extend my deep sense of gratitude to Dr. T. S. K. Meenakshisundaram, Chancellor, Avinashilingam Institute for Home Science and Higher Education for Women, Coimbatore, Tamil Nadu, India, for the constant support in bringing out this book.

I extend my heartiest gratitude to Dr. Sheela Ramachandran, Vice Chancellor, Avinashilingam Institute for Home Science and Higher Education for Women, for her constant encouragement and support at different stages of publishing this book.

I submit my gratitude to Dr. Gowri Ramakrishnan, Registrar, Avinashilingam Institute for Home Science and Higher Education for Women, for her support in bringing out this book.

I am grateful to Dr. Saroja Pabhakaran, former Vice Chancellor, Avinashilingam Institute for Home Science and Higher Education for Women, for her encouragement and motivation to publish this book.

I am very grateful to Dr. Shantha B. Kurup, former Dean, Faculty of Business Administration, Avinashilingam Institute for Home Science and Higher Education for Women, for her valuable suggestions. It is her constant interest and immense help that have made this book possible.

It is my proud privilege to express my deep sense of gratitude and indebtedness to my revered teacher, guide and source of inspiration, Dr. U. Jerinabi. M.Com., Dip. Ed., M. Phil., Ph.D., Dean, Faculty of Business Administration, Avinashilingam Institute for Home Science and Higher Education for Women, without whose encouragement it would not have been possible for me to bring out this book. Despite her very busy work schedule and engagements she always found time to help me.

I extend my sincere thanks to Dr. S. Kalamani, M.A., M. Phil., Ph.D., Associate Professor, Department of English, Avinashilingam Institute for Home Science and Higher Education for Women, for her valuable suggestions, moral support and immense help provided in framing this book.

I would like to express my deep sense of gratitude to Dr. E. Raja Justus, Professor, MBA (Finance), Department of Management Studies, Manonmaniam Sundaranar University, Tirunelveli, Tamil Nadu, India, for his expert opinion and suggestions.

I would also like to place on record my profound sense of gratitude to the Proprietor, Discovery Publishing House Pvt. Ltd., New Delhi, who readily agreed to take up the assignment of publishing this book and executed the task within the shortest possible time.

I would like to express my sincere thanks to Tmt. D. Shobha Pai and Tmt. D. Sujatha Pai of Fast Forward, No. 55, Bharathi Park Road, Coimbatore, for their excellent service rendered in checking the draft of the manuscript and having typed it with great care.

I wish to thank all the members of my family for their unstinted support and co-operation.

Any errors, omissions and valuable suggestions for the improvement of this book brought to my notice, will be thankfully acknowledged.

Dr. K. Kanniammal

CONTENTS

ABBREVIATIONS

ADB	:	Asian Development Bank.
AKRSP	:	Agha Khan Rural Support Programme.
APRACA	:	Asia and Pacific Regional Agricultural Credit Association.
ASSEFA	:	Association of Sarva Seva Farms.
BAAC	:	Bank for Agriculture and Agricultural Co-operatives.
BASIX	:	Baratiya Samrudhi Investments and Consulting Services.
BIRD	:	Bankers Institute of Rural Development.
BRAC	:	Bangladesh Rural Advancement Committee.
BRI	:	Bank Rakyat Indonesia.
BSS	:	Bharat Sevak Samaj.
CBO	:	Community Based Organizations.
DPIP	:	District Poverty Initiative Programmes.
DRDA	:	District Rural Development Agency.
DWCRA	:	Development of Women and Children in Rural Areas.
FAO	:	Food and Agricultural Organization.
FDC	:	Foundation for Development Co-operation.
FI's	:	Financial Institutions.

FUNDAP's	:	Fund Development of Port Activities.
GB	:	Grameen Bank.
GOI	:	Government of India.
GOME	:	Group-Owned Micro Enterprises.
GOMS	:	Government Order Miscellaneous.
IFAD	:	International Fund for Agricultural Development.
IRDP	:	Integrated Rural Development Programme.
MATHI	:	Mahalir Tittam.
MDG	:	Millennium Development Goals.
MF	:	Micro Finance.
MFI	:	Micro Finance Institution.
MRCP	:	Maharashtra Rural Credit Project.
MYRADA	:	Mysore Resettlement and Development Agency.
NABARD	:	National Bank for Agriculture and Rural Development.
NERD	:	Non-Conventional Energy and Rural Development.
NGOs	:	Non-Governmental Organizations.
NHGs	:	Neighbourhood Groups.
NIBM	:	National Institute of Bank Management.
PRADAN	:	Professional Assistance for Development Action.
PVGB	:	Panchmahals Vadodara Grameen Bank.
RBI	:	Reserve Bank of India.
RGVN	:	Rashtriya Gramin Vikas Nidhi.
RMK	:	Rashtriya Mahila Kosh.
RNFE	:	Rural Non-Farm Employment.
RRB	:	Regional Rural Bank.
SCs	:	Scheduled Castes.
SEVAI	:	Society for Education, Village Action and Improvement.
SEWA	:	Self-Employed Women's Association.

SGSY	:	Swaranajayanthi Gram Swarozar Yojana.
SHARE	:	Society for Helping Awakening Rural People through Education.
SHG	:	Self-Help Group.
SHPIs	:	Self-Help Group Promoting Institutions.
SIDBI	:	Small Industries Development Bank of India.
SIDCO	:	Small Industrial Development Corporation.
SKS	:	Swayam Krishi Sangam.
SOME	:	Single-Owned Micro Enterprises.
STs	:	Scheduled Tribes.
TNCDW	:	Tamil Nadu Corporation for Development of Women.
TRYSEM	:	Training for Rural Youth for Self-Employment.
VA	:	Village Administrator.
WFP	:	World Food Programme.
WWF	:	Working Women's Forum.

INTRODUCTION

> *"I did something that challenged the banking world. While conventional banks look for the rich, we look for the absolutely poor. All people are entrepreneurs, but many don't have the opportunity to find that out".*
>
> **– Prof. Mohammed Yunus**

"Access to financial markets is important for poor people. Like all economic agents, low-income households and micro enterprises benefit from credit, savings and insurance services. Such services help to overcome the risk and to have smooth consumption, thereby allowing the people to take advantage of profitable business opportunities and increase their earning potential. The special features of the financial markets, often serve poor people very badly since they have insufficient traditional forms of collateral assets to offer. Unfortunately they are often excluded from traditional financial markets. Transaction costs are very high for small loans, typically demanded by poor people. And in areas where population density is low, physical access to banking services has been very difficult" (World Bank, World Development Report, 2001).

India has a population of 1.21 billion with 83.3 crore living in rural areas (Census of India, 2011). About 33.8 per cent of the rural population and 20.90 per cent of the urban population are estimated to be living below the poverty line (Tendulkar Committee Report and Press Note, Planning Commission 2011). Finance is an extraordinarily effective tool in spreading economic opportunity and fighting poverty. The main emphasis on antipoverty programmes directed through formal financial institutions was to provide the poor with access to credit and improve their income and standard of living.

In order to reduce poverty among the rural poor, various programmes such as food for work, targeted wage employment and other rural developmental programmes were undertaken by the government. This smoothened the consumption expenditure, creating jobs, developing skills and at times redistributing income from the wealthier to the poor (Ravallion, 1991). Even then, lack of capital among the poor makes it difficult to undertake productive activities which could generate employment opportunities. In this situation, provision of credit seems to be an important means to generate self-employment opportunities for the poor in rural areas (Khandker, 1998). Government plays a major role in extending credit to the poor by sponsoring several programmes, which provides financial assistance through capital subsidy and bank credit. All these were possible mainly because of excellent rural financial institutions in the country created through nationalisation of commercial banks and expansion of rural branch network (Rao and Zeller, 1998).

The formal financial institutions have failed to provide credit and other services to rural poor (Braverman and Guash 1989; Hoff and Stiglitz, 1990 and Desai and Namboodiri, 1996). Most of the studies on poverty alleviation programmes revealed that only 27 per cent of rural credit was deployed to rural population (Rangarajan, 1995). There was little post disbursement follow up since banks did not consider these programmes as their own (Government of India, 1985). Further if consumption needs of the poor were not met, they had a strong tendency to divert whatever loans they received, for consumption purposes. The above reasons resulted in the misuse of credit leading to poor recovery of loans (Rath, 1985).

Problems of Rural Poor

Despite the vast expansion of formal credit system in India, the dependence of the poor particularly in the rural sector on the money lenders continues in many areas especially for meeting the emergent requirements of the family. The money lenders provide timely credit without any collateral security for all purposes (Bouman and Houtman 1988; Hoff and stiglitz, 1990 Udry, 1990 and Foundation for Development Corporation, 1992). The anti poverty programmes directed through formal financial institutions have not reached the rural poor and improved their status substantially (Naidu, 1985; Tripathy, 1984; Feder *et al.* 1989 and Huppi and Feder, 1990). The rural poor mostly demanded credit for their consumption purposes but banks perceived theses demands for credit were for non-productive purposes (Desai, 1987 and Namboodiri and Shiyani, 2001). The most germane fact is the difficulty in dealing effectively and economically a large number of small borrowers who require credit frequently and in small quantities. In view of this, banks felt that banking with poor is not economically viable and a high risk phenomenon. As a result, the rural credit delivery system was burdened with poor quality loans, high level of overdues, non-performing assets, subsidised and uneconomic rate of interest and high transaction costs (Tiwari and Fahad, 2000 and Meyer, 2001). The transaction cost included expenses on repeated visits to the government offices and banks, opportunity costs in terms of wages foregone during such visits and costs associated with strict documentation procedures. It is estimated that on an average, the poor incurred an expenditure of about 18.90 per cent of the total amount towards the transaction cost (House, 1995). Rural credit markets are plagued with asymmetric information and imperfect enforcement (Hoff and Stiglitz, 1990 and Binswanger and Rosenzweig, 1986) which create inefficiency in both production and consumption and disproportionally affects the poor in rural areas (Damayanthi, 1999).

Hence in most of the developing countries attempts were made to develop co-operative credit societies but the societies achieved only limited success. Often people see the co-operative as government agencies and not as their own institutions (Nanda, 1994). So, in order to meet the credit requirements of the rural poor women and at the same time to reduce the transaction cost for both formal financial institutions and borrowers, some other institutional innovations need to be created (Zeller and Sharma, 1998). The inadequacies of the formal financial system to cater to the needs of the poor and the realisation of the fact that the key to success lies in the evolution and participation of community based organizations at the grass roots level led to the emergence of new generation of Micro Finance Institutions.

Evolution of Micro Finance Institutions

The task force on supportive policy and regulatory frame work for micro finance has defined micro finance as provision of thrift, credit and other financial services and products for very small amounts to the poor in rural, semi-urban or urban areas for enabling them to raise their income levels and improve living standards. Micro credit emphasises more on loans while micro finance stresses support services like market assistance, technical assistance, capacity building, insurance, social and cultural programmes and promotion of thrift along with loans. Micro finance programme was launched to improve the standard of living of the poor people. This is directed through Self-Help Groups (SHGs) to the poorer section of the society for taking up income-generating activity.

Micro finance institutions have emerged as an effective alternative to formal credit institutions in alleviating poverty with high rate of loan recovery and potential for self-sustainability. Several informal and innovative approaches in financing the poor were promoted in a sustainable manner in developing countries over the past 20 years. It can help to reduce poverty by increasing the poor's income and purchasing power, enabling them to accumulate assets and thus promote economic growth. It has also been demonstrated to empower poor women by giving them more control over financial services (Nelson and Gupta, 2003).

Prof. Mohammed Yunus, Professor of Economics in Chittagong University of Bangladesh was the founder of micro finance model and 'access to credit as human rights' forms the basis and foundation for micro finance model in Bangladesh (Jha, 2002). Bangladesh Grameen Bank has been followed as a model for the development of micro finance institutions in India and other countries. The important feature of this bank was 98 per cent recovery rate and provision of credit without any collateral security. Some other successful micro finance institutions in other countries are Bangladesh Rural Advancement Committee (BRAC) of Bangladesh, Bank Raykat Indonesia (BRI) in Indonesia and bank for Agriculture and Agricultural co-operatives (BAAC) in Thailand, Micro Finance Institutions in South East and South Asia remain successful in terms of outreach and performance in delivering credit services to the poorest of the poor women and the rural artisans in rural and urban areas, selection of borrowers and offering cost effective approaches to formal institutions (Yaron, 1994 and Besley, 1994).

Micro finance institutions offer a sustainable approach to poverty alleviation and empowerment for the economically active poor and resulted in holding assets by woman other than land, changes in labour supply, household expenditure (Pitt and Khandker, 1998) and empowerment of women (Kabber, 2001; Satish, 2001 and Meyer, 2001). Moreover, banking linkage results in low transaction cost and good repayment contributing for profitability and reduction in non-performing assets of the banks (Swarup, 2001 and Rengarajan, 2001). Unlike infrastructure intensive development spending, micro lending directly benefits the disadvantaged. In the long-term, coupled with the investment in human resource development as advocated by Amartya Sen, it is sure to create a global population well-equipped to participate in every sector of the economy (Somanath, 2009).

One of the major differences between micro finance approach and direct credit approach is that micro finance institutions strive to attain long-run sustainability. Of the 20 crore target poor households in the Asia Pacific Region, less than five per cent have access to financial services. Outreach of micro finance institutions was less in Nepal, Sri Lanka and negligible in Pakistan, Malaysia and Thailand. World Micro Credit Summit at Washington D.C., February 1997 announced a global target of supporting 100 million of the world's poor families especially the women, with micro credit for self-employment and other financial and business services by the year 2007 (Yunus, 1997; Micro Credit Summit Report, 1997; Morduch,. 1999; Nair, 2001 and Patel, 2002). Recent study reported that around 2,931 reporting institutions are working globally on micro finance programme and it has reached about 80.90 million people till the end of 2003 and out of these, 67.70 per cent are accounted as the poorest clients in the world (Nair, 2005). Micro finance through SHG-Bank Linkage Programmes is being propagated as an alternative system of credit delivery for the poorest of the poor groups. In other words, micro finance is a programme for the poor and by the poor to mobilise the savings and use them to meet their financial needs (Pandey, 2008). Micro finance includes the entire range of financial services rendered to the poor other than providing credit. It includes skill up-gradation and entrepreneurial development which would enable them to overcome poverty (Puhazhendi and Satyasai, 2002 and Banerjee, 2002). Micro finance is a small amount of money with collateral free loan to jointly liable groups in order to foster income-generation and poverty reduction through enhancing self-employment (Chowdhry, 2003).

Evolution of Self-Help Groups (SHGs)

Informal agencies oriented to savings and credit functions are not a new phenomenon in India (Desai and Namboodiri, 2001). Some forms of credit operations existed even before 1904 when the Co-operative Credit Society Act was passed. Credit instruments such as Nidhis and Chit funds are popular especially in South India. They have several distinguishing features such as encouraging thrift, mobilising small savings and inculcating the habits of punctuality and planning. The useful role played by these institutions in rural areas as an important source of credit to people with moderate needs was well recognised (Namboodiri and Shiyani, 2001).

After realising the limitations of existing formal system, the obvious need for an efficient alternate credit delivery system was felt in the country. Asia and Pacific Regional Agricultural Credit Association (APRACA) discussed this issue in a workshop conducted during 1986 and it resulted in financing of SHGs. SHGs are considered as an important institution at local or village level, through which members of the group save and lend among themselves. Initially, SHGs was intended to bring together people particularly economically weaker sections and to undertake activities of mutual interest. Later, it was evolved as an institutional arrangement for collective saving, consumption credit as well as integrating social and economic goals among small groups. Now SHG concept is evolved to cater to the needs of the rural poor by providing finance and other services to attain social and economic empowerment especially of rural women. SHGs in India are informal groups comprising mostly of women (90%) with 15-20 members in a group.

The SHG approach assumed significance when National Bank for Agriculture and Rural Development (NABARD) recognised the SHGs as people's institution and canalised micro finance programme through SHGs especially to rural women (Puhazhendi and Satyasai, 2002). NABARD has pioneered the concept and implemented the SHG-Bank Linkage Programme since 1992 and the SHGs have become a predominant component of the Indian financial system. The most significant initiative taken by the Indian banking sector which has the potential to transfer the rural economy is SHG-Bank Linkage Programme. The concept of micro finance for SHGs has proved that even the poor are worthy of bank loans. Among the real and potential clients of micro finance, women are the most appropriate targeted beneficiaries, since it is argued that the entire household benefits from the loans, when given to women. As part of poverty alleviation measures, the Government of India has implemented self-employment programmes like Swaranajayanthi Gram Swarozgar Yojana (SGSY), District Poverty Initiative Programmes, Development of Women and Children in Rural Areas (DWCRA) and SWASHAKTI where, the major emphasis has been laid upon SHG formation, social mobilisation, training and capacity building of women and their access and control over economic resources.

Concept of Self-Help Group

The SHGs are voluntary associations of people formed to attain a collective goal. People who are homogeneous with respect to social background, heritage, caste or traditional occupation come together for a common cause to raise and manage resources for the benefit of the group members.

The process by which the group of people with common objectives are facilitated to come together in order to participate in developmental activities *i.e.*, savings, credit, income-generation, etc., is called group formation.

Although the SHGs can be formed for any developmental activity, for the financial institutions to use them as a conduit for banking activities, the SHGs should be practicing thrift and credit and be familiar with money management (Gupta, 1993).

Characteristics of Self-Help Groups

- The group should be homogeneous, which may be in terms of heritage, caste, creed, religion, economic status, occupation, activity, common interest and social background in addition to that the members should be in the age group between 18 and 60 years.
- The group should be an 'Affinity Group' – affinity may be in terms of like: mindedness, mutual trust, confidence and concern for the poor.
- The system of caste, creed and religion is not a bar to SHG formation.
- Group should be voluntarily formed with 'self-select' members and there should not be any political interference.
- Members should have the mentality to function democratically to have proper repayment ethics and one member in one group only.

- Group should democratically select three representatives among themselves.
- The responsibilities of the leaders are to convene meetings, maintain records, resolve conflicts among members and deal with banks, government and other agencies.
- Leaders should be given designation such as Animator, Representative – I and Representative – II, normally rotated once in a year and the period may be extended if all the members desire and for the benefit of the group.
- Meetings should be conducted at regular intervals in a specific place at specified time and penalty may be imposed for late coming and absence.
- The conduct of the meetings and resolutions passed should be recorded in the minutes book. Members should decide on regular savings at regular interval and savings should be collected in group meetings. Savings bank account should be opened in the name of the group.
- Among the three representatives selected, any two of them should be authorised to operate the bank account and the savings amount should be lent to the needy members. The group should decide on the priority, quantum of loan, repayment period and rate of interest.
- After six months of good performance, the group should decide on availing loan from banks. The amount of group corpus and the bank loan should be lent to the members based on their need and repaying capacity. All the members are jointly and severally responsible for the proper utilisation of loan amount and prompt repayment.
- Collection of savings, disbursement of loan, repayment of loan and other financial activities should take place only in group meetings.
- Inclusion and deletion of members should be recorded properly and all members should participate in group discussions.

On the strength of these features, the functions of the SHGs have been decided.

Functions of Self-Help Groups

(a) *Savings and Thrift*

- All SHG members regularly save a small amount. The amount may be small, but the savings have to be regular with a continuous habit pursued by all the members.
- 'Savings First Credit Later' should be the motto of every SHG member.
- SHG members take a step towards self-dependence when they start small savings. They learn financial discipline through savings and internal lending.

(b) *Internal Lending*

- The SHGs should use the savings amount for giving loans to members.
- The purpose, the rate of interest, schedule of repayment etc., are to be decided by the group itself.
- Proper accounts have to be kept by the SHGs.

(c) *Conduct of Meetings*

- Regular meetings should be conducted weekly or fortnightly or monthly at scheduled times in specific places.
- In every meeting, the SHG should be encouraged to discuss the problems and find solutions to the problems faced by the members of the group. Individually, the poor people are weak and lack resources to solve their problems. The group can help its members to ease the difficulties and come up with solutions.

(d) *Availing Bank Loan*

- The SHG takes loans from the bank and lends it to its members.

(e) *Others*

- Selection of office bearers.
- Rotational leadership.
- Evolving norms/bye laws on their own.
- Opening of bank account.
- Book keeping and maintenance of records.

- Credit management.
- Linkage with banks, government etc.
- Awareness programmes/trainings.
- Sorting out issues concerning family, women, children, habits etc.
- Other social activities.

The great merit of SHGs has been their ability to inculcate among members the sound habits of thrift, savings and banking. The strength of SHG-Bank Linkage Programme in mobilising small savings of the poor, utilising funds optionally through collective wisdom, transparent and democratic participation, ensuring excellent repayment through group dynamism and peer pressure and reduction in transaction costs both for the banks and the SHG members has been demonstrated amply in various parts of the country. In its endeavour for economic empowerment of the poor through improved access to bank credit, NABARD collaborates with non-governmental organizations and micro finance institutions in promotion of SHGs and linking them with banks.

Due to the encouraging results of SHGs under Bank Linkage Programme, Reserve Bank of India included financing to SHGs as a mainstream activity of banks under priority sector lending in 1999. This programme was expected to cover over five lakh SHGs with cumulative loans exceeding ₹ 1,200 crore reaching over eight million households (Tripathy, 2003; Kroop and Suran, 2002 and Seibel and Dave, 2002). The typical characteristics of SHG are presented in Figure 1.1.

Women and Micro Finance

Women are an integral part of every economy. All round development and harmonious growth of a nation would be possible only when women are considered as equal partners in progress with men. Women's contribution to national development is crucial. "Women represent 50 per cent of population, make up 30 per cent of the official labour force, work 60 per cent of all working hours but receive only 10 per cent of the world's income and own less than one per cent of the world's property" (Sahay, 1998). Women are deprived of

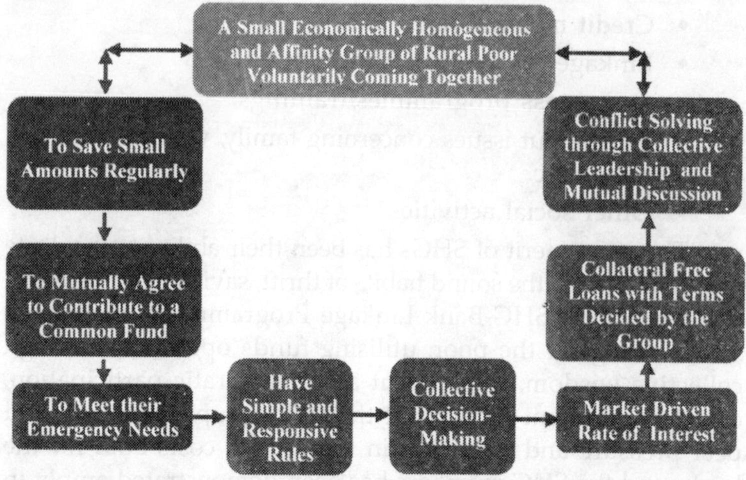

Fig. 1.1: Concept of Self-help Group

Source: NABARD (2004).

their economic status especially in rural areas and absence of adequate opportunities act as obstacles on the path of women towards economic and social progress (Dwarakanath, 2002).

The status of women can be improved by organizing them at the grass root level (Agarwal, 1985). Moreover, women's access to credit is an important criterion to assess the performance of rural financial institutions. It is based on the premise that women are less liable to default and that they utilise credit in a more prudent way. The direct access to credit accompanied by savings could become a catalyst for change that brings benefits to rural women as well as their families and communities (Monica and Perrett, 1991). Micro finance provided through SHGs enables the members to satisfy their consumption needs as well as other production needs. The members and leaders are the decision-makers and the decisions and behaviour are guided by agreements (Uphoff, 1992 and Chavan and Kumar, 2002).

Together with access to credit for women, SHGs are important for sustainable rural development and food security. They not only mobilise economic and social capital and regulate their use in a most efficient and sustainable manner, but also encourage people to take a long-term view by creating common expectations and a basis for co-operation that goes beyond individual interest. SHGs play a crucial role in implementing policies aimed at eliminating market failures such as asymmetric information, moral hazard and high transaction cost. They ensure joint liability and consequent peer monitoring of member borrowers (Stiglitz, 1990; Singh, 1995 and Chakrabarti, 2003). Micro finance through SHG-Bank Linkage Programme has in recent times come to be recognised and accepted as one of the new development paradigms for alleviating poverty through social and economic empowerment of the poor with focus on empowering women.

Indian Experience on Micro Finance

The demonstrative success of micro credit in Bangladesh, made many developing countries, including India, to introduce the concept with modifications. In India, innovative approach in SHG movement was made by NABARD by the introduction of a pilot project in 1991. SHGs are formed either spontaneously or promoted by certain agencies such as government and non-governmental agencies. Under Central Government, Ministry of Urban Employment is involved in the promotion of SHGs among the urban poor. At the State level, District Rural Development Agency (DRDA) and Mahalir Thittam (MATHI) are organizing SHGs among rural poor women with the support from NGOs. Apart from this, Nationalised Banks and Regional Rural Banks are also involved in organizing SHGs. NGOs are the pioneers in organizing SHGs and linking of groups with banks for taking up income-generating activities (Kumaran, 2001). The growth of SHGs had been in areas where they received support from NGOs. They support not only in the formation of SHGs but also in identifying activities, imparting training and even financial support at the initial stage. Subsequently the SHGs are linked with banks for savings and credit operations. The bank linkage model which evolved as a core strategy could be used by the banking system for increasing its outreach to the poorest of the poor (Nanda, 1999).

In India, Self-employed Women's Association (SEWA) in Gujarat and Madhya Pradesh, Mysore Resettlement and Development Agency (MYRADA) in Karnataka, Professional Assistance for Development Action (PRADAN) in Rajasthan, Association of Sarva Seva Farms (ASSEFA) in Tamil Nadu, New Public School Society in Uttar Pradesh and other organizations took up the initiative. The credit needs of groups are met in a convenient, flexible and cost effective way.

Presently over 800 NGOs are actively engaged in micro finance intermediation in the country. India has the world's largest micro finance programme in terms of outreach, benefiting more than 46.96 million poor households, to gain access to micro finance from the formal banking system in 2007-08 (NABARD, 2008). India has committed to bring 2.5 crore of poor women under micro finance programme and to provide about ₹ 15,000 crore as loans to ensure reasonably good living conditions to them in the next five years.

Linkage Models in India

The SHG-Bank Linkage Programme supported by NABARD has emerged as the single largest micro finance programme in the world in terms of outreach. Linking of SHGs with banks is approached in three different models in India (Figures 1.2, 1.3 and 1.4).

Model I : NABARD - Bank – SHG (Direct financial assistance to SHG).

Model II : NABARD - Bank – NGO/SHPI[1] (as a facilitator) – SHG.

Model III : NABARD - Bank – NGO/SHPI - (as financial intermediary) – SHG.

The bank linkage aims at intermediation of the SHGs between the banks and the rural poor for cutting down the transaction costs for both banks and their rural clients. The objectives of linkage programme could be:

1. SHPI: Self-Help Promoting Institution also termed as Non-Governmental Organization.

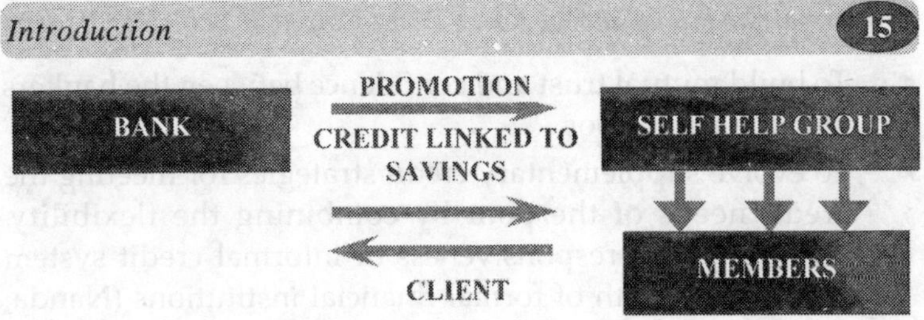

Fig. 1.2: SHG – Bank Linkage Model I

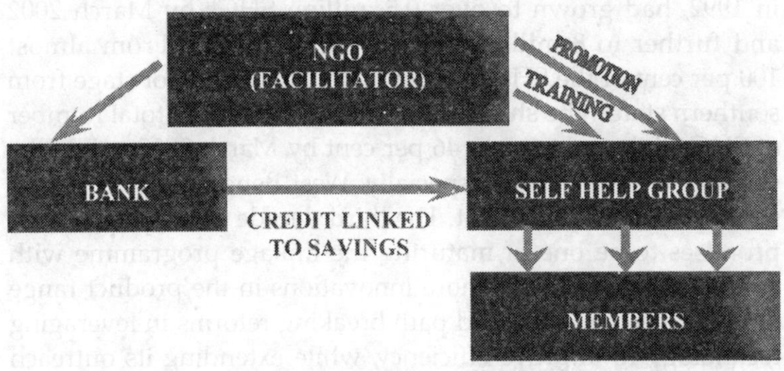

Fig. 1.3: SHG – Bank Linkage Model II

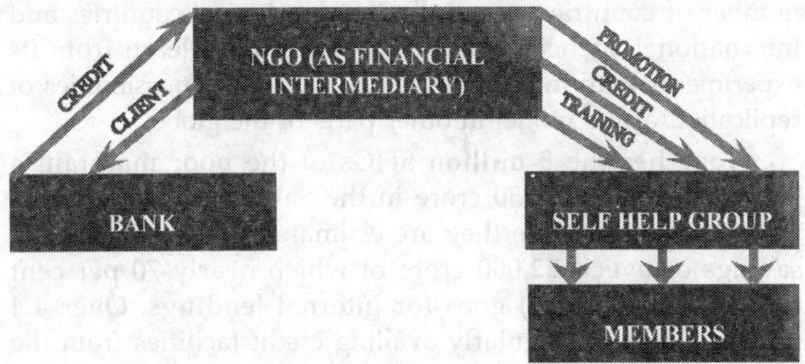

Fig. 1.4: SHG – Bank Linkage Model III

Source: NABARD, Annual Report (2003-04).

- To build mutual trust and confidence between the bankers and the rural poor.
- To evolve supplementary credit strategies for meeting the credit needs of the poor by combining the flexibility, sensitivity and responsiveness of informal credit system with the strength of formal financial institutions (Nanda, 1994).

Growth of SHG-Bank Linkage

The small beginning of linking only 500 SHGs to banks in 1992, had grown to over 0.5 million SHGs by March 2002 and further to 8 million SHGs by March 2012. From almost 100 per cent of the SHGs linked to Banks at the pilot stage from southern states, the share of southern States in the total number of SHGs linked shrank to 46 per cent by March 2012, while the share of eastern States (especially, West Bengal, Odissa, Bihar) shot up to over 20 per cent. The third decade of the programme promises to be one of maturing the linkage programme with livelihoods support, lot more innovations in the product range offered through SHGs and path breaking reforms in leveraging technology to improve efficiency, while extending its outreach to more geographical regions, especially the most resource poor regions of the country. It is widely believed that the SHGs of the poor will be the vehicles leading the march of India's emergence as a super economic power in the next decade. A number of countries, especially the developing countries and international agencies are turning to India to learn from its experiments with micro finance and to explore possibilities of replication of the model in other parts of the globe.

Together the 8 million SHGs of the poor maintain a balance of over ₹ 6,550 crore in the Savings Bank accounts with the Banks, while they are estimated to have harnessed savings of over ₹ 22,000 crore of which nearly 70 per cent (over ₹ 15,000 crore) goes for internal lendings. Over 4.4 million SHGs are regularly availing credit facilities from the Banks. During 2011-12 alone, over 1.15 Million Groups availed loans amounting to ₹ 16,535 crore from Banks and together 4.4 million Groups have loans to the extent of ₹ 36,340 crore outstanding against them with the financing banks as on 31.3.2012. As the credit availed by the groups along with their internal savings are revolved many times within the group for shorter durations, the multiplier effect makes the process much larger than the basic figures indicate. Figure 1.5 shows a graphical presentation of the savings, fresh loans and the loan outstanding of SHGs with banks for the last four years.

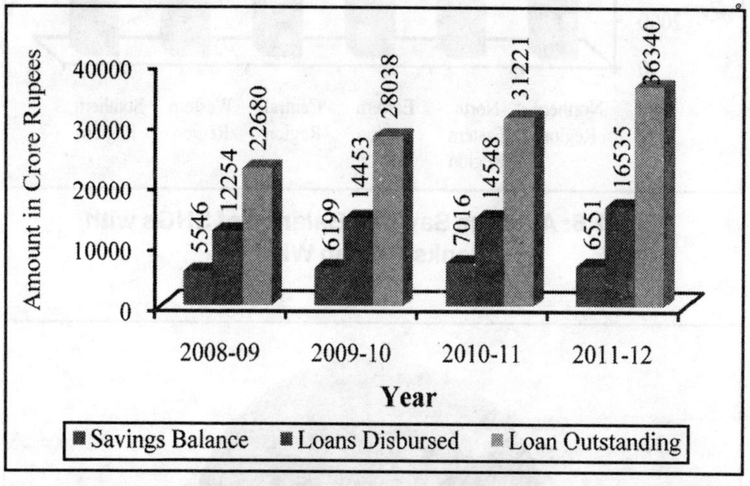

Fig.1.5: SHGs as on 31.3.2012 – Savings and Credit

The balance in the savings accounts of the banks as at the end of March 2012 stood at ₹ 6,551.41 crore. Among the major States, Karnataka SHGs maintain the highest S. B., balance of over ₹ 16,000 per SHG followed by Punjab of nearly ₹ 12,500 per SHG. Among the regions, southern region is highest at ₹ 10,080 per SHG and north eastern region recorded the lowest balance of ₹ 4,159 per SHG (Figure 1.6). On an average, the SHGs maintain a balance of ₹ 8,230. Commercial Banks account for 58 per cent of the savings account maintained by SHGs and RRBs 27 per cent and Co-operative Banks the remaining 15 per cent (Figure 1.7).

Further, over 4.36 million SHGs have now access to direct credit facilities from the banks and the total bank loans

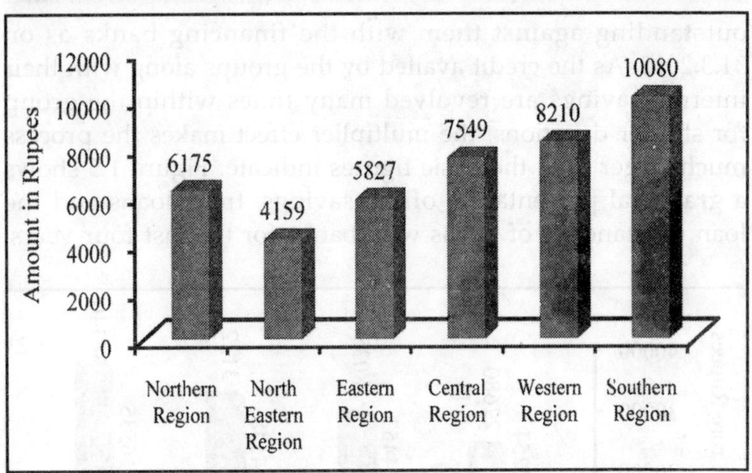

Fig. 1.6: Average Savings Balance of SHGs with Banks-Region Wise

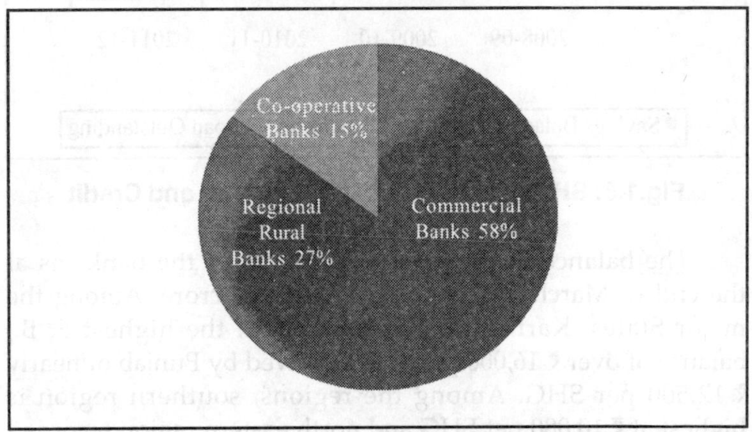

Fig. 1.7: Saving Linked SHGs (Number): Agency Wise

outstanding against these groups is over ₹ 36340 crore as on 31 March 2012 *i.e.*, an average of ₹ 83500 per group. About 1.15 million SHGs were extended fresh loans to the extent of ₹ 16535 crore during 2011-12 by all banks averaging ₹ 1.44 lakh per group.

Status of Micro Finance in Tamil Nadu

In Tamil Nadu 5,56,311 SHGs with 85.70 lakhs members are functioning as on 31st March 2012: out of which 3,72,092 were rural SHGs and the remaining urban SHGs. The total savings of SHGs were ₹ 3,374.60 crores and the total credit availed is ₹ 15,633.83 crores.

Impact of Micro Finance

The experience of micro finance through SHGs in India showed that it was one of the successful interventions in rural credit market. It proved that the poor are bankable (Patel, 2002) and poverty alleviation was possible without subsidies (Khandker, 1998). The studies on micro credit policy in India indicated that group lending through SHGs reduced the lending and transaction cost of public banks (Puhazhendi, 1995 and Zeller *et al.* 1997) and improved the repayment rates (Karmakar, 1999). The SHG-banking is highly profitable to banks and beneficial to SHGs and their members (Karduck and Seibel, 2004). The SHG lending is more profitable and has lower default rate for banks (less than one per cent as compared to 11-12 per cent of their regular portfolios) (Basu and Srivastava, 2005). Recovery rates for SHG loans stand above 99 per cent (Gupta, 2008 and Rajan, 2009).

The impact was found to be cost effective when SHGs are functioning under non-governmental organizations (Patel, 2002). SHG-Bank linkage project under NABARD was considered as part of the new micro finance emphasising flexibility, responsiveness and sensitivity in providing financial services to the rural poor women (Kaladhar, 1997).

The important features that contributed to the success of SHGs *i.e.,* group lending were socio-economic homogeneity of the group, small size, active participation, voluntary mode, joint liability (Huppi and Feder, 1990), non-political nature, similarities of the needs and problems of group members (Singh, 1995 and Rao, 2002), peer monitoring and group pressure (Wydick, 1999a). Studies related to the impact of micro finance on the economic and social conditions of the members proved that the income, savings and loan had increased due to the intervention of SHG-Bank Linkage Programme (NABARD, 2000; Harper, 2002; Manthri, 2004; Anjugam, 2005; Jerinabi, 2006 and Pandey, 2008).

Micro credit has given women in India an opportunity to become agents of change. Poor women, who are in the forefront of the micro credit movement in the country, use small loans to jumpstart a long chain of activity. Keeping in view the immense inherent potential in SHGs in mobilising savings and in credit multiplication, the banks are considering micro credit as one of their important marketing avenues. The importance of micro credit has created a universal acceptance for the concept, the world over, declaring the year 2005 as the 'International year of Micro Credit'.

In recent years, in its wider dimension micro credit known as micro finance has become a much-favoured intervention for poverty alleviation in the developing countries and least developed countries (Jerinabi, 2008).

The role of micro finance as the most suitable and feasible alternative in accomplishing the goals of growth and poverty alleviation is now well recognised. Micro finance embodies the basic democratic ethos of self-development through a participatory approach. The experiment of micro finance in India through the conduit of SHGs has demonstrated considerable democratic functioning and group dynamism. Their adroitness in assessing and appraising the credit needs of members, their business like functioning and efficiency in recycling the funds often with repayment rates nearing cent per cent have proved that this is among the best alternatives in improving the credit delivery to the poor. Recognising their importance, both the Reserve Bank and NABARD have been spearheading the promotion and linkage of SHGs to the banking system through refinance support and initiating other proactive policies and systems. The programme of micro finance has made rapid strides in India (Gupta, 2008).

Statement of the Problem

In the last two decades, micro finance programme has shown an increasing trend in terms of both linkages and disbursement of loans to the rural poor. Banks are pumping credit enormously because they find it profitable to provide credit to the poor. The evaluation of micro finance institutions has revealed that they are successful in outreach with the clients.

There are empirical evidences which show that the involvement of women associated with the micro finance SHG-Bank Linkage Programmes has been on the rise, resulting in a greater awareness and confidence amongst them. The various studies conducted proved that the women had developed abundant self-confidence and self-esteem through SHG movement. Not only poverty but also social and gender issues could be tackled effectively through this process. Further the SHGs are fast emerging agencies for the socio-economic development of the rural areas. The government is also keen in raising the standard of living of those rural poor through various developmental schemes. Women's participation in the SHG-Bank Linkage Programme has paved the way for the speedy development of economic and productive activities.

In general, micro finance is a path towards empowering the most marginalised among the poor to take charge of their life's requirements. It has been believed that through micro finance, they are better positioned to access not only financial services but also the resources such as group support, accessibility to markets and other related benefits. While micro finance is looked upon as a financially viable approach to address economic vulnerability, it has demonstrated the potential of building up the social capital of the poorest communities. To find out concrete and suitable facts to the above mentioned views, a systematic study was needed. The results of the empirical evidences could be used in making necessary changes in the developmental programmes for women empowerment. Finance is fundamental for any programme and plays a vital role in all developmental activities. Hence a study on "Microfinancing of Rural Women Through SHG and Bank Linkage (A Study in Coimbatore District of Tamil Nadu)" was undertaken.

Scope of the Study

The financing of SHG is a significant factor that contributes to the development of the SHG member's initiatives. The SHG is a social and an economic organization that relies on its members' own resources and gradually supplements its resources from the banking system. It builds on the collective decision-making abilities of the members and their capacity to utilise effectively the available resources for the all round development of the members and the people around them. The growth and linkage of SHGs are found to be growing in an enormous way at the grass root level, after the introduction of SGSY programme.

In this context, an attempt has been made to analyse the economic impact of the programme on income-generation, savings, employment generation, asset creation of the members and their social empowerment. The study also focuses on the functional pattern of SHGs and their members from the financial perspectives, *viz;* in terms of savings mobilisation, delivery of credit, management of funds, training, income-generating activities, marketing problems and repayment of loans. The overall result that emerges from the study would provide a scope for formulating the policies relating to the effectiveness of the SHGs functioning and to enhance its scope to cover more sections of the society under the SHGs' umbrella.

Objectives of the Study

The objectives of the study are:

1. To understand the organization, management and financial performance of SHGs in the rural areas of selected blocks in Coimbatore District.
2. To analyse the socio-economic factors influencing the members in the choice of ownership of the micro enterprises.
3. To examine the extent of participation of SHG members in microfinancing.
4. To study the impact of micro finance through SHG-Bank Linkage Programme on income, savings, employment generation, asset creation, decision-making skills and overall empowerment of the members.

Hypotheses Framed

- There is no functional relationship between the choice of enterprises and socio-economic conditions of the members.
- There is no significant difference in the level of income, savings, personal assets, business assets, indebtedness and decision-making capacity of the members before and after SHG period.

Operational Definitions

(a) *Group Owned Micro Enterprises (GOME) and Single Owned Micro Enterprises (SOME):* GOME denotes Group-Owned Micro Enterprises. If two or more members join together to start a business within the group and share the returns, it is termed as GOME. SOME denotes Single-Owned Micro Enterprises. If the SHG members initiate micro enterprises on their own without joining with other group members, it is termed as SOME.

(b) *Investments:* The amount contributed by the members in the business including their own and borrowed.

(c) *Income:* Income denotes income earned through the micro enterprises.

Limitations

1. As the study is based on the primary data collected through interview method, the reliability depends on the true response of the SHG office bearers and members. However, adequate care has been taken to elicit true response through cross checks.
2. The study was confined to one district and it may have some limitations of comparison across boundaries. Nevertheless, all efforts have been put forth to make the study as objective as possible.
3. Only women SHGs have been taken for the study though a number of men SHGs also exist.
4. Only those SHG members who are engaged in income-generating activities have been considered for the study.

Organization of the Study

The study is organized under the following five chapters.

Chapter I: Introduction

Problem focus, scope, objectives, hypotheses and limitations of the study are presented.

Chapter II: Review of Literature

A brief review of various related studies is presented.

Chapter III: Methodology

The locale of the study, profile of the study area, sampling design, period of the study and analytical tools used in the study are presented.

Chapter IV: Results and Discussion

The results obtained from the analysis of data and specific inferences drawn from the results are presented.

Chapter V: Summary and Conclusion

A summary of findings and practically viable suggestions are presented.

REVIEW OF LITERATURE

The literature pertaining to the study on 'Microfinancing of Rural Women through SHG and Bank Linkage (A Study in Coimbatore District of Tamil Nadu)' are reviewed under the following headings:

- Status of Rural Women.
- Role of Women in Poverty Alleviation Programme.
- Role of Micro Finance Institutions in Poverty Alleviation.
- Impact of Micro Finance and Self-Help Group (SHG)-Bank Linkage Programme on Rural Women.
- Socio-economic Status of SHGs.
- Functions and Performance of SHGs.
- Empowerment of Women through SHGs.

Status of Rural Women

India has been a land of diverse cultures and traditions. The customs, norms and values affecting women of today have their roots in the past and they have crucial influence on the shaping of the feminine identity.

Kalpagam (1986) in her study on the 'Status of Rural Women' found that women, particularly the rural women are subjected to wrong discrimination between male and female in matters of wages. It has already been pointed out that a large part of women's work, family labour which has received no value in economic analysis is unpaid. A number of explanations have been given in various studies for the existence of male-female wage differences and low economic status to which women labours in general are subjected to. The absence of collective initiative is sometimes advanced as the main reason for discrimination in terms of access to employment and wages of women in the labour market, and such a lack of organization is universally present in informal sectors like: agriculture and unorganized agricultural sector. Their family responsibilities and obligations, the attitude and reactions of other family members towards them and the prevalent socio-cultural atmosphere, negatively affect the organized effort of women workers and hence they face wage discrimination. Moreover, in family labour-based household and agricultural households, division of labour is solely based on patriarchy and this largely affects the status of rural women in the agrarian economy.

Singh and Singh (1987) in their study 'Impact of Rural Development Programme on Economic Status of Women in Uttar Pradesh' stated that the economic status of more than 50 per cent of women with regard to standard of living, food and employment has increased. The study also showed that women enjoyed an important role in decision-making in matters related to household activities, selection of crops, technology, credit and marketing arrangements.

Rao (1991) in his study on 'Promotion of Entrepreneurship in Andhra Pradesh' reported that poor financial status of women was found to be very critical in the promotion of entrepreneurship among women. Want of co-operation from family, ignorance about the programmes like Development of Women and Children in Rural Areas (DWCRA), Integrated Rural Development Programme (IRDP), Training for Rural Youth for Self-employment (TRYSEM), insufficient managerial skills, apathy, sense of fear and high degree of illiteracy, outdated customs and traditions were some of the hindrances to female entrepreneurship. He also found that a vast majority of women in the state are interested in organizing SHGs. Women have opted for schemes like: fishponds, vegetable cultivation, horticulture, garment shop, petty trade, weaving and breeding mythos to be taken up through SHGs. Financial assistance from the government is required to implement these schemes on an experimental basis. This would go a long way to improve the socio-economic status of women.

Chikara (1993) studied the 'Impact of Institutional Credit on the Weaker Section' and has found that there existed a wide gap between the credit requirements and the credit supplied by the financial institutions which had led to repeated borrowing from private agencies. This had created a problem of indebtedness and had brought these people under the clutches of private money lenders.

Rao (1995) in his study on 'Dimensions of Rural Non-Farm Employment of Women' examined the intra district trends in share, growth and composition of Rural Non-Farm Employment (RNFE) of women in west Godavari District for the period 1971-91. The share of RNFE of women increased in delta taluk from 1971 to 1991 whereas it declined in the upland taluk and the agency taluk. At taluk level, Narsapur, Tanuku and Tadepalli Guden occupied the first three positions among themselves. The growth of RNFE of women in delta and upland taluks was attributed to initial support and vast change in agriculture during 1980s and the establishment of female based agro-industries like: cashew kernel processing, tobacco handling and fruit juice manufacturing industries. Female employment in delta area was high in household and non-household manufacturing units, transport, storage and communication whereas in upland area, the female employment was high in construction, trade and commerce. RNFE of women in the district level showed rising trends in all the regions with some discerning differences in growth levels, due to agro economic conditions. Implementation of employment generation programmes by the government and adoption of agro climatic regional planning approach are the suggestions offered for the removal of disparities in women's earnings.

Devadas (1998) examined 'Economic Development of Indian Women' and stated that women's participation in SHGs is believed to increase their status and decision-making power. Employed women do not remain as just objects of social change but become agents of it.

Kohili (1998) examined 'Women Entrepreneurs in India' and stated that a majority (73%) of the members did not attend any entrepreneurial training programme or got any financial support from outside. Twenty seven per cent are getting financial support from outside and thirty eight per cent faced discrimination in business. But the majority (63%) of them are aware of Government programmes for self-employment.

Rani (1998) in her study 'Towards Empowerment of Women: Organizational and Managerial Perspectives of Women Co-operatives' suggested that women form an important segment of the labour force and that the economic role played by them cannot be isolated from the total framework of development, as the role and degree of integration of women in economic development had always been an indicator of economic independence and social status.

Sahay (1998) in her study on, 'Women and Empowerment: Approaches and Strategies' highlighted that "Women represent fifty per cent of population, make up thirty per cent of the official labour force, perform sixty per cent of all working hours, but receive ten per cent of the world's income and own less than one per cent of the world's property". They share multiple responsibilities and perform important roles as producers of food, managers of natural resources, earners of income and caretakers of household affairs. Moreover, they are the active agents of change, the dynamic promoters of social transformation and play a vital role in shaping the destiny of future generations. Yet, in the gendered social formations, they are placed below the hierarchy of men.

Rajeswari and Sumangala (1999) in their research on 'Women Entrepreneurs a Scan on their Problems and Prospects in Women Entrepreneurship' explored the problems and prospects in women entrepreneurship and stated that women entrepreneurship enabled the pooling of small capital resources and skills available with women. It paved the way for fuller utilisation of capital and also mobilised the female human potential.

Hill (2001) had undertaken a study to evaluate the 'Women in the Indian Informal Economy: Collective Strategies for Work Life Improvement and Development' and found that informal sector workers in developing countries are currently dominated by resource-based approaches like the micro credit movement. This policy framework is predicated upon certain liberal assumptions about individual human action and the relationship between human behaviour and economic development. This article concludes that these assumptions are inappropriate when they are applied to informal sector workers and their economic activities.

Reddi and Reddi (2003) conducted a research on 'Women in Agriculture: A Sociological Study in Southern India' in Andhra Pradesh by taking a sample of 276 agricultural women from villages, where agriculture has been the main source of livelihood.

The major findings of the study were: *(i)* nearly half of the respondents ranged between the age of 20 and 40 *(ii)* as the social class and economic status go hand in hand, generally lower caste women's participation has been greater than upper caste women, because caste system plays a prominent role in rural India. Despite working together on the same fields for years together, discrimination among castes still exists in rural areas; and *(iii)* women have very little access to education particularly in rural areas and hence most of them suffer from illiteracy. This may probably be due to the fact that there has been no sincere attempt to raise the position and status of rural women and a social stigma continues to exist towards their education. The study concluded that the socio-economic conditions under which these women live are traditional and exploitative which in turn impede their development and go on lowering their socio-economic status day-by-day.

Women are the most vulnerable group affected by the poverty and thus paved the way for the emergence of various poverty alleviation programmes.

Role of Women in Poverty Alleviation Programmes

Over the years a plethora of poverty alleviation programmes in various forms has been implemented in the country and huge amounts on social and financial investments have been made available to achieve the sole aim of poverty alleviation.

Mohiuddin (1987) in his comparative study on 'Integrated Rural Development Programme (IRDP) and Development of Women and Children in Rural Areas (DWCRA)' stated as follows: a significant percentage of women beneficiaries are in agriculture sector, both in the IRDP and DWCRA programmes and higher percentage of IRDP beneficiaries belongs to the middle income group and the lower income group, but in DWCRA, a higher percentage of women are from the lower income group, followed by middle income group. As these women have selected the schemes which have an assured market, marketing has not turned out to be a problem to them and the status of the IRDP beneficiaries have greatly increased compared to the respondents of DWCRA.

Alosyus (1991) in his study on 'DWCRA – Working Wonders for Kashmiri Women' assessed the impact of DWCRA on the Kashmiri women. Women workers have been trained in various schemes of readymade garments, shawls, knitting and related work. The DWCRA programme extended its supportive services such as education, health, nutrition, immunisation, family welfare and balwadis in addition to their economic betterment of rural women. The programme proved to be a success as it has generated and infused a sense of confidence into the women folk.

Mukherjee (1993) in her paper on 'Women's Participation and Jawahar Rozgar Yojana' studied two selective objectives of Jawahar Rozgar Yojana, one creating assets in favour of the rural poor for their direct and continuing benefit and the other improving the overall quality of life in rural areas. The major findings of the study were as follows: the effectiveness of such programme depends on who decides on how a programme is going to benefit the rural women and the role played by the rural women in such a programme. The author concluded that if the rural women are able to participate in planning, decision-making and implementing of different programmes, they will get an opportunity to express themselves and to exercise their choice in deciding upon their priorities and even influencing male dominated decisions.

Sithalakshmi and Jothimani (1994) in their article 'Organizational Behaviour as a Means of Empowerment' presented an analysis of organizational behaviour exhibited by women in the DWCRA programme. According to them, if permanent changes are to take place in the status of women, they must be given intervention programmes (income-generating projects) or they must engage in income-generating activities/run institutions individually or collectively, in an organized way. But they should be backed by structural and institutional changes that give them economic independence and allow them to develop their skills, leadership qualities and decision-making authority. They arrived at the conclusion that organizational behaviour of DWCRA groups directly influenced the active status of the groups concerned. In other words, organizational behaviour of the women acted as a means of empowerment.

Ray and Vasundhara (1996) in their study 'Like My Mother's House: Women's Thrift and Credit Co-operatives in South India' attempted to assess Co-operative Development Foundation's efforts to empower women economically, socially and politically. They showed how the Co-operative Development Foundation, an NGO established in 1982 by the Paddy Farmers' Co-operative Society helped local women (who were excluded from the Co-operative because they did not have title to own land) to establish their own thrift and credit groups. The study has shown that there was a spectacular growth in membership of the women's group and how women had benefited economically through access to loans to set up small enterprises and gained economic independence combined with self-confidence. It has undoubtedly resulted in an increase in the well being of the women themselves and of their communities in general.

Apparao (1999) in an article, 'Rural Women and Poverty Alleviation' explored the various developmental and poverty alleviation programmes launched by the Central Government since independence to help the rural masses for the improvement of the socio-economic conditions and standard of living through elimination of poverty, inequality in income, inadequate infrastructure, small and scattered unorganized rural enterprises. Apparao found that the achievements of the various programmes did not cover all the rural women. In his opinion, the rural women are to be associated with poverty alleviation programmes right from the planning stage to make the programmes need based. Awareness should be created among rural women on various activities of different poverty alleviation programmes of Central and State Governments. Women oriented projects need to be given priority even under limited budget for the development of rural women and to make women part and parcel of development.

Sreelakshanamma (2000) conducted a study on 'Empowerment of Rural Women in Rural Non-Farm Activities through the DWCRA Programme' in the Chrial Mandal of Prakasam district of Andhra Pradesh and found that after joining the DWCRA, half of the beneficiaries were sensitised about their level of rights and village politics. Apart from this, one-fourth of the beneficiaries had reported that they have realised the importance of health and nutrition only after becoming members of DWCRA. There is a substantial increase in the family income of the sample beneficiaries after they have joined in the activity. Majority of the respondents have found that the DWCRA programme is highly beneficial in a number of ways.

Varma and Nath (2004) in their study on 'Women in Development Programmes under Different Five-year Plans: A Critical Approach' concluded that the *First* five-year plan was mainly welfare oriented as far as women's issues were concerned, the *Second* five-year plan concentrated on organizing Mahila Mandals (Women's Groups) at grass root levels to ensure better implementation of welfare schemes. The *Third, Fourth* and other Interim plans accorded high priority to women's education. In the Fifth plan there was a shift in the approach from welfare to development. An exclusive scheme for the social and economic upliftment of women belonging to families below the poverty line DWCRA was launched in 1982 as a sub-component of IRDP.

In the Seventh plan beneficiary oriented programmes, which extended direct benefits to women were introduced and in the Eighth plan, there was a shift from development to empowerment of women. By pointing out these, they concluded that the policy directives issued by the Government of India for the increased share for women in the development programmes and the promotion of participatory approach, do not provide for corresponding development in the infrastructure, extension, training information, support and strong monitoring system which is particularly lacking at the state level.

The failure of the earlier poverty alleviation schemes of the Government and the approach of the financial institutions to reach the really needy, found the path for the introduction of the micro finance and SHGs.

Role of Micro Finance Institutions in Poverty Alleviation

To meet the gaps in the implementation of the erstwhile self-employment programme called Integrated Rural Development Programme, the Central Government announced a holistic programme called Swarnajayanthi Gram Swarozgar Yojana. This programme was based on a group approach to rural development where the rural poor were organized into SHGs, provided micro credit and took up viable economic activities on their own. SHGs were also formed under Swayam Siddha, Mission Shakti, Rashtriya Mahila Kosh (RMK), SHG-Bank Linkage scheme of NABARD and Small Industries Development Bank of India (SIDBI) etc.

Yaron (1994) in his study on 'What Makes Rural Financial Institutions Successful' concluded that the micro finance institutions remain the most successful ones in terms of outreach and performance in delivering credit services to the poorest of the poor women and small artisans in the rural and urban areas, reduction in adverse selection of borrowers, development of collateral substitutions and offering cost effective approaches to formal institutions.

Bankers Institute for Rural Development (1996) has analysed 'The Bank Performance Improvement study under the Maharashtra Rural Credit Project (MRCP)' and observed that with the SHG intermediation, the transaction and the risk costs of the advances of the rural branches could be brought down and that could help to turn around many loss-making rural branches into profit-making ones.

Wydick (1999b) in his article 'Can Social Cohesion be Harnessed to Repair Market Failures: Evidence from Group Lending in Guatemala' observed that many institutions prefer to lend traditional loans to SHG groups instead of individuals, due to the reduction in collection costs. His study revealed that the repayment rate for Fund Development of Port Activities (FUNDAP's) group loan had been around 97 per cent, which has several times higher than the rate of recovery of individual loans.

Kallur and Biradar (2000) in their micro level study based on secondary data aimed at examining "The New Paradigm of Micro Finance and the Role of Non-Governmental Voluntary Agencies in its Promotion: A Few Reflections" and to comment on their sustainability in the years to come. The study had thrown light on the origin and the nature of micro credit organization and its superiority over macro one in catering to the needs of farmers. It also revealed that as a result of continuous efforts of NABARD, 255 groups linked together as on 31st March 1998 had been increased to 14,317 groups covering 30 commercial banks, 260 NGOs in 19 states and two Union Territories involving bank loan of ₹ 23.62 crore and NABARD refinance of ₹ 21.38 crore. The study also discussed the role of micro credit organizations with particular reference to the Indo-Swiss project and their sustainability and concluded that the NGOs have succeeded in promoting SHGs.

Bansal (2003) in his article 'SHG-Bank Linkage Programme in India: An Overview' stated that the formal financial institutions in India have ventured into micro finance in a massive way by adopting the SHG-Bank Linkage mode. The paper had reviewed the performance of the programme in different states of India, across three major institutions – *(i)* Commercial Banks, *(ii)* Co-operatives and *(iii)* the Regional Rural Banks (RRBs). The author stated that since its initiation, the programme had shown severe spatial preferences, predominating in certain states, namely: Andhra Pradesh, Uttar Pradesh, Tamil Nadu and Karnataka, in particular had accounted for 40 per cent of the programme's outreach. The author had identified the following reasons for the programme's success in Andhra Pradesh: *(i)* special project sponsored by UNDP called South Asia Poverty Alleviation Programme had promoted 2,700 groups in the state; *(ii)* credit movement in South India led to the evolution of community based development finance institutions, comprising of SHGs promoted by NGOs and by district rural development agencies; *(iii)* district collectors, NABARD district development managers and lead bank managers had supported the SHG-Bank Linkage Programme in the state; *(iv)* leading NGOs in the micro finance sector in India had also worked in Andhra Pradesh; and *(v)* 40 per cent of the SHGs that have been credit linked under DWCRA were concentrated in Andhra Pradesh alone. The author also made the following observations on institutional involvement in the linkage programme: *(i)* commercial banks have been predominant in relatively better off states; *(ii)* RRBs have been more dominant in poorer states and are more successful while acting as Self-Help Group Promoting Institutions (SHPIs); and *(iii)* co-operatives in India have not yet ventured into SHG financing in a significant manner.

Mujumadar (2004) viewed in his article 'Resurrection of Rural Credit' that the rural credit should take a new avatar in terms of the credit delivery mechanism. He also pointed out that the two core causes for the present sickness of the rural credit institutions had been the high transaction cost and the poor recovery performance. He stated that the experiment of micro finance through the conduit of SHGs had shown that transaction costs could be reduced drastically and repayment rates could be as high as 90 per cent. The RBI and NABARD had been the leading force in the promotion and linkage of SHGs to the banking system through refinance support and other pro active policies. The programme initiated in 1992 has covered, 31,000 rural households linking with 500 banks, with a loan amount of ₹ 2,000 crore (31st March 2003). Thus the programme had enabled the formal banking system to reach 11.6 million poor households through the conduit of 7.17 lakh SHGs. Therefore micro credit would be the most appropriate and economically feasible alternative in attaining the objectives of growth and poverty alleviation.

Kunjukunju (2005) in his study on 'Role of Institutional Finance in Rural Development of Kerala' analysed the role of Commercial Banks, Primary Agriculture Credit Societies and Primary Co-operative Agriculture and Rural Development Banks in rural upliftment of Kerala state. He had analysed the extent of credit requirements, credit disbursement and the prevailing credit gap. The study had given an insight into the hurdles encountered by borrowers in obtaining credit, *viz;* cost of borrowings and delay in getting the credit. The problems related to utilisation of loan, repayment performance and impact of credit on borrowers income, employment, asset position and standard of living had also been dealt within the study. To measure the impact, 'The before and after' approach had been employed. Paired 't' test and chi-square test had been used to analyse the data. The findings of the study revealed that there had been an increase in rural credit, but the requirements of the borrowers had not been fully met. Borrowers had incurred 1.60 per cent of the amount of loan as 'borrowing cost' and the average time taken by banks to disburse the loans worked out to be 33 days. Regarding the impact of credit, the average total income and the average annual employment of the borrowers had increased compared to that of the pre-loan period. The study had concluded that the loans advanced by financial institutions to the rural poor for productive purposes and its proper utilisation by them had a positive impact on their economic and social conditions.

Venkatesh and Rao (2007) conducted a study on 'Micro Finance Institutions and Credit Accessibility to the poor in Karnataka' and found that the organizations like: Bharat Sevak Samaj (BSS), Sangamithra, Grameena Koota and Janodaya Foundation had proved beyond doubt that the micro finance helped the poor not only to increase their income level but also acts as a viable business model. There is a huge potential for micro finance to emerge as a successful model to address the problems of unemployment, women backwardness and poverty in India.

Kumar and Sharma (2007) in their study 'Micro Finance on Mountainous States (Disparities in Outreach)' analysed the disparities in growth and outreach of micro finance of the states with an emphasis on Himachal Pradesh, based on secondary data for the period 2002-04. They had found that there is an increase in the share of the number of SHGs linked to the banks and the Bank Linkage Groups were more active in districts with low poverty. This shows that micro credit institutions are indeed effective weapons in the war against rural poverty.

Impact of Micro Finance

Micro credit and SHG-Bank Linkage Programme have brought positive changes in the lives of SHG members. SHGs are the powerful community-based institutions that could enable the community to realise several benefits. The impact of micro credit and SHG-Bank Linkage Programme have been reviewed under the following headings:

- Socio-economic Status of SHGs.
- Functions and Performance of SHGs.
- Empowerment of Women through SHGs.

Socio-economic Status of SHGs

Major impact among the SHG members could easily be said to be the general awareness and awakening to various aspects of their lives. Right from developing the habit of savings, understanding various environmental and social problems, developing communication skills, the prompt repayment of debts, the tendency to help others and the like had brought about vast changes among the individuals.

Khandker (1998) in his study 'Fighting Poverty with Micro Credit Experience in Bangladesh' had analysed the household data collected in 1991-92 and 1997-98 in Bangladesh to find out the long-term impact of micro finance on household consumption and poverty. The study addressed the following issues: *(i)* whether the poor who lack both physical (such as land) and human capital (such as education) actually participate more in micro finance programmes; *(ii)* whether the long-term poverty impact of micro finance are due to sustained income impact or simple income redistribution; and *(iii)* whether the aggregate impact of micro finance is actually affecting the poor beyond programme participation. The results had confirmed that micro finance matters a lot for the very poor borrowers and also for the local economy, because it had led to a rise in the per capita consumption, mainly non food and household non-land assets. In particular, this paper had revealed that: *(i)* the probability that the participants of the programmes might be able to lift themselves out of poverty had increased; *(ii)* the welfare impact of micro finance had also been positive for non-participant households, indicating that micro finance programmes had helped the poor beyond income redistribution with a contribution to local income growth; *(iii)* micro finance programmes have spilt over effects in local economies, thereby increased local village welfare; and *(iv)* micro finance had also helped in reducing extreme poverty more than moderate poverty at the village level. Finally, he suggested that in order to have a stronger impact on poverty reduction, micro finance institution should find ways to develop the skills of their poor borrowers, improve their productivity and income and assist them in marketing and improving the quality of their products.

Puhazhendi and Jayaraman (1999) analysed the 'Increasing Women's Participation and Employment Generation Among Rural Poor: An Approach through Informal Groups'. He observed that SHGs in Tamil Nadu had been performing well towards social change and transformation. The emerging trends were leading to positive direction of empowerment of members and promotion of micro finance.

Dahiya *et al.* (1999) made an attempt to study the 'Socio Economic Upliftment through Self-Help Groups in Solan District at Himachal Pradesh'. The objective of the study was to evaluate the socio-economic conditions of the SHGs. The study concluded that the social impact was deep in empowering women folk, educational development of children and emancipation from social evils.

Ahmad (1999) through a case study on 'Women Empowerment: Self-Help Groups' highlighted that women were coming to the administration directly for their just rights and to address their grievances boldly. It proved that SHGs were successful in North East India even in the midst of insurgency.

Bhatia and Bhatia (2000) through a few case studies on 'Women and Micro Credit' highlighted that recovery of SHGs was higher than other credit sanctioned to borrowers. Moreover, involvement of SHGs had helped the bank branches in the recovery of old dues. They observed that there had been perceptible changes in the living standards of the SHG members, in terms of ownership of assets, increase in savings and borrowing capacity, income-generating activities and income levels as well.

Nedumaran *et al.* (2001) undertook a study with a specific objective of analysing the 'A Study on the Performance and Socio Economic Impact of the Self-Help Groups'. A total of 30 SHGs and 150 members in Erode and Tiruchirappalli districts under two NGOs, namely: *(i)* MYRADA and *(ii)* LEAD had constituted the sample for the study. The results revealed that about eighty seven per cent of the groups were exclusively women groups and thirteen per cent were of men and mixed groups. The size of the group ranged from 10 to 25 members. The agricultural labourers accounted for seventy per cent, followed by fifteen per cent of labourers engaged in non farm activities, ten per cent rural artisans and five per cent of marginal farmers. The average annual savings per member had been ₹ 550 in 2-3 year old groups and had almost doubled after a period of four years. The average annual loan amount per member had been ₹ 5,317 in 2-3 year old groups, ₹ 5,620 in 3-4 years and ₹ 10,900 in four years and above age groups.

Nearly 70.47 per cent members availed loans for production purposes and 29.53 per cent for consumption purposes. The scoring technique results indicated that sixty per cent of the groups were rated as good performers and the rate of savings and share of productive loan to total loan had been the major factors which in turn influenced the good performance of the groups. The average net income per household of SHG members had increased from ₹ 15,146 to ₹ 18,658. The study had concluded stating that the informal groups with active intervention of NGOs had significantly improved the participation of the poor people in group activities and they had an easy access to formal credit through SHGs. The group activities had a positive impact on income, assets position and social conditions of the members.

Caroline (2002) in her study on 'Assessing the Household Impact of Micro Finance on Rural Nigerian Women' had indicated that the micro credit had positively changed the clients' self-esteem, confidence, leadership qualities and decision-making power; had contributed to their household's well-being and increasingly sought solutions to their own problems and those of the community.

Misra *et al.* (2001) made an attempt to study the 'Socio-Economic Analysis of Rural SHG's Scheme'. The objectives of the study were to examine the socio-economic characteristics of SHGs, the functions and impact on generation of income and employment, to identify the major constraints and problems of the groups. The study concluded that the major problems faced by the members of SHGs were lack of training, inadequate credit and marketing facilities, lack of entrepreneurial qualities, social evils and high rate of interest. It is suggested that the banks and credit societies should come forward to help the rural poor through the SHGs and provide liberalised credit facilities at cheaper rate of interest.

Singh *et al.* (2004) conducted 'A Study on Working and Impact of Rural SHGs in Hisar District of Hariyana'. The objective of the study was to improve the standard of living of rural SHG members through micro credit. The study concluded that the members did not mind paying a high rate of interest of twenty four per cent per annum to the groups which borrowed from the banks at twelve per cent rate of interest. Earnings from the members were deposited in the bank at a higher interest rate or distributed among the members of the group on repayment of bank loan.

Chandrakavate (2006) in her study on 'The SHG Model of Micro Finance: A Silent Movement towards Empowering Women' had analysed the SHG model of micro finance and found that the linkage of SHGs with bank had brought many changes such as: increased savings, access to credit, regular repayment of loans, commercialisation of economic link and change in attitude and the life styles of poor women. But the impact of micro financing on the income, employment and standard of living of their members was marginal.

Gangaiah *et al.* (2006) conducted a primary study on 17 SHG groups at Karkambadi Village, in Renigunta Mandal of Chittoor District during the month of December 2005, focusing on the 'Impact of Self-Help Groups on Income and Employment in Rural Areas'. The study observed that the number of SHGs is substantially increasing and that they were able to mobilise and manage thrift. The groups also generated awareness among rural women about government development programmes, transformation of social outlook, sense of equality of status of women as participants in decision-making and becoming beneficiaries in the democratic, economic and social spheres of life.

Gupta and Gupta (2006) attempted to study the functioning of three SHGs formed under a project started at Chandigarh by Punjab Engineering College to analyse the 'Economic Empowerment of Women Through Self-Help Groups'. The study had revealed that the organized working of the women through these SHGs had increased the income of the families involved. Most of them had been able to repay their old debts and started asset building. The enterprises run by the SHGs had been better managed. These SHGs had not only improved the economic status of the women but there had also been a drastic change in their social status. Positive changes in the socio economic status would be the crux for better financial performance.

Functions and Performance of SHGs

Thrift and credit activities had emerged as driving force to mobilise the members in groups. The below studies proved that linking the SHGs with the banks would become financially self-sustainable.

Puhazhendi (1995) in his study on 'Transaction Cost of Lending to the Rural Poor' analysed 19 SHGs and five bank branches in Karnataka and Tamil Nadu and had concluded that the intermediation of SHGs reduced the time spent by bank personnel in identification of borrowers, documentation, follow up and recoveries effecting forty per cent reduction in the transaction cost of banks as compared to direct lending to individual borrowers. The transaction cost of borrowers was reduced by eighty five per cent.

Indian Bank (1995) had conducted a study on 'Performance of Indian Bank Branches in SHG Lending' in Tamil Nadu, covering 45 branches of their bank and 101 SHGs. The study examined only the transaction cost of the branches under different models for credit delivered for medium team loans upto ₹ 25,000. It concluded that lending to SHGs, with NGOs acting as non-financial intermediary, resulted in saving of transaction cost to the extent of forty five per cent as compared to lending under government sponsored programmes and other direct lending projects.

Girija and Satish (1999) in their study on the 'Impact of SHG Lending on the Profitability of Branches' found that the SHG lending constituted more than five per cent of the loan portfolio. They concluded that lending to SHGs and NGOs carried the least cost when compared with other models of lending. Lending to the SHGs reduced the cost by eighty five per cent and through a federation, reduced the cost by ninety five per cent as compared to direct lending. The default risk was negligible in the case of lending to SHGs and NGOs/ Federations.

Shylendra (1999) in his study on 'Micro Finance and Self-Help Groups', made an attempt to explore and understand the functioning and performance of the SHGs promoted by two leading NGOs namely: Self-Employed Women's Association (SEWA) and Agha Khan Rural Support Programme (AKRSP) in Gujarat. Both the NGOs had implemented the concept of SHGs in a fairly successful manner. The study had revealed that SHGs were capable of playing an effective role as financial intermediaries for the poor. Besides helping members in mobilising funds, SHGs had also been able to tap external funds to meet the credit requirements of their members. The members opined that their SHGs had been much superior to other sources of credit both for formal and informal. The SHGs of both SEWA and AKRSP had attained higher loan recovery rates. In general, the study had proved that the SHGs could serve as an alternative instrument of financial intermediation for the poor and NGOs can certainly play a major role in making their promotion successful by ensuring the presence of elements critical to the success of SHGs.

Modekey (1999) in his article 'SHGs and Micro Credit: Sustaining Rural Women' observed that: *(i)* the SHGs usually generated a common fund out of small savings from persons or groups collected on a regular basis by curtailing unproductive expenditure. The internal savings thus generated were supplemented by external resources or donated by voluntary agencies involved in promoting and strengthening the SHGs; *(ii)* the credit needs of the members were usually assessed at monthly meetings; and *(iii)* the SHGs collectively ensured repayment of bank loans. Thus, the SHGs had been a tool for providing access to credit for the poor and the transaction cost was also low for the banks.

The National Bank For Agriculture and Rural Development (NABARD, 2000) conducted a study on the 'Impact of Micro Finance on the Living Standards of SHG members'. The study aimed at finding out how far the SHG Bank Linkage Programme had lightened the life burden for the average member of SHG and to analyse the betterment of household by gaining access to micro finance. The study covered 560 SHG member households from 223 SHGs spread over 11 states and showed positive results. There were perceptible and wholesome changes in the living standards of the SHG members, in terms of ownership of assets, increase in savings and borrowing capacity, income generating activities and income levels. The study revealed that almost all the members developed saving habits in the post-SHG situation as against twenty three per cent of households who had this habit earlier and the average borrowings per year of the household increased from ₹ 4,282 to ₹ 8,341. The study concluded that the involvement in the group significantly contributed in improving the self-confidence of the members. The feelings of self-worth and communication with others improved after their association with the SHGs and the members were relatively more assertive in confronting social evils and problematic situations. As a result, there was a fall in incidence of family violence.

Jain (2000) in his study on 'Empowerment of Women through NGOs – The SEWA Bank Experience' observed that the bank (SEWA) had been providing banking services to the poor, illiterate, self-employed women and had become a viable financial venture. The case study revealed that there were 67,113 women depositors with a working capital of ₹ 1,916.72 lakh in 1966. It further observed that the banks helped the women to acquire skills to make new products and identify work opportunities. It was also found that the repayment rate had been excellent, which was between ninety three and ninety six per cent due to close monitoring by the bank and the link between the bank and the village groups. The conclusion was that from the women's point of view, their involvement in group activities and ownership of a successful institution enhanced their collective strength and empowerment that came with organization. From a wider perspective, member-owned controlled micro credit institution could help to strengthen the country's democratic system.

Manimekalai (2000) in her study on 'NGO's Intervention through Micro Credit for Self-Help Women Groups in Rural Tamil Nadu' had attempted to analyse the working of the Society for Education, Village Action and Improvement (SEVAI) in empowering women and the rural poor through micro credit. The objectives of the study were to find out the characteristics and working of the micro credit institution namely: Villuthukal. This was a bank established for the benefit of SHGs to assist them by extending micro credit and to highlight the strategies adopted to mobilise the women to form SHGs. The study was based on primary and secondary data. The secondary data were collected from 70 women who were the members and who had availed credit from the bank. The analysis of the study revealed that the women in rural areas were really longing for supplementary income and the intervention through micro credit was a boon to them. The study also proved that, after the micro credit and intervention of SEVAI, the education of the children had been better cared for and the women beneficiary households were able to manage the budget without deficit. The study concluded with the suggestion that micro credit strategies could be followed by other institutions working for the upliftment of women and could prove that micro credit would be instrumental in realising the proposed objectives.

Nagayya (2000) in his article 'An Informal Arrangement for Credit Supply to the Poor through SHGs' has expressed that an informal arrangement for credit supply to the poor through SHGs is fast emerging as a promising tool for promoting income-generating enterprises. He reviewed the initiatives taken at the national level with a view to promote institutional arrangements to support this programme for alleviation of poverty among the poor, with focus on women. He maintained that NABARD and SIDBI were playing a prominent role at various stages of implementation of this programme. There are other national level bodies also supporting NGO's/Village Administrators (VAs), *viz;* Rashtriya Mahila Kosh (RMK), Rashtriya Gramin Vikas Nidhi (RGVN) etc. He called for an imperative need to enlarge the coverage of SHGs in advance portfolio of banks as part of their corporate strategy, to recognise perceived benefits of SHGs financing in terms of reduced default risk and transaction cost.

Malhotra (2000) in his study on 'Women and Empowerment – Approaches and Strategies' covered 174 women beneficiaries, in Rai Bareilly of the state of Uttar Pradesh, drawn and covered randomly from formal agencies of credit *i.e.* Commercial Banks,

Regional Rural Banks and the Primary Agricultural Co-operative Societies. The study revealed that less than half per cent of female population against 3.50 per cent of male population in the study area had been the clients of the banks. Furthermore, only 7.64 per cent of the total number of cases financed and only 6.96 per cent of the total quantum of credit extended have gone to women. It has also been observed that though eighty three per cent of loans have been availed by women, male members were primarily responsible for the end use of credit.

Dasgupta (2000) in his study 'Micro Finance in India: Empirical Evidence, Alternative Models and Policy Imperatives' had expressed that micro financing through informal group approach had effected quite a few benefits *viz*:

(i) Savings were mobilised by the poor.

(ii) Access to the required amount of appropriate credit by the poor.

(iii) Matching the demand and supply of credit structure and opening new market for Financial Institutions (FI's).

(iv) Reduction in transaction cost for both lenders and borrowers.

(v) Tremendous improvement in recovery.

(vi) Heralding a new realisation of subsidy and corruption less credit.

(vii) Remarkable empowerment of poor women.

He stressed that SHGs should be considered as one of the best means to counter social and financial problems of the poor.

Barbara and Mahanta (2001) in their study on 'Micro Enterprises for Income-Generation' indicated that the SHGs have helped to set up a number of micro enterprises for income-generation. Rastriya Gramin Vikas Nidhi's credit and saving programme in Assam had been found successful as its focus is exclusively on the rural poor. It adopted a credit delivery system designed specially for them with the support of a specially trained staff and a supportive policy with no political intervention at any stage in the implementation of the programme.

Singh (2001) in his study on 'Bank Performance Improvement in Uttar Pradesh Rural Credit Project' highlighted that the SHGs is now functioning in place of moneylenders because loan could be taken at any time as and when needed for any purpose. There are no formalities involved and the transaction cost is low.

Choudhury *et al.* (2001) conducted a study to document the experience of SHGs in promoting micro enterprises through micro credit interventions and the efficacy of Self-Help Promoting Institutions (SHPI) in 'Micro Credit for Micro Enterprises'. The study analysed the core issue of poverty reduction and efficacy of SHGs route for micro enterprise promotion. The main objectives of the study were to analyse the operating system in SHGs, to explore the effectiveness of SHGs in identifying the micro enterprises and to suggest appropriate policy intervention for effective performance of SHGs. The study was carried out in selected cluster spread over regions in the states of Tamil Nadu, Karnataka, Andhra Pradesh and Maharashtra. The study covered 76 SHGs, 450 members and 135 micro entrepreneurs from five regions. It was observed that group enterprises on a big scale would involve greater risks but would yield better returns to the entrepreneurs. The study revealed the fact that, out of three SHPIs namely: NGOs, banks and government, NGOs were better equipped for capacity building of SHGs and promotion of micro enterprises. The study also showed that SHGs were still in a state of flux and their sustainable development depended on a number of factors which were internal and external to the organization.

Namboodiri and Shiyani (2001) conducted a study on 'Potential Role of SHGs in Rural Financial Deepening' to find out the basic features and financial operations of SHGs promoted by both SHPI and NGOs served by the Panchmahals Vadodara Grameen Bank (PVGB). A sample of five branches of PVGB was selected, out of which three were located in Dahod district and two in Panchmahals district of Gujarat state. The main findings that emerged from this study were that, while the percentage of women groups promoted by the

SHPI was fifty two per cent, it was as high as eighty four per cent for those promoted by the NGOs. The percentage of SHGs linked by the SHPI was sixty five per cent and that of NGO was forty two per cent. The average amount advanced to SHGs varied from ₹ 7,000 to ₹ 30,000 for those promoted by the NGOs. The SHGs that were promoted by the NGOs had a better saving performance compared to that of SHPI, in terms of amount saved per SHGs as well as in terms of credit savings ratio. The repayment performance of the SHGs promoted by the SHPI was superior to that of NGOs.

Dadhich (2001) conducted a study on 'Micro Finance – A Panacea for Poverty Alleviation: A Case Study of Oriental Grameen Project in India' for assessing the benefit of the project and economic viability. Out of a total 450 SHGs covered by the project, 447 were women groups and only three were men SHGs. The main findings of the study indicated that a large number of women had taken up subsidiary occupation and consequently their family incomes had substantially increased. An analysis of figures relating to income and expenditure of a specialised micro credit branch revealed that the branch had become a profit centre right from the second year of its operation. There was 100 per cent recovery of loan. The study also revealed that the borrowers under Oriental Bank Grameen Project had both the advantages of fine rate of interest, as well as hassle free credit, whereas their counterparts elsewhere were paying exorbitant rates of interest.

Satish (2001) in his study on 'Some Issues in the Formation of Self-Help Groups' made an attempt to answer the following questions:

(i) Are there a large number of pre existing groups in the rural areas and if so can they evolve into suitable SHGs?

(ii) Are the really poor accepted as members of SHGs?

(iii) What are the processes in SHG formation?

(iv) Do the SHGs face resistance at the time of their formation. If so how has the resistance been overcome?

This study covered groups formed by the NGOs and banks. The number of groups formed by the NGOs and banks were five and four respectively in Karnataka, four and nil in Maharashtra and seven and two in Uttar Pradesh. These groups had constituted the sample and the study was based on the secondary data, collected over the period from 1997 to 2000 from the Bankers Institute of Rural Development (BIRD), Lucknow. The study revealed that several SHGs included very poor members and the process of SHG formation had to be systematic whether it was formed by a bank or an NGO. It also observed that most of the SHGs had faced initial resistance in their efforts. The study concluded that the NGOs were more suited for forming and nurturing the SHGs.

The National Institute of Bank Management (NIBM) (2001) had studied SHGs in four districts in Maharashtra promoted under 'Maharashtra Rural Credit Project (MRCP)'. The study observed that sixty nine per cent of the groups were of the size 11-20, in which fifty per cent of the members were illiterate. The study further observed that fifty five per cent of the office bearers had at least a secondary level of education. The study revealed that the average savings of the SHGs in MRCP was ₹ 24 per month per member. This rate was more for new groups than for the old groups. The study also found that the average amount of savings mobilised amounted to ₹ 10,658 per group and that the SHGs and MRCP had started lending their own thrift capital from the eighth month of their formation.

Kundu (2003) made an attempt to study the 'Sustainable Micro Finance through Self-Help Groups: A Case Study of Gurugon District'. The objectives of the study were to examine the characteristics and performance of SHGs and the major constraints in habiting the sustainability of the SHGs. The study concluded that the SHGs not only developed confidence in the rural poor but also cultivated the habit of thrift/saving and utilisation of collective wisdom to tackle their problems. If the rural poor were properly organized and given the proper set up, microfinancing as a supplement to the existing rural credit operations would help to ensure increased access to credit for them.

Srinivasan *et al.* (2004) made an attempt to study the 'Financial Performance of Rural and Urban Self-Help Groups' with the objective of analysing the comparative financial performance of rural and urban SHGs. The results of the study showed that the average total membership and the average total defaults were found to be higher in rural SHGs than in urban SHGs. The average thrift credit ratio of urban SHGs was lower than the rural SHGs which implies that the overall financial performance of the urban SHGs was better than the rural SHGs.

Soundarapandian (2006) had attempted to analyse the 'Role of Micro Finance in the growth of SHGs'. The specific objectives of the study were to study the growth and trend of the SHGs and micro finance in India and to review the problems faced by the micro entrepreneurship development in rural areas. Secondary data and primary data were used to analyse the role of micro finance for rural entrepreneurship development. As per the study, women SHGs mostly concentrated on powder preparation, tailoring, typewriting, milch animal rearing and fair price shops and were able to earn a considerable amount of income.

The objectives of Jerinabi's (2006) study on 'Micro Credit Management by Women's Self-Help Groups' was to initiate SHGs in the rural and urban areas, motivate the SHGs to undertake income-generating activities, availing micro credit facilities and to study the impact of the efforts of the SHGs in quantitative and qualitative dimensions. Accordingly 20 SHGs were formed in the Coimbatore Corporation slums (urban) and Karamadai Panchayat union (rural) and a total of 254 members initiated micro enterprises. The training programme *viz;* vocational skill training, preparation of simple business plans and credit management were given to the micro entrepreneurs. This action research had brought high perceptible changes in the working of the SHGs. A large number of women had taken up income-generating activities like: manufacturing food items, running dairy and grocery shops and adopting agricultural activities. Consequently, family incomes had substantially increased. Apart from the economic changes, tremendous social changes had also been evident in the project areas. Women had begun to command more respect, found due affection and a rightful place in the family. Their involvement in the family decisions had substantially enhanced. As a member of a group, woman had gained more confidence and power. An analysis of income mobility among the micro entrepreneurs disclosed that due to initiation of micro enterprises, they shifted from lower income bracket to higher income bracket indicating positive impact of micro credit on SHG members.

Pandey (2008) conducted a case study on 'Micro Financing: A Blessing for the Poor: A Case Study of Eastern Uttar Pradesh' in Eastern Uttar Pradesh with the objectives of examining the performance of micro financing in rural areas and to find out the role of SHGs in micro finance. The study covers the Varanasi, Jaunpur, Mau, Azamgarh, Gazipur, Balia and Gorakhpur districts of Uttar Pradesh. The data had been collected through random samples of 250 respondents, who had been members of SHGs in the aforesaid districts. The study revealed that 54 per cent of the respondents were satisfied with interest rate policy, 76 per cent with repayment policy and 68 per cent were satisfied with the consultation facility. It was observed that performance of micro finance is satisfactory in almost all districts but Varanasi, Gorakhpur, Azamgarh and Janupur had shown better performance in regard to micro finance.

Several studies of micro enterprises had brought home the fact that the profitability as well as viability of these enterprises can be greatly enhanced if they are provided access to credit at fair terms.

Empowerment of Women through SHGs

The efforts of empowering women were to help the SHG members to exercise their rights in decision-making at all levels both within and outside their households and to enable them to be equal partners in the society.

Prasad (1997) of the National Institute of Rural Development, Hyderabad carried out two case studies, one in Salem District of Tamil Nadu and another in Tribal Development

Project areas of Andhra Pradesh to understand the process of economic empowerment of women in her study on 'Women's Development Programme for Economic Empowerment'. In Salem district 11 blocks were covered under International Fund for Agricultural Development (IFAD) Programme. This project broadly envisaged empowering rural women by expanding their resources, improving access to credit, raising the level of awareness, providing better access to health and establishing a viable model for women's development.

The findings of the study revealed that the intermediate objective of social enhancement through group dynamics and bringing of rural women into the mainstream of credit delivery seemed to had been achieved with reasonable success. In Andhra Pradesh a case study on 'Thrift Society and Grain Bank for Economic Empowerment of Tribal Women' was conducted at Vampaliguda village, Srikakulam district. The main objective of this study was to improve the household food security and to promote sustainable self-reliance amongst the participant groups. The study observed that the making of women's societies responsible for construction of school buildings, check dams and satellite nurseries resulted in the capacity building of the women concerned. The long-term objective of inculcating the saving habit and building up of food security have, however, not been achieved.

Jain (2000) conducted a case study on 'Empowerment of Women through NGOs – The SEWA Bank Experience' and observed that the bank SEWA had been providing banking services to the poor, illiterate and self-employed women. The case study revealed that there were 67,113 women depositors with a working capital of ₹ 1916.72 lakh in 1966 and the banks had helped the women to acquire skills to make new products and to identify work opportunities. It has also found that the repayment rate had been excellent, (between 93 and 96%) due to close monitoring by the bank, the good link between the group leaders and borrowers and a constant communication between the bank and the village groups. The study had concluded that, from the women's point of view, their involvement and ownership of a successful institution had enhanced their collective strength and empowerment. From a wider perspective, member owned/controlled micro credit institution could help to strengthen the country's democratic system.

Mayoux (2000) has critically analysed fifteen case studies on 'Micro Finance and the Empowerment of Women – A Review of the Key Issues' and concluded that women's empowerment needs to be an integral part of policies. Empowerment cannot be assumed to be an automatic outcome of micro finance programmes, whether designed for financial sustainability or poverty alleviation. More research and innovation on conditions of micro finance delivery are needed. Cost effective ways of integrating micro finance with other empowerment interventions, including group development and complementary services were still lacking. Unless empowerment was an integral part of the planning process, the rapid expansion of micro finance is unlikely to make more than a limited contribution to empowerment.

Puhazhendi and Satyasai (2001) in their study on 'Economic and Social Empowerment of Rural Poor through Self-Help Groups' attempted to evaluate the performance of SHGs with special reference to social and economic empowerment. Primary data collected with the help of structured questionnaire from 560 sample households in 223 SHGs functioning in 11 states representing four different regions across the country formed the basis of the study. The findings of the study revealed that the SHGs as institutional arrangement could positively contribute to the economic and social empowerment of rural poor and the impact on the later was more pronouncing than on the former. Though there was no specific pattern in the performance of SHGs among different regions, the southern region could edge out other regions. The SHGs programme had been found more popular in the southern region and its progress in other regions is quite low, thus signifying an uneven achievement among the regions. Older groups had relatively more positive features like better performance than younger groups.

Manimekalai and Rajeswari (2001) had studied the 'Nature and Performance of Informal Self-Help Groups in Rural Areas of Tamil Nadu' taking 150 SHG members. They found that the SHGs helped to initiate micro enterprises including farm and non-farm activities, trading and service units. It had been reported that there was a significant difference in the mean performance of the entrepreneurs based on their age, education and previous experience. The micro finance had facilitated the women to have economic and social empowerment, a sense of leadership, organizational skill and management of various activities of a business, right to obtain finance, identifying raw materials, marketing etc., by themselves.

Sharma (2001) in his study on 'Women Self-Help Groups and Empowerment' viewed that SHGs are a means for women empowerment. Their participation in the economic activities and decision-making at the household and society level is increasing and making the process of rural development participatory, democratic, sustainable and independent of subsidy. Thus, microfinancing through SHGs is contributing to the development of the rural people in a meaningful way.

The objective of the Madheswaran and Dharmadhikary's (2001) study on 'Empowering Rural Women through SHGs: Lessons from Maharashtra Rural Credit Project' was to examine the SHG mechanism of the micro credit scheme as an effective and financially viable tool in channelising credit to the rural poor. In this study an attempt had been made to analyse the impact of SHGs in providing credit to rural women, to help them uplift their economic status. The analysis was based on a survey of three villages of Pune district, conducted during 1999, where the Maharashtra Rural Credit Programme was being implemented. The study revealed that the Maharashtra Rural Credit Programme was successful to some extent in its objective due to a combination of factors such as: *(i)* SHG-Bank linkage; *(ii)* credit being made available for consumption purposes; *(iii)* easy and periodic availability of credit due to rotation of savings; and *(iv)* active participation of the NGOs. The study further revealed that peer monitoring could be used as a channel to provide credit at a low transaction cost which in turn frequently reduces the rural poverty. The study concluded that micro credit should be used to meet the current demands of the rural women and this should lead to gradual improvement in the quality of their life and would enable them to identify activities for economic betterment.

Lalitha and Nagarajan (2002) conducted a critical study on the 'Functioning of the SHGs in Selected Districts of Tamil Nadu'. The study had undertaken to document the efforts of NGOs in promoting SHGs. The objectives of the study were to trace the structure and modalities of the SHGs, study the functioning of the SHGs, examine the role of SHGs in empowerment of women, investigate the group dynamics of SHGs, identify the factors which contributed to the success/failure of the groups and study the income-generating programmes promoted by SHGs. The study was based on multistage sampling technique and it had been carried out in three districts. NGOs who had organized SHGs for more than four years had been identified. Out of the 14 institutions, nine NGOs had been selected and two SHGs from each NGO had been selected on the basis of non-proportionate random sampling method. The study had been based on survey method and had covered both primary and secondary data. The study had highlighted the facts that SHGs are people's institutions and with their support, the women could march towards empowerment and that the groups could promote individual and group ventures of income generating activities under the effective guidance of NGOs. The study also revealed that effective leadership, group cohesiveness, savings, regular meetings, peer group pressure, linkage with other institutions and effective supervision by the NGOs had been the factors which contributed to the success of the groups.

Dwarakanath (2002) had analysed the 'Rural Credit and Women Self-Help Groups – A Profile of Ranga Reddy District in Andhra Pradesh' and found that the SHGs using the loan facilities from the Co-operative Credit Banks, Commercial Banks, Mahila Bank and Maheswaran Banks had produced more than 50 varieties of products. Among them, the brass items, hosiery, candles, carpets, coir items and pickles have been important products. In addition, the study had observed that the women groups had started to educate their own group members as they realised the importance and significance of literacy, while a lot of enthusiasm had been generated and the SHGs had a greater vision in empowerment of rural women and for overall human development.

Anand (2002) had made an exploratory study of the 'Self-Help Groups in Empowering Women: Case Study of Selected SHGs and NHGs' to examine the 'Impact of SHGs as micro credit programme on women empowerment'. The study revealed that the leaders who got re elected repeatedly seem to have got the most 'empowerment' and 'benefit'. Though not undesirable, confinement of empowerment to themselves also had given them the opportunity to dominate others in the group. Unless the group leaders educate the entire team to manage the group and maintain accounts and other records of the group, it may lead to lop sided empowerment.

Rani *et al.* (2002) had undertaken a study to evaluate the social status of women in house management, their leadership qualities, health and sanitation and economic status after participation in the SHGs in their research on 'SHGs Micro Credit and Empowerment'. Out of 600 SHGs established by Padmavathi Mahila Mandal, Tirupati, Andhra Pradesh, 50 SHGs were randomly selected for the study. From each group two women members were selected randomly. The study was based on primary data and a specially designed rating scale was administered to the sample to collect the information. The findings of the study revealed that, in all the four aspects there was positive correlation between the women's educational status and empowerment. The study observed that the participation in SHGs enhanced the empowerment of women in these four aspects and the self-confidence among the women increased. Their decision-making power also had a welcome change during the period of participation.

Rasure (2002) made an attempt to study the 'Empowerment of Women through SHGs'. The objectives of the study were to shape their social activities and voluntary organizations for taking up the cause of women's just rights and to fight against corruption in the implementation of different government schemes in the development of villages. To develop women's awareness in health, hygiene and nutrition, necessary training should be given. The study concluded that the micro finance through SHGs covered all uncovered groups with credit and in the process could help borrowers to come out of the vicious circle of poverty.

Puhazhendi and Badatya (2002) assessed the 'Impact of the SHG Bank-Linkage Programme of NABARD, in three Eastern Districts in the States of Orissa, Jharkhand and Chattisgarh'. It had covered the following aspects: *(i)* structure and performance assessment of SHGs promoted under the SHG Bank Linkage Programme; *(ii)* quantification of the changes in the savings and borrowing patterns amongst group members; *(iii)* impact of the programme on the income and employment of members; and *(iv)* changes in the social conditions of member households as a result of their involvement in the SHGs. The scheduled castes, scheduled tribes and backward classes have constituted eighty three per cent of the sample covered during the study. The main findings of the study were: *(i)* different types of saving products enhanced savings of the members in the groups; *(ii)* the average loan per SHG member had been 123 per cent, higher than the pre-SHG situation; *(iii)* in the post-SHG situation, consumption oriented loans had been replaced by production oriented loans, mainly due to the skill training provided through the SHGs; *(iv)* recovery performance from members to SHGs had been ninety five per cent whereas it had been 86.60 per cent from SHGs to the banks; and *(v)* the empowerment per sample household had increased between the pre and post SHG situations. Social empowerment of SHG members had improved significantly in terms of self-confidence, involvement in decision-making and better communication.

Vyas's (2003) research on 'Influence of Micro Finance Programme of SEWA Bank in India on Women's Financial Decision-Making within the Household' had confirmed that clients had gained from programme membership and improved their knowledge, skill, attitude and decision-making power in matters of finance.

Singh and Singh (2003) in their study on 'Economic Participation of Rural Women in Informal Sector through Self-Help Group' reported that the only best solution for improving the present pitiable position of women is the formation of SHGs by women themselves, thereby making them economically self-reliant and allowing them to take their own decisions independently. The strength of SHGs is based on the fact that people who are facing problems are likely to be committed to solving them. The authors have concluded that the economic participation of women through SHGs will *(i)* enhance women's confidence and decision-making ability; *(ii)* develop in them leadership qualities; *(iii)* help them control and manage resources available to them *(iv)* improve their inter personal relationship and *(v)* help women counter their unequal context and improve the quality of their lives on several fronts.

Lal (2005) in her article 'Information Technology Initiatives: Impact on Self-Help Groups in India' had reported that the systematic linkages of informal and formal systems had been created by intermediary organizations like the NGOs. The SHGs had been further federated to tackle higher order functions in order to improve their functioning. The SHGs had created critical self-awareness, solidarity and self-confidence. The collective initiatives had enhanced in their risk taking ability, appreciation of micro enterprises, management and survival strategies. The SHG intermediation had become relevant more for the concept of women empowerment than for mere poverty alleviation.

Panda (2005) had conducted a study on 'Women's Empowerment through SHG Revolution in Orissa: An Analysis through Case Studies' by taking six SHGs from Keonjbar and Mayurbhanj districts of Orissa covering all 102 SHG members by following a three stage stratified sampling and delphi technique. The study was conducted to assess the empowerment of SHGs based on the linkage with other institutions, organizations and individuals. The study clearly showed that the SHG concept not only provided financial services to the rural poor but also acted as a launching pad for livelihood intervention, proper capacity building and linkage of SHGs to mainstream organizations that have really succeeded in poverty alleviation and social upliftment.

Revathi and Sumathi (2006) in their study on 'Self-Help Groups Promote Growth' analysed the working of SHGs in Trichy District covering 50 SHGs had revealed the following results: *(i)* ninety five per cent of the members had been in the age group of 25 to 45 years; savings per member had been around ₹ 50 per month *(ii)* nearly fifty per cent of the members had belonged to the most backward class; *(iii)* fifty per cent of the members had been below poverty line; *(iv)* loans taken had been used for dairy activities; and *(v)* loan repayment had been nearly hundred per cent. The major implications of the study had been that women get empowered through the SHGs; the annual average savings had increased and they have played an active role in getting loans and handling cash effectively.

Gaiha and Nandhi (2007) had conducted a study on 'Micro Finance, Self-Help Group and Empowerment in Maharashtra' to assess the benefits of micro finance through SHGs and to assess some key dimensions of women's empowerment. The study is based on primary data collected from six villages in Pune District in Maharashtra *viz;* Fursungi, Fulgaon, Zargadwadi, Dorlewadi, Godre and Botarde. After selection of villages, a list of SHGs in these villages was obtained. From the members' list, a random selection of participants who had availed of at least one loan was made. Thus, from each village, 12 participants were interviewed. Non participants were also randomly picked from these villages making sure that Scheduled Castes and Scheduled Tribes (SCs/STs) and other deprived groups were included. Altogether, 24 non-participants four from each village constituted the control group. The study revealed that empowerment was corroborated by different sources in varying degrees. The members were empowered in terms of greater self-confidence, assertive role in domestic sphere, greater respect for family, more assertive role in children's health and education, reduction in domestic violence, greater participation in community affairs, more active participation in Panchayats, increased self-confidence to improve family and community lives, better buying and selling skills, better prices for products, independent marketing and better agricultural practices.

The various studies enumerated above covered various dimensions. Based on the literature reviewed and inference drawn by an in-depth study, the researcher found that the earlier studies had not concentrated much on the impact of the micro finance on rural women. This research gap made the researcher analyse the 'Microfinancing of Rural Women through SHG and Bank Linkage (A Study in Coimbatore District of Tamil Nadu)'.

3 METHODOLOGY

A systematic and careful analysis of information is inevitable in any research. In order to obtain reliable results, it is essential to evolve scientific method of data collection and apply appropriate and reliable techniques for the analysis of information. The methodology followed in the current study was discussed under the following heads:

- Locale of the Study Area.
- Profile of the Study Area.
- Selection of the Sample Self-Help Groups (SHGs) and Sample Members.
- Period of the Study and Collection of Data.
- Tools for Analysis.

Locale of the Study Area

The present study was confined to the selected group of rural SHGs and the members in the Coimbatore District of Tamil Nadu.

Till recently women under rural groups were not able to actively participate in income-generating activities. There is an urgent and basic necessity to take agent oriented approach to women. National Bank for Agriculture and Rural Development (NABARD) had pioneered the concept and implemented the

SHG-Bank Linkage Programme since 1992 for providing easy access of institutional credit to the rural poor. According to the NABARD Report (2008), over 90 per cent of the bank linked groups were women groups and about 80 per cent were situated in rural areas, a traditionally under served area. The Census Report (2001) indicated that 58.33 per cent of the rural female population in Coimbatore District are non-workers, consisting of aged persons, housewives, children and people engaged in their personal service. Coimbatore district was one of the districts in Tamil Nadu implementing more number of SHG-Bank Linkage Programme among rural women. Hence the researcher had selected rural areas of Coimbatore district to analyse the "Microfinancing of Rural Women through SHG and Bank Linkage (A Study in Coimbatore District of Tamil Nadu)".

Profile of the Study Area

The Coimbatore city is situated on the banks of the river Noyyal. Coimbatore existed even prior to the second century A. D., as a small tribal village capital called Kongunad until it was brought under Chola control in the 2nd or 3rd century A. D., by Karikalan, the first of the early Cholas. The other great rulers of this city were the Rashtrakuttas, Chalukyas, Pandyas, Hoysalas and the Vijayanagara kings. The small village was also named as 'Covanputhur' after the leader of the local group, whose name was 'Covan'. According to the 'Cholan Poorva Pattayam' in the Madras Oriented Manuscript Library, Covanputhur later changed to Coimbatore. When Kongunad fell to the British along with the rest of the state, its name was changed to Coimbatore and it is by this name that it is known even today, except in Tamil, in which it is called Kovai. Surrounded by the fairy queen Nilgiris, the blue hills, in the north, the western ghats of Kerala in the west and the tobacco and vegetable Dindigul District in the east, there lies Coimbatore, the highly progressive, entrepreneurial and commercial District of Tamil Nadu. The District lies between 10-10 and 11-30 northern latitude and 76-40 and 77-30 eastern longitude with salubrious climate throughout the year. The selected district of Coimbatore in Tamil Nadu is given in Figure 3.1.

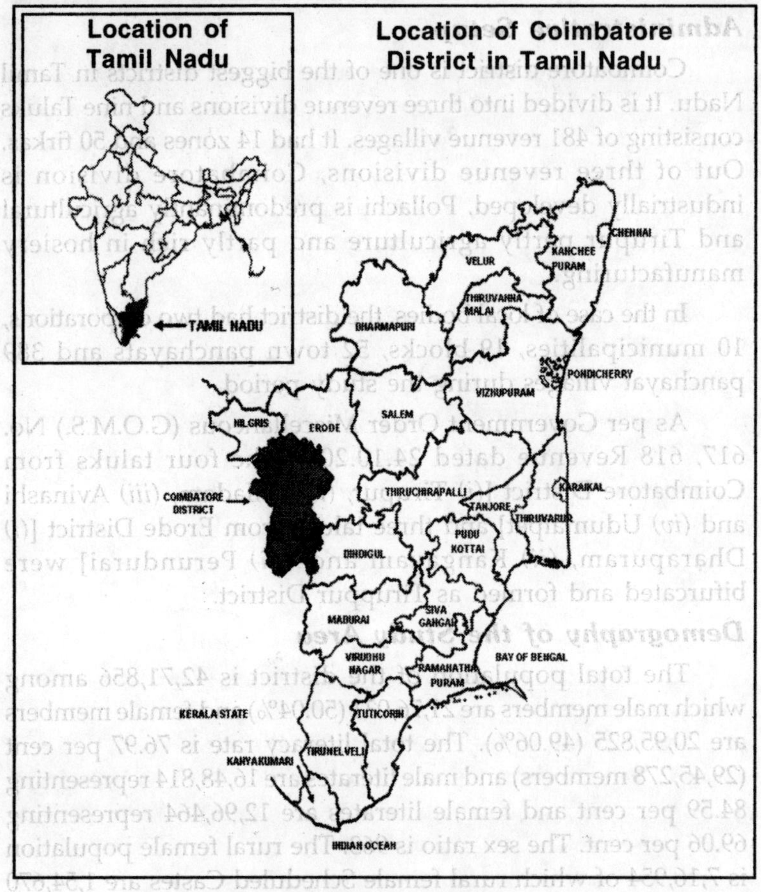

Fig. 3.1: Coimbatore District in Tamil Nadu

The profile of the district was discussed under the following headings:

- Administrative Set-up.
- Demography of the Study Area.
- Banking Institutions.
- Industries.
- Economy.
- Performance of SHG-Bank Linkage Programme in Coimbatore District.

Administrative Setup

Coimbatore district is one of the biggest districts in Tamil Nadu. It is divided into three revenue divisions and nine Taluks consisting of 481 revenue villages. It had 14 zones and 50 firkas. Out of three revenue divisions, Coimbatore division is industrially developed, Pollachi is predominantly agricultural and Tirupur partly agriculture and partly rich in hosiery manufacturing.

In the case of local bodies, the district had two corporations, 10 municipalities, 19 blocks, 52 town panchayats and 389 panchayat villages during the study period.

As per Government Order Miscellaneous (G.O.M.S.) No. 617, 618 Revenue dated 24.10.2008, the four taluks from Coimbatore District [*(i)* Tirupur, *(ii)* Palladam, *(iii)* Avinashi and *(iv)* Udumalpet] and three taluks from Erode District [*(i)* Dharapuram, *(ii)* Kangayam and *(iii)* Perundurai] were bifurcated and formed as Tiruppur District.

Demography of the Study Area

The total population of the district is 42,71,856 among which male members are 21,76,031 (50.04%) and female members are 20,95,825 (49.06%). The total literacy rate is 76.97 per cent (29,45,278 members) and male literates are 16,48,814 representing 84.59 per cent and female literates are 12,96,464 representing 69.06 per cent. The sex ratio is 963. The rural female population is 7,16,954 of which rural female Scheduled Castes are 1,54,670 and rural female Scheduled Tribes are 9,880. Rural female literates are 3,53,339 and rural female workers are 2,98,733 (Census of India, 2001). The block wise demographic details are given in Table 3.1.

Banking Institutions

The district has 447 banks and 185 primary co-operative banks to provide banking facilities to the customers. The district has a good number of bank branches to provide SHG-Bank Linkage Programme. The commercial banks have ₹ 14,871.88 crore as deposits and advances of ₹ 24,129.11 crore

Table 3.1: Demographic Profile of the Coimbatore District

S. No.	Name of the Block/Municipality	Density (sq. km.)	Sex Ratio	Population (%)		Literacy Rate (%)		Population (%)	
1	2	3	4	5		6		7	
				Urban	Rural	Male	Female	S.C.	S.T.
1.	Anaimalai	400.59	998	75.0	25.0	56.8	43.1	19.0	0.72
2.	Annur	347.79	979	74.5	25.5	39.6	60.3	25.2	0.48
3.	Avinashi	428.58	966	75.9	24.1	39.5	60.4	21.1	0.06
4.	Gudimangalam	239.37	1000	73.6	26.4	58.4	41.5	23.4	1.76
5.	Karamadai	367.86	976	80.2	19.8	40.5	59.4	14.5	0.56
6.	Kinathukadavu	307.56	1014	75.6	24.4	57.2	42.7	19.0	0.72
7.	Madathukulam	422.08	986	77.6	22.4	57.6	42.3	23.8	0.01
8.	Madukkarai	1023.98	969	86.3	18.2	55.3	44.6	16.1	1.90
9.	Palladam	459.49	954	80.5	19.5	57.6	42.3	18.4	0.03
10.	Periya Naicken Palayam	605.86	952	75.7	24.3	55.5	44.4	10.8	1.60
11.	Pollachi (North)	675.67	989	83.2	16.8	57.8	42.1	21.6	0.48
12.	Pollachi (South)	540.93	974	81.1	18.9	57.9	42.0	20.3	0.17
13.	Pongalur	218.89	965	70.9	29.1	58.5	41.4	18.3	0.005

Contd...

1	2	3	4	5		6		7	
14.	Sarkar Sama Kulam	561.33	971	83.7	16.3	55.9	44.09	15.9	0.03
15.	Sulur	646.95	951	85.1	14.9	57.1	42.8	7.9	0.04
16.	Sultanpet	234.19	893	74.6	25.4	58.6	41.3	21.9	0.001
17.	Thondamuthur	353.26	976	80.9	19.1	56.1	43.9	18.2	5.90
18.	Udumalpet	243.19	985	81.6	18.4	57.9	42.0	54.3	0.86
19.	Tiruppur	2083.30	957	87.5	12.5	58.5	41.4	20.2	0.02
20.	Coimbatore Corporation	8815.17	948	100.0	100	54.1	45.8	8.3	0.05
21.	Mettupalayam (M)	9249.31	994	100.0	100	38.9	61.07	12.5	0.06
22.	Pollachi (M)	6371.00	988	100.0	100	53.9	46.0	11.7	0.01
23.	Tiruppur (M)	7616.89	914	100	100	56.7	43.2	5.7	0.09
24.	Udumalpet (M)	7294.38	1034	100	100	52.5	47.4	9.2	0.05

Source: Census of India, 2001.

M - Municipality

upto 2007-08 and the Co-operative Banks have ₹ 97.03 crore as deposits and ₹ 74.82 crore as advances. The District Central Co-operative Bank had given loan to 756 SHGs to the extent of ₹ 27.38 million and 7,414 SHGs were given loan to the extent of ₹ 5,492.10 crore by the Commercial Banks as on 31st March 2008. The following banks are engaged in SHG credit linkage programme. (Table 3.2)

Table 3.2:

S. No.	Public Sector Banks	Private Sector Banks	Co-operative Banks
1.	Allahabad Bank	Dhanalakshmi Bank	Primary Co-operative Bank
2.	Andhra Bank	Karur Vysya Bank Ltd	Repco Bank
3.	Bank of Baroda	Lakshmi Vilas Bank Ltd	
4.	Bank of India	South Indian Bank Ltd	
5.	Canara Bank	Tamilnadu Mercantile Bank Ltd	
6.	Central Bank of India	HDFC Bank Ltd	
7.	Corporation Bank	ICICI Bank Ltd	
8.	Indian Bank		
9.	Indian Overseas Bank		
10.	Punjab National Bank		
11.	State Bank of India		
12.	Syndicate Bank		
13.	Union Bank of India		
14.	Vijaya Bank		

Industries

Industrial growth in Coimabtore has always been at the forefront. The State Government had created several organizations and institutions to provide infrastructural support to the private enterprises. Industrial estates have been set up by the Government, Small Industrial Development Corporation (SIDCO), Co-operatives and private persons.

Important industries in the district are Ancillary units, Cement, Dairy, Flourmill, Hosiery, Motor pumps, Paper, Sugar, Soya and Textile. There are 256 medium scale industries, 49,084 small scale industries and 7,500 cottage industries. Existence of these industries provides a good scope for starting micro enterprises in the district.

Economy

Coimbatore known as the 'Manchester of South India' has more than 50,000 small, medium and large scale industries and textile mills. Coimbatore is also famous for the manufacture of motor pump sets and varied engineering goods, due to which it has earned the title 'Detroit of the South'. The development of hydro-electricity from the Pykara falls in the 1930s led to a cotton boom in Coimbatore. The result has been a strong economy and a reputation as one of the greatest industrial cities in South India. Coimbatore is known for its technical manpower and innovative entrepreneurship. The city finds its place in the top bracket in rapid industrialisation and also as a booming trading place for manufacturers and investors.

Performance of SHG-Bank Linkage Programme in Coimbatore District

Under Mahalir Thittam Scheme 16,479 groups were linked with the banks as on 31.3.2008. Since the inception of this programme, loans to the extent of ₹ 14,016 lakh were given to 16,479 SHGs. In urban areas 1,265 SC/ST groups were given loans to the extent of ₹ 417.54 lakh and in rural areas 4,834 SC/ST groups were given loans to the extent of ₹ 1,937.05 lakh. Block wise credit linked groups are given in Table 3.3.

Selection of the Sample Self-Help Groups and Sample Members

In the first stage, a list of affiliated Non-Governmental Organizations (NGOs) engaged in the promotion of SHGs was obtained from Mahalir Thittam Office, Coimbatore. Out of the list, ten NOGs who act as a facilitator in the promotion of SHGs were identified and approached to get the details of SHGs. The selected NGOs are:

Table 3.3: Block Wise Distribution of SHGs in Coimbatore District (31st March 2008)

S. No.	Name of the Block	Number of SHGs Linked with the Banks
1.	Anaimalai	1,010
2.	Annur	928
3.	Avinashi	1,068
4.	Gudimangalam	771
5.	Karamadai	1,250
6.	Kinathukadavu	802
7.	Madathukulam	669
8.	Madukkarai	662
9.	Palladam	670
10.	Periya Naicken Palayam	882
11.	Pollachi (North)	882
12.	Pollachi (South)	896
13.	Pongalur	591
14.	Sarkar Sama Kulam	471
15.	Sulur	762
16.	Sulthanpet	707
17.	Thondamuthur	835
18.	Tirupur	1,122
19.	Udumalpet	1,501
	Total	**16,479**

Source: Mahalir Thittam Office, Coimbatore

1. Centre for Social Education and Development – Avinashi
2. Coimbatore Multipurpose Social Service Society – Coimbatore
3. Coimbatore Rural Development Association – Caltonpet, Coimbatore
4. Deepam Social Education Trust – Sulur

5. Foundation for Infrastructure Reconstruction and Employment – Sirumugai, Coimbatore
6. High Class Women Welfare Social Service – Anaimalai
7. Non-Conventional Energy and Rural Development (NERD) Society – Vadavalli, Coimbatore
8. Nesakkarangal – Udumalpet
9. Sri Avinashilingam Educational Trust – Coimbatore
10. Rural Extension Service Trust – Singanallur, Coimbatore

In the second stage, based on the information provided by the NGOs, 10 blocks were randomly selected in the district covering 50 per cent of blocks and is given below (Figure 3.2).

1. Anaimalai.
2. Annur.
3. Avinashi.
4. Gudimangalam.
5. Karamadai.
6. Madathukkulam.
7. Palladam.
8. Sulur.
9. Thondamuthur.
10. Udumalpet.

In the third stage six villages in each selected block were further identified randomly constituting 60 villages. In the fourth stage two SHGs with five years of experience as on 2007-08 had been identified from each selected village. Thus 120 SHGs were selected. To assess the impact of SHG-Bank Linkage Programme on women, five respondents engaged in income-generating activities, including one group leader, one representative and three ordinary members who were available at the time of data collection from each of the 120 sample SHGs were randomly selected. Thus the sample of 600 SHG members consists of 120 group leaders, 120 representatives and 360 members.

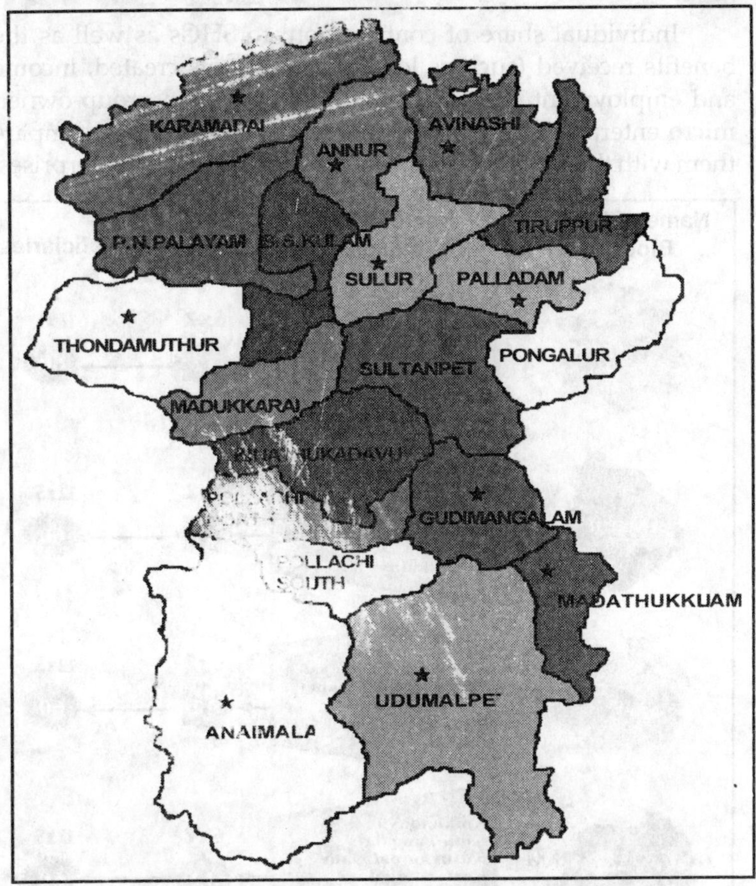

Fig. 3. 2: Selected Blocks in Coimbatore District

Among them, 333 members were engaged in group business and 267 members were engaged in individual business.

The analysis was carried out to study the performance of members engaged in Group-Owned Micro Enterprises (GOME) and Self-Owned Micro Enterprises (SOME). The coverage of the area and the sample size are given in Figure 3.10.

NGOs	Blocks	Villages	SHGs	Beneficiaries
10	10	Six in each block (10 x 6) 60 villages	Two from each village (60 x 2) 120 groups	Five from each groups (120 x 5) 600 members

Individual share of contribution[1] to SHGs as well as the benefits received (such as loan availed, assets created, income and employment generated) by the members in group-owned micro enterprises were taken into account in order to compare them with those of the members in self-owned micro enterprises.

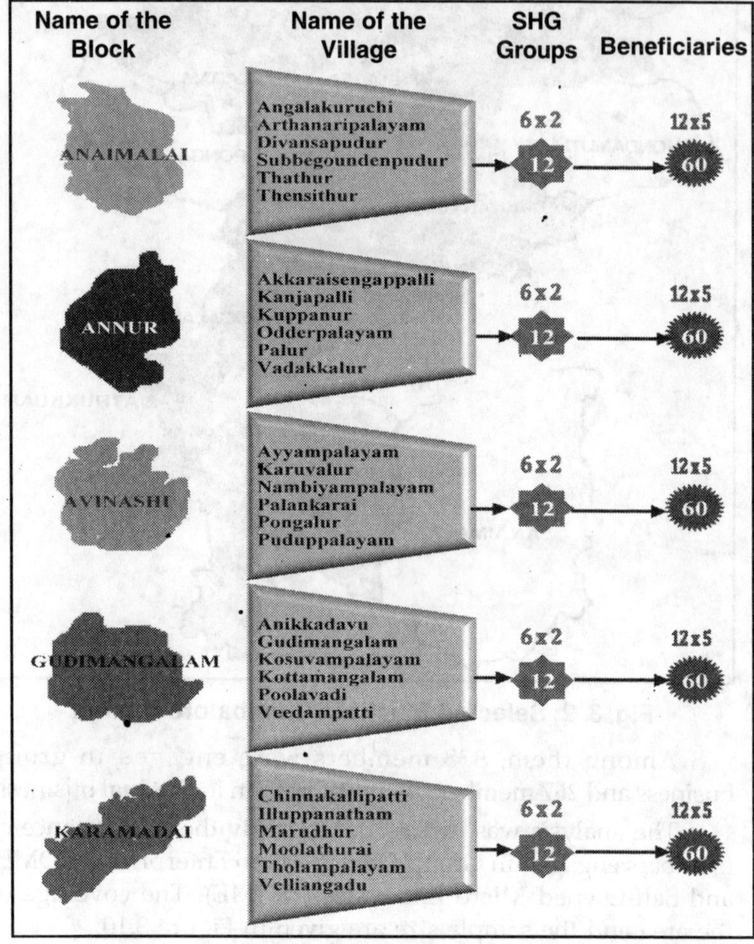

Fig. 3.3: Selected Villages and the Samples

1. The individual contribution of the members of the group is derived by dividing the total amount by the number of members in the group.

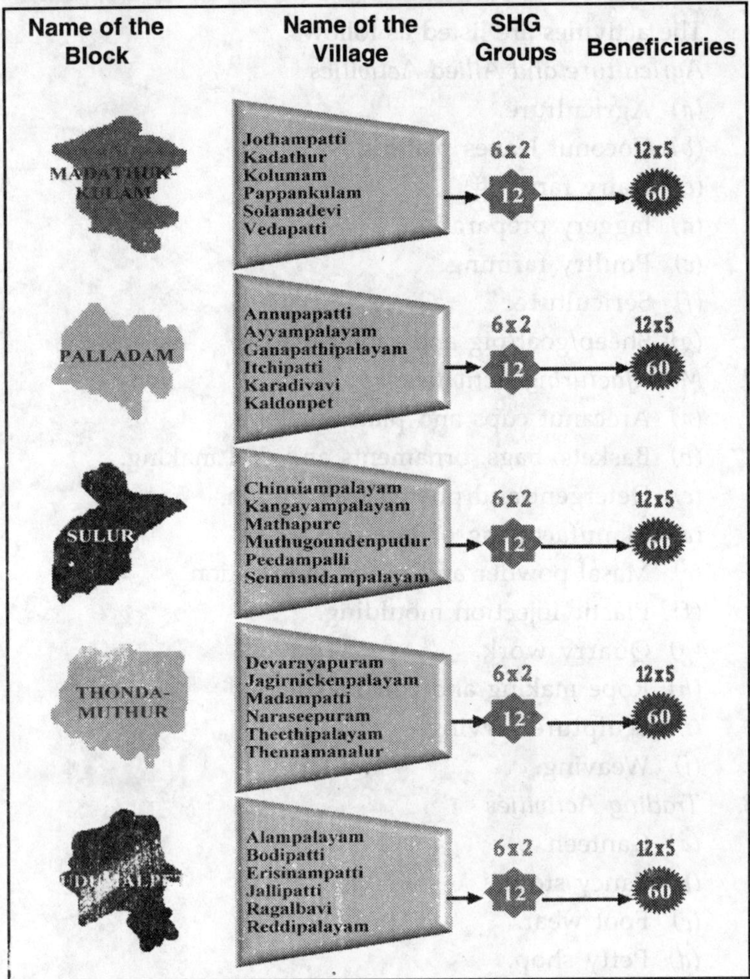

Fig. 3.4: Selected Villages and the Samples

Types of Micro Enterprises

Micro enterprises carried out by the SHG members were brought under four groups.

1. Agriculture and allied activities.
2. Manufacturing activities.
3. Trading activities.
4. Service activities.

The activities are listed as follows:

1. *Agriculture and Allied Activities*
   - (*a*) Agriculture.
   - (*b*) Coconut leaves plaiting.
   - (*c*) Dairy farming.
   - (*d*) Jaggery preparation.
   - (*e*) Poultry farming.
   - (*f*) Sericulture.
   - (*g*) Sheep/goat/pig and rabbit rearing.
2. *Manufacturing Activities*
   - (*a*) Arecanut cups and plates making.
   - (*b*) Baskets, bags, ornaments and doll making.
   - (*c*) Detergent and phenyl preparation.
   - (*d*) Manufacturing of hundials.
   - (*e*) Masal powder and pickle preparation.
   - (*f*) Plastic injection moulding.
   - (*g*) Quarry work.
   - (*h*) Rope making and coir making.
   - (*i*) Sculpture carving.
   - (*j*) Weaving.
3. *Trading Activities*
   - (*a*) Canteen.
   - (*b*) Fancy store.
   - (*c*) Foot wear.
   - (*d*) Petty shop.
   - (*e*) Provisional stores.
   - (*f*) Ration shop.
   - (*g*) Sale of cloth.
   - (*h*) Vegetables vending
4. *Service Activities*
   - (*a*) Beauty parlours.
   - (*b*) Boat service.
   - (*c*) Furniture and utensils lending to functions.

(d) Grinding.
(e) Laundry.
(f) Renting concrete machines.
(g) Tailoring.

Period of the Study and Collection of Data

Period of the Study

Period of the study was five years from 2003-04 to 2007-08.

Data Collection

To fulfill the objectives of the study both primary and secondary data were collected.

Primary Data

The primary data was collected from 600 respondents through a detailed, interview schedule-personally administered, observation from surveying the locality and from personal interviews.

Two interview schedules were prepared.

1. To collect information about the groups by contacting the group leaders/representatives.
2. To collect information from the members.

Schedules meant for groups contained questions related to structure, organization, governance of SHGs, management practices, financial management, savings and lending activities of the groups.

Schedule meant for members contained questions on the socio-economic background of the respondents, their position, participation in the group, training and experience, savings, loan details, income generating activities and impact of the micro finance on the socio-economic status of the members.

Secondary Data

The secondary data were collected from the records of SHGs, the annual reports and administrative guidelines of Coimbatore Mahalir Thittam Office, NGOs, Publications of RBI, NABARD, MFIs, District Statistical Office and also from the related books, journals and web sites.

Income-Generating Activities of SHG Members

Plaiting Coconut Leaves

Poultry Farming

Mat Preparation

Arecanut Plates and Cups Preparation

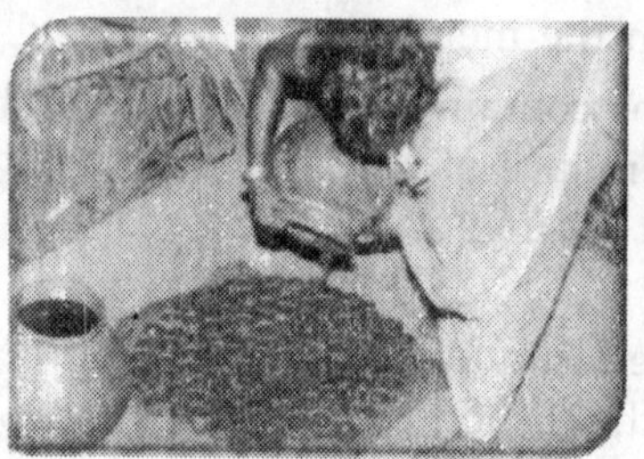

Jaggery Preparation

Amla Sales

Masala Powder Preparation

Snacks Preparation

Weaving - Handloom

Weaving - Power Loom

Plastic Injection Moulding

Quarry Work

Utensils Lending

Tailoring

Appalam Preparation

Cashew Nut Process

Plate 1

Pilot Study

The schedules were prepared and pre-tested through a pilot survey carried out on a sample of 12 groups and 60 members in six villages covering three blocks, during May and June 2007. Based on the pilot survey, the schedules were modified and the revised schedules were administered to the selected sample of the study.

Reference Period

As the study aims at analysing the impact of micro finance through SHG-Bank Linkage Programme on Rural Women in the pre and post SHG period, it was felt that, the reference period selected should be such that it would allow sufficient time for the programme to have its full impact on the economic conditions of the beneficiaries. Considering this, the reference period had been fixed as 2007-08. The members who had joined the SHGs during the year 2002-03 and started income-generating activities had been selected for the study. Therefore, the year 2003-04 had been considered as the base year to assess the pre-SHG position and the year 2007-08 as the reference period to assess the post SHG position.

The required data were collected through personal interview method from April 2008 to September 2008.

Data on various economic aspects like: asset structure, net income, savings, loans, investment patterns, employment patterns and social aspects such as: improvement in self-confidence, communication skills, behavioural changes, etc., were collected to assess the impact of the programme.

Tools for Analysis

To draw meaningful inferences, a sound methodology accompanied by appropriate tools and techniques of analysis was necessary. The statistical tools and techniques used in the analysis were:

- Summary statistics.
- Fixed index numbers.
- Compound growth rate.
- Ratio analysis.

Interviewing the SHG Members

Plate 2

- Garret ranking technique.
- Chi-square test.
- Factor analysis.
- Paired 't' test.
- 'z' test for proportions.
- Likert scaling technique.

Summary Statistics

Summary statistics like average, standard deviation and co-efficient of variation were used to analyse and compare the data in addition to frequencies and percentages.

Mean

Mean also known as arithmetic average is the most common measure of central tendency and may be defined as the value which is divided by the total of the value of various given items in a series by the total number of items.

$$\overline{X} = \frac{\Sigma x}{n}$$

Σx – Sum of values of all the items

n – Number of items

Standard Deviation

Standard deviation is the most widely used measure of dispersion of a series and is commonly denoted by the symbol " σ". It is calculated by applying the following formula.

$$\text{Standard deviation } (\sigma) = \sqrt{\frac{\Sigma (x - \overline{x})^2}{n}}$$

$\Sigma (x - \overline{x})^2$ = Sum of squares of deviation taken from arithmetic average number of items.

Co-efficient of Variation

Co-efficient of variation is a relative measure of dispersion. It is computed to compare the relative variation in savings. The Least co-efficient of variation implies greater consistency and higher co-efficient of variation implies greater disparity. Coefficient of variation was computed as follows:

$$\text{Co-efficient of variation} = \frac{\text{Standard deviation}}{\text{Arithmetic means}} \times 100$$

Fixed Index Numbers

To calculate the changes in savings, investments and income during the study period, index numbers were calculated by taking the initial year as the base year and the subsequent years were expressed as a percentage of the base year.

Compound Growth Rate

Compound growth rate was calculated to anlayse the annual growth rate of savings. The growth rate was calculated by using the following functional form.

$$Y = AB^{X}$$

where

Y = Dependent variable – Savings

X = Time period

A	=	Constant
B	=	Co-efficient of X
Growth rate	=	[Anti log (log B) - 1] x 100

Ratio Analysis

The following ratios were used for assessing the performance and financial viability of SHGs.

(i) Credit Saving Ratio

Credit saving ratio or velocity of internal lending is the product of total internal loans against total savings of the group and a high ratio shows better fund management practices of the group.

$$\text{Credit saving ratio} = \frac{\text{Average internal loans disbursed}}{\text{Average savings moblised}}$$

(ii) Recovery Index

The recovery index arrived at is as follows:

$$\text{Recovery index} = \frac{\text{Amount recovered}}{\text{Demand for recovered}} \times 100$$

(iii) Loan Saving Ratio

Loan saving ratio shows the net rotation of bank loans among members against the progressive savings of the group since its inception. A high ratio indicates the better accessibility of the groups to institutional funds.

$$\text{Loan saving ratio} = \frac{\text{Average bank loans}}{\text{Average savings moblised}}$$

(iv) Return on Investment

Return on investment is used to measure the performance of the SHGs.

$$\text{Return on investment} = \frac{\text{Net income}}{\text{Total investment}} \times 100$$

Garrett Ranking

Garrett ranking technique was used to find out the motivating factors in order of merit that led women to join SHGs. The sample respondents were asked to rank the given factors from 1-8, giving one to the highest motivating factor and eight to the least motivating factor. The given factors were as follows:

(i) Unemployment.
(ii) To mobilise savings.
(iii) To avail internal loans.
(iv) To avail bank loans.
(v) To develop socio-economic status.
(vi) NGOs encouragement.
(vii) To initiate income-generating activities.
(viii) To set off old debts.

The order of the merit as given by sample respondents were changed into per cent position by using the following formula:

$$\text{Percent position} = \frac{100\,(R_{ij} - 0.5)}{N_j}$$

where

R_{ij} – Is the rank given for the ith factor by the jth respondent

N^j – Number of factors ranked by j^{th} respondent

The per cent position of each rank thus obtained was converted into scores by referring to table given by Garrett (1969). For each factor the scores of individual sample respondents were added together and divided by the total number of sample respondents Based on these mean scores, ranks were assigned.

The mean scores of all the factors for the entire study group were arranged and the ranks were given for the analysis.

Chi-square Test

To establish the relationship between the nature of activity and the personal factors a chi-square test had been applied with the necessary hypothesis as under:

Ho - There has been no significant association between the choice of enterprises and the personal variables namely, age of the members, education, community, size of the family, occupation, annual income, marital status, education of the husband, employment of the husband, position of the member and period of membership.

Ha - There has been a significant association between the choice of enterprises and the personal variables.

$$x^2 = \sum \frac{(O_{ij} - E_{ij})^2}{E_{ij}}$$

where

O_{ij} = Observed frequency of the cell in ith row and j^{th} column

E_{ij} = Expected frequency of the cell in ith row and j^{th} column

The χ^2 values obtained as such should be compared with relevant table value of χ^2 and the inference could be drawn. If the calculated value is greater than the table value, the null hypothesis framed would be rejected, otherwise accepted.

Factor Analysis

To assess the impact of the training undergone by the members on the following factors, a factor analysis was carried out. The factors were X^1 – Confidence building; X^2 – Skill development; X^3 – Marketing linkage; X^4 – Bank linkage; X^5 – Linkage with Government Officials; X^6 – Knowledge on rights, entitlements and development programmes; X^7 – Managerial efficiency for micro enterprise development; X^8 – Enhanced income and savings; X^9 – Active participation in decision-making in family; X^{10} – Active participation in developmental programmes and X^{11} – Active participation in decision-making outside the family.

Factor analysis is a multivariate statistical technique used to condense and simplify the set of larger number of variables to smaller number of variables called factors. This technique is helpful to identify the underlying factors that determine the relationship between the observed variables and provides an empirical classification scheme of clustering of variables into groups called factors. The specific terms related to Factor Analysis are given below:

Factor

A factor is an underlying dimension that account for several observed variables. There can be one or more factors, depending upon the nature of the study and the number of variables involved in it.

Factor-loading

Factor-loading are those values which explain how closely the variables are related to each one of the factors discovered.

Communality (h^2)

Communality, symbolised as h^2, shows how much of each variable is accounted for by the underlying factor taken together. A high value of communality means that not much of the variable is left over after whatever the factors represent is taken into consideration.

Eigen Value or Latent Root

Eigen value is the sum of square values of factor loading relating to a factor. It indicates the relative importance of each in accounting for the particular set of variables under study.

Total Sum of Squares

When Eigen values of all factors are totalled, the resulting value is called the total of squares.

Rotation

Rotation is done (*i.e.,* a factor matrix is subjected to rotation) to attain what is technically called 'simple structure' in data. Factor scores represent the degree to which each respondent gets high scores on the growth of item that load high on each factor.

Paired 't' Test

Paired 't' test was applied to find out the significant changes in the selected variables of the members before and after SHG period.

The variables tested were:

1. Average annual income.
2. Savings.
3. Increase in the decision-making capacity.

Ho - There is no significant change in the average annual income, savings and decision-making capacity of the members after joining SHGs.

Ha - There is a significant change in the average annual income, savings and decision-making capacity of the members after joining SHGs.

The 't' test based on paired observations was calculated by applying the following formula:

$$t = \frac{\bar{d}\sqrt{n}}{S}$$

where $\bar{d}$ = The mean of the differences.

S = The standard deviation of the differences.

The value of S is calculated as follows:

$$S = \sqrt{\frac{\Sigma (d-\bar{d})^2}{n-1}} \quad \text{or} \quad \sqrt{\frac{\Sigma d^2 - n(\bar{d})^2}{n-1}}$$

'z' Test

'z' test was applied to test the proportion of increase in the selected variables during pre SHG and post SHG period. The variables examined were:

1. Institution wise changes in the savings.
2. Changes in the indebtedness of members.
3. Changes in the personal assets.

Ho - There is no significant change in the institution wise savings, personal assets acquired and indebtedness of members after joining SHGs.

Ha - There is a significant change in the institution wise savings, personal assets acquired and indebtedness of members after joining SHGs.

The 'z' test was calculated by applying the following formula.

$$z = \frac{P_1 - P_2}{SE(P_1 - P_2)}$$

P_1 Refers to the proportion of members in the pre SHG group.

P_2 Refers to the proportion of members in the post SHG group.

Likert's Scaling Technique (Five Point Scaling Technique)

The impact of SHG Bank Linkage Programme on personality development of women was analysed by following five point scaling technique. The scores were assigned as follows:

Significantly improved	:	5
Improved	:	4
No change	:	3
Not improved	:	2
Significantly not improved	:	1

The respondents were asked to opine their level of improvement based on which the scores were allotted. The total score and main score were found out for analysis.

RESULTS AND DISCUSSION

The findings of the current study on the "(Microfinancing of Rural Women through SHG and Bank Linkage (A Study in Coimbatore District of Tamil Nadu)" are discussed in two sections.

In the *first section* the functions and performance of Self-Help Groups through Bank Linkage Programme are discussed under the following headings:

- Organization and Management of Self-Help Groups.
- Performance of Self-Help Groups.
- Entrepreneurial Activities of the Groups.

In the *second section* the impact of micro finance through SHG-Bank Linkage Programme on Rural Women is discussed under the following headings:

- Socio-Economic Profile of the Sample Members.
- Participation in Microfinancing Activities.
- Capacity Building of Members.
- Income-Generating Activities and Economic Returns.
- Impact of Micro Finance on Income, Savings, Asset creation, Employment Generation and Social Empowerment of the Members.
- Problems faced by the Members.

SECTION ONE

FUNCTIONS AND PERFORMANCE OF SELF-HELP GROUPS THROUGH BANK LINKAGE PROGRAMME

The purpose of forming SHGs is to make financial services available to those who are otherwise likely to be bypassed by the formal banking system. This reduces the dependence of the members of the group on money lenders who generally charge exorbitant rates of interest. The SHGs provide the members with a launch pad to gain confidence, skills and power to promote their interest towards entrepreneurial activities. The objectives of the linkage programme are:

- To evolve supplementary credit strategies for meeting the needs of the poor by combining the flexibility, sensitivity and responsiveness of the informal credit system with the technical, administrative capabilities and financial resources of formal financial institutions.
- To build mutual trust and confidence between bankers and the rural poor.
- To encourage banking activity in both the savings and credit aspects in a segment of the population to whom the formal financial institutions usually find difficult to reach.

In this section the following aspects are discussed:

- Organization and Management of Self-Help Groups.
- Performance of the Self-Help Groups.
- Entrepreneurial Activities of the Groups.

Organization and Management of Self-Help Groups

The SHGs originally conceived are not just groups but intend to promote savings and provide credit. They are also intended to become institutions that promote human development and empower their members. The organization and management of Self-Help Groups are discussed under the following sub-headings:

- General characteristics of SHGs.
- Governance of SHGs.
- General management practices of the groups.
- Financial management practices.

General Characteristics of SHGs

The profile of SHGs based on the member's socio-economic characteristics throws light on the back ground of SHGs and is shown in Table 4.1.

Table 4.1: Profile of Sample SHGs

S. No.	Socio-Economic Characteristics		Number	Percentage
1	2		3	4
1.	Group size (No. of members)	10-11	6	5.00
		12-13	98	81.66
		14-15	16	13.34
		Total	**120**	**100.00**
2.	Age of the members (in years)	Less than 25	163	10.98
		26-35	770	51.88
		36-45	338	22.78
		46-55	170	11.46
		55 and above	43	2.90
		Total	**1,484**	**100.00**
3.	Educational Status of the members	Illiterate	437	29.45
		Primary	162	10.92
		Middle	432	29.11
		Secondary	219	14.76
		Higher Secondary	205	14.82
		Graduates	29	0.94
		Total	**1,484**	**100.00**
4.	Marital status of the members	Married	1,341	90.36
		Unmarried	21	1.42
		Separated/Divorced	88	5.93
		Widowed	34	2.29
		Total	**1,484**	**100.00**
5.	Community of the members	Backward	676	45.55
		Most Backward	190	12.80
		Scheduled Caste	495	33.36
		Scheduled Tribes	123	8.29
		Total	**1,484**	**100.00**

Contd...

1	2		3	4
6.	Annual income of the members (₹)	Below 12,000	136	9.16
		12,001-18,000	724	48.79
		18,001-24,000	596	40.16
		24,001-30,000	16	1.08
		Above 30,000	12	0.81
		Total	**1,484**	**100.00**

Source: Field Survey, 2008.

NABARD stipulated that the SHGs might have 12-20 members and the size should not exceed 20 since that would warrant registration under the Societies Act. The cohesion of the group may also get weakened and may go beyond management when the size is above 20. It was found that 81.66 per cent of the groups had members of twelve to thirteen. NABARD has prescribed that individuals above the age of 18 years and below 60 years could join the SHG. In this present study, 51.88 per cent were in the age group of 26-35 years, 22.78 per cent in 36-45 years and the last 2.90 per cent were above 55 years.

Though no specific educational qualification had been prescribed by the NABARD for those who wish to enroll themselves in SHGs, a minimum level of education could help to acquire necessary technical skills and knowledge for empowerment and economic enlistment. It is clearly understood that 29.11 per cent possessed middle level education, 14.82 per cent of the respondents had higher secondary education, 10.92 per cent had primary education and only 0.94 per cent remained graduates. It is specified that the SHG members should preferably be married women and women who are the bread winners of the family but those who remain unmarried could also be included in the SHGs. Preference is accorded to the poorest women (below the poverty line) amongst the target groups with particular focus on widows, divorcees, deserted and disabled women and women belonging to the down-trodden communities. Out of 1,484 members, 90.36 per cent (1,341) members were married, 5.93 per cent (88) were separated/ divorced, 2.29 per cent (34) were widowed and the rest 1.42

per cent (21) were unmarried. The proportion of scheduled caste members was 33.36 per cent indicating their involvement in groups and backward community represented 45.55 per cent.

The members were classified into five categories on the basis of their annual income before joining the SHGs. Table 4.1 indicates that 48.79 per cent of the members belonged to an income group of ₹ 12,001-₹ 18,000, 40.16 per cent in ₹ 18,001-₹ 24,000, 9.16 per cent of the members were in the income group of below ₹ 12,000, 1.08 per cent in ₹ 24,001- ₹ 30,000 and the remaining 0.81 per cent above ₹ 30,000.

The detailed analysis of socio-economic profile of SHGs clearly depicting the prevailing stature of development scenario in the country today is overwhelmed by the growth of Self-Help Groups formed with the twin objectives of women's empowerment and poverty alleviation.

Governance of SHGs

Proper functioning, sustainability and success of SHGs depend upon the efficiency of the leader. The role of sincere and dynamic leader is one of the foremost factors responsible for a group's success or failure. Further, for the smooth functioning of SHGs, there should be a change in leadership periodically so that every member will get an experience in managing the group. The system of governance of SHGs is given in Table 4.2.

Table 4.2: Governance of SHGs

S. No.	System of Governance of SHGs		No. of SHGs	Percentage
1.	System of selecting leader	Election	12	10.00
		Nomination	108	90.00
		Total	**120**	**100.00**
2.	Period of change in leadership	Once in a year	6	5.00
		Once in two years	22	18.33
		Once in three years	11	9.17
		Not changed	81	67.50
		Total	**120**	**100.00**

Source: Field Survey, 2008.

It could be noted that in a majority of 90 per cent of the groups, the leaders were nominated by the members and only in 10 per cent of the groups, the leaders were elected by the members. The concern for smooth functioning in day to day operations could be an important reason for the high percentage of leaders chosen by nomination by the members of the SHGs. Again it could be noted that in 67.50 per cent of the groups, the leaders were not changed due to unwillingness of the other members, in five per cent of the groups, the leaders were changed every year, while in 18.33 per cent of the groups the leaders were changed once in two years and in 9.17 per cent of the groups once in three years.

General Management Practices of the Groups

SHGs have to function in a democratic manner. Regular meetings of group members are one of the activities of the SHGs that ensure effective participation of members. In these meetings, they undertake financial transactions of both collection of savings and disbursement of loans. Meetings are also an occasion for the members to discuss their common problems and other issues that need to be sorted out through the intervention of the group or other members. The general management practices of the groups are discussed under the following headings:

- Conduct of meetings.
- Conduct of emergency meetings.
- Participation in meetings.

Conduct of Meetings

The details of conduct of meetings are given in Table 4.3.

Meetings on weekly basis were observed to be the common phenomena for 63.33 per cent of the groups, followed by the monthly meetings of 21.67 per cent and fortnightly meetings of 15 per cent. In 73.33 per cent of the groups, the meetings were conducted regularly. However, the groups with irregular conduct of meetings were observed to be particular in collecting the savings, recovery and disbursing loans in an informal manner. The study reported that in 53.33 per cent of the groups

Table 4.3: Distribution of Sample SHGs by Conduct of Meetings

S. No.	Conduct of Meetings		No. of SHGs	Percentage
1.	Frequency	Weekly	76	63.33
		Fortnightly	18	15.00
		Monthly	26	21.67
		Total	**120**	**100.00**
2.	Regularity	Regular	88	73.33
		Irregular	32	26.67
		Total	**120**	**100.00**
3.	Initiation	Group members	64	53.33
		Animators	42	35.00
		Representatives	14	11.67
		Total	**120**	**100.00**

Source: Field Survey, 2008.

the meetings were organized by the group members, in 35 per cent of the groups by the animators and in 11.67 per cent of the groups the meetings were organized by the representatives.

Conduct of Emergency Meetings

In an effective organization, a situation may arise for conducting emergency meetings. This would help to identify the solution to the problem which requires an immediate attention. Table 4.4 examines the reasons for conducting an emergency meetings.

Table 4.4: Conduct of Emergency Meetings

S. No.	Reasons	No. of SHGs*	Percentage
1.	To discuss official proceedings	62	51.67
2.	To discuss urgent loans	79	65.83
3.	To discuss operational problems of the group	19	15.83
4.	To discuss the social and surrounding problems	52	62.40

Source: Field Survey, 2008.

* Multiple response.

Among the sample SHGs, 65.83 per cent viewed that emergency meetings were conducted to discuss urgent loan requirements of the members, 62.40 per cent of the SHGs viewed that the emergency meetings have been organized to discuss about social and surrounding problems, 51.67 per cent of the SHGs viewed that emergency meetings were conducted to discuss the official proceedings and 15.83 per cent viewed the reason as, to discuss the operational problems of the groups.

Participation in Meetings

One of the important parameters to assess the changes in group behaviour is to analyse the change in personal traits, qualities and attributes that are viewed from their perspectives. SHGs acquire strength and power not merely through plans or programmes but through a process of continued functioning, close interaction, concerned unity and collective efforts in accomplishing certain tasks. This is achieved by attending and participating in the meetings.

The details of SHG members' participation in meetings are given in Table 4.5.

Table 4.5: Distribution of SHGs by Member's Participation in Meetings

S. No.	Participation in Meetings		No. of SHGs	Percentage
1.	Attendance	Below 70%	2	1.67
		71% - 80%	10	8.33
		81% - 90%	22	18.33
		Above 90%	86	71.67
		Total	**120**	**100.00**
2.	Fine for not attending	Imposed	86	71.67
		Not imposed	34	28.33
		Total	**120**	**100.00**
3.	Participation in meetings	High	72	60.00
		Medium	32	26.67
		Low	16	13.33
		Total	**120**	**100.00**

Source: Field Survey, 2008.

Compulsory attendance of members in the meetings is one of the pre-requisites for smooth functioning of the groups. It is one of the indicators that ensures the active participation of members in the business of the group in a democratic manner. The level of attendance was more than 90 per cent in 72 per cent of the groups, it was 81 90 per cent in 18 per cent of the groups, 71 80 per cent in 8 per cent of the groups and less than 70 per cent in two per cent of SHGs. The higher percentage of attendance could be attributed to imposing penalty or fine for late attendance or absenteeism in the meetings. Further it is seen that about 72 per cent of the groups imposed fine for not attending the meetings and the rest did not impose any fine on the members but strictly advised them to attend the meetings in future. The fines collected for not attending the meetings were added to group capital. However, there were provisions in almost all SHGs for waiving the penalty and fine for genuine reasons like sickness and urgency of work. To voice the problems and achievements, meeting place gives forum. Further 60 per cent of group members were highly interacting and participating in the group meetings, 26.67 per cent members' participation was medium and 13.33 per cent members' participation was low.

Financial Management Practices

The core strength of SHGs lies in building financial capabilities. The SHGs have proved to be an effective medium of delivering and ensuring timely repayment, hence maintaining and handling the books of accounts are the necessary tasks. The SHGs have to maintain various ledgers for savings, loan, minutes, attendance, subscriptions, cash and members' passbooks. Maintenance of records and books of accounts details are given in Table 4.6.

It could be inferred from Table 4.6 that 63.33 per cent of the groups were regular in maintaining the accounts and updating the records. As against this in 36.67 per cent of the groups, the records were not properly maintained, due to pre occupation with household activities and business activities of the group members, animators and the representatives.

Table 4.6: Maintenance of Records and Books of Accounts

S. No.	Financial Management Practices		No. of SHGs	Percentage
1.	Maintenance of records and books of accounts	Regular	76	63.33
		Irregular	44	36.67
		Total	**120**	**100.00**
2.	Responsibility for records and books of accounts	Animator	62	51.67
		Representatives	36	30.00
		Members	22	18.33
		Total	**120**	**100.00**
3.	Verification of records and books of accounts by members	Always	84	70.00
		Occasionally	36	30.00
		Total	**120**	**100.00**
4.	Frequency of group auditing by NGOs	Quarterly	64	53.33
		Half yearly	37	30.83
		Annually	19	15.84
		Total	**120**	**100.00**

Source: Field Survey, 2008.

Further in 51.67 per cent of the groups, the accounts were maintained by animator; in 30 per cent of the groups, the representatives maintained the accounts and in 18.33 per cent of the groups the members maintained the accounts. Verification of records ensures transparency and cross-checking among members. Again it was reported that in 70 per cent of the groups, the members were very particular in verifying the records and in 30 per cent of groups, the members verified the records only occasionally. Further it could be noted that in majority of SHGs (53.33%) books of accounts, records and ledgers were audited quarterly, in 30.83 per cent of SHGs, the records were audited half-yearly and in 15.84 per cent, the records were audited annually.

Performance of Self-Help Groups

The SHGs became a regular component of the Indian financial system since 1996. The SHGs are small, informal and homogenous groups. These groups have proved as cyclic agents of development in both the rural and urban areas. The SHGs after being formed start collecting a fixed amount of savings from each member regularly. After accumulating a reasonable amount of savings, the group starts lending to its members for petty consumption needs. If the bank is satisfied with the group in terms of: *(i)* genuineness of demand for credit; *(ii)* credit handling capacity of the members; *(iii)* repayment behaviour within the groups; and *(iv)* the accounting system and maintenance of the records, it extends a term loan of smaller amount to the groups. Thus, financing through SHGs effects quite a few benefits like: *(i)* savings mobilised by the poor; *(ii)* access to the required amount of appropriate credit by the poor; *(iii)* meeting the demand and supply of credit structure and opening of new market for financing institutions; *(iv)* reduction in transaction cost for both lenders and borrowers; *(v)* tremendous improvement in recovery; *(vi)* heralding a new realisation of subsidy less and corruption-less credit; and *(vii)* remarkable empowerment of poor women. The performances of the groups are discussed under the following sub-headings:

- Saving activities of the groups.
- Lending activities.
- Bank linkage pattern among SHGs.
- Repayment behaviour of the groups.
- Financial viability of SHGs.

Saving Activities of the Groups

The SHG-Bank Linkage Programme distinctly differs from other micro finance programmes across the world mainly in terms of its greater emphasis on savings. The basic philosophy of savings first and credit next is assumed to be the principle of the programme. The programme rests on the premise that members will develop the habit of savings so that during the post SHG phase they can avail loan. This, besides increasing their self-reliance in meeting the credit needs of the group members, will also help in efficient deployment of credit among the members as their own money is at stake. The existing savings and lending products mainly from institutional sources are not adaptable to the rural poor. Keeping this in view, the programme had shifted the entire responsibility of innovating the saving and lending products to SHGs with a broader framework suggested in their guidelines.

The saving activities of the groups are discussed under the following sub-headings:

- Periodicity of savings and operation of bank accounts.
- Quantum of savings.

Periodicity of Savings and Operation of Bank Accounts

Periodicity of savings and operation of bank accounts are given in Table 4.7.

Table 4.7: Periodicity of Savings and Operation of Bank Accounts

S. No.	Activities		No. of SHGs	Percentage
1.	Periodicity of savings	Weekly	70	58.33
		Fortnightly	18	15.00
		Monthly	32	26.67
		Total	**120**	**100.00**
2.	Operation of accounts	Animator and Representatives	55	45.83
		Animator and Representatives and one or two members in rotation	65	54.17
		Total	**120**	**100.00**
3.	Frequency of bank transactions	Fortnightly	44	36.67
		Once in a month	76	63.33
		Total	**120**	**100.00**

Source: Field Survey, 2008.

Table 4.7 indicates that majority of the surveyed SHG groups (58.33%) collected the savings money on a weekly basis from their members and 26.67 per cent of the groups collected the money on a monthly basis. The rest of the 15 per cent adopted a fortnightly term for the collection of savings money from the members. On formation of SHGs, it is mandatory that bank accounts are opened and operated to ensure financial monitoring, especially when micro credit has been availed. In this context it was found that 54.17 per cent of SHGs operated their accounts with animators and representatives and also group members in rotation and in 45.83 per cent of the SHGs the accounts were operated by animators and representatives only. The mobility of the SHGs completely relied upon the amount of savings made and utilised. It is clearly understood that 63.33 per cent of the SHGs operated their bank accounts monthly and 36.67 per cent of them fortnightly.

Quantum of Savings

The quantum of money saved by the group members ranged from ₹ 40 - ₹ 200 per month per member during the study period. The details of the savings of the members are given in the following Table 4.8. Growth index of SHGs by group savings are given in Figure 4.1.

Table 4.8: Distribution of SHGs by Group Savings

Quantum of Savings (Range) \ Year	2003-04	2004-05	2005-06	2006-07	2007-08
Below ₹ 5,000 (N)	98 (81.67)	60 (50.00)	24 (20.00)	–	–
₹ 5,001 - ₹ 10,000 (N)	22 (18.33)	44 (36.67)	52 (43.33)	46 (38.33)	28 (23.33)
₹ 10,001 - ₹ 15,000 (N)	–	16 (13.33)	40 (33.33)	52 (43.33)	46 (38.33)
₹ 15,001 - ₹ 20,000 (N)	–	–	4 (3.34)	22 (18.34)	32 (26.67)
₹ 20,001 - ₹ 25,000 (N)	–	–	–	–	14 (11.67)
Total (N)	**120 (100.00)**	**120 (100.00)**	**120 (100.00)**	**120 (100.00)**	**120 (100.00)**
Year wise savings (Value in ₹ Lakh)	7.80	11.76	17.50	23.94	32.10
Growth Index (%)	100	150.77	224	306.92	411.54
Cumulative savings (Value in ₹ Lakh)	7.80	19.56	37.06	61.00	93.10
Average savings per group (Value in ₹)	6,500	16,300	30,880	50,830	77,580

Source: Calculations based on Field Survey, 2008.

N: Number of groups.

Figures in parentheses indicate the percentage to the column total.

Mean savings	₹ 18.62 lakh
Standard deviation	9.6877
Co-efficient of variation	52.03%
Growth rate	42.48%

Table 4.8 reveals that the savings of the group constantly increased during the study period. The year wise index reveals that the savings has been increased by 50.77 per cent in 2004-05 compared to the previous year 2003-04 and in 2005-06 it is increased by 124 per cent, 206.92 per cent in 2006-07 and by 311.54 per cent in 2007 08. The total savings of sample groups during the study period was ₹ 93.10 lakh and the average savings per group was ₹ 77,580. There was an increasing trend of incremental savings corresponding to the age of the group. The average savings of the groups for the study period was ₹ 18.62 lakh. The co-efficient of variation was 52.03 per cent showing moderate variance and the compound growth rate was 42.48 per cent indicating the consistency in the increasing trend. This was expected, since over the years the members recognised the need for savings and had the tendency to increase the rate of savings corresponding to the loan amount.

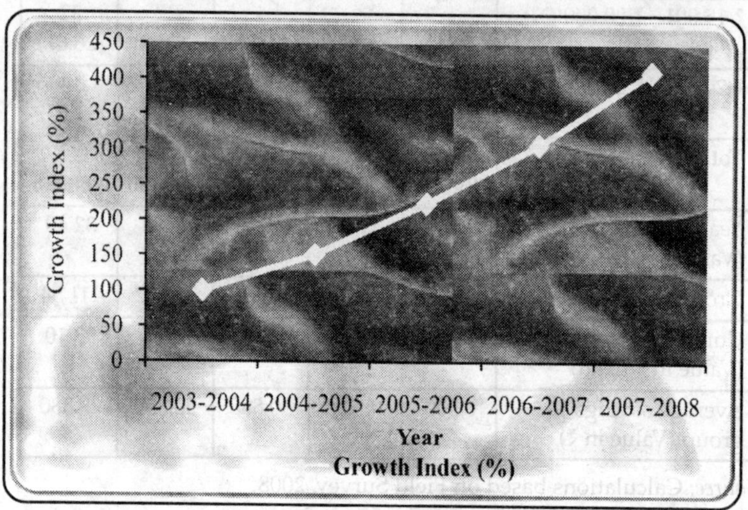

Fig. 4.1: Growth Index of Savings of SHGs

Lending Activities

Internal lending is that, which the SHGs lend to its members from the amount saved and deposited by its members with the SHGs. The lending commences after six months of savings. The members take internal loans from the amount of group savings for different purposes. They are able to take easy loans from their own savings for their usual expenses as well as at time of emergencies at low rate of interest compared to that of money lenders and loan sharks. Internal lending has become an important activity of the SHGs. SHGs have been thought of by its member as an alternative to banks. The group, after estimating the loan requirements from its members, passes a resolution, withdraws the amount from the bank and pays the amount to the members. The repayment of the loan by the borrowers is prompt and the repayment rate ranges from 97.50 per cent to 100 per cent.

The decision-making powers are vested with the members. The maximum repayment period for the loan was fixed at 12 months. In extreme cases, if the loan was not repaid in the scheduled month, at least the interest due was to be paid for the month. Discussions with the members showed that group pressure would be brought, though not amounting to coercion, upon the defaulting members. The interest rate charged did not vary among the groups. Though they were entrusted with the power of fixing their own rate of interest and were aware of using it as a regulatory tool of rationing credit, they did not want to cause much inconvenience to their members by hiking interest rates. The SHGs charged a uniform rate of 24 per cent interest per annum, irrespective of the loan amount until 2006-07 and since 2007-08 it is reduced to 12 per cent per annum.

The SHGs viewed the interest as a source of income and ensured that the interest is collected promptly. The SHGs have promoted unity among the members by giving preference to those members who are urgently in need of loans. The number of installments for the repayment of the loan was usually fixed by the groups. The repayment of loan started in the month following the loan disbursement. The process helps them to imbibe the essentials of financial intermediation including prioritisation of needs, setting terms and conditions and account keeping. This gradually builds financial discipline among them. The lending activities of the groups are discussed under the following sub-headings:

- Internal lending.
- Changes in the savings and lending activities of SHGs since bank linkage.

Internal Lending

The details of internal lending by the groups are given in Table 4.9 and Figure 4.2.

Table 4.9: Internal Lending by the Groups

Year	Total Amount Lent (₹ in lakh)	Average per Group (₹ in lakh)	Repayment (in%)
2003-04	6.48	0.054	100.00
2004-05	29.76	0.248	97.80
2005-06	46.44	0.387	98.50
2006-07	57.72	0.481	97.50
2007-08	64.80	0.540	98.50
Total	**205.20**	**1.710**	

Source: Calculations based on Field Survey, 2008.

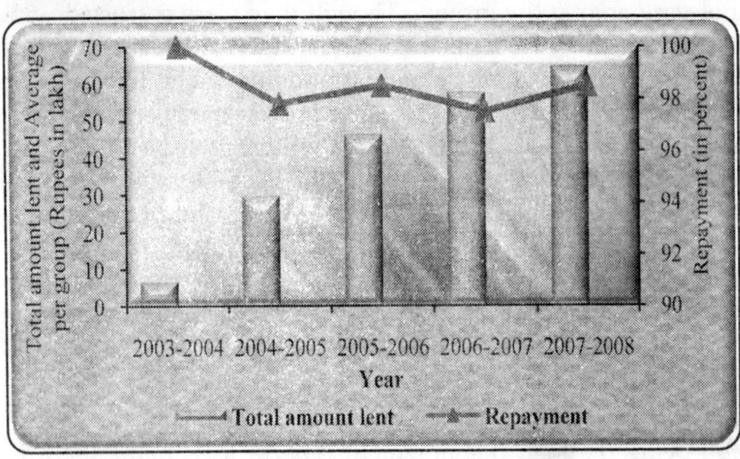

Fig. 4.2: Internal Lending by the Groups

Table 4.9 reveals that the internal loan given by the groups increases year after year corresponding to savings. The average internal loan given by the group has increased from ₹ 0.054 lakh in 2003-04 to ₹ 0.540 lakh in 2007-08 during the study period. The average loan given by the group was ₹ 1.71 lakh during the study period indicating the several cycles of loan given to members to overcome poverty and to climb up the socio-economic ladder. Mostly, the funds were utilised for consumption purposes rather than income-generating activities because the amount required in small quantity is used frequently for meeting out the emergency needs.

Changes in the Savings and Lending Activities of SHGs since Bank Linkage

Changes in the savings and lending services offered to members by SHGs are given in Table 4.10.

Table 4.10: Changes in the Savings and Credit Services Offered to Members

Changes in the Savings/ Credit Services	2003-04 (base year) (percentage)	2007-08 (percentage)
Saving Activities		
Weekly	72.00	58.33
Fortnightly	17.00	15.00
Monthly	11.00	26.67
Credit Services		
Weekly	31.00	68.00
Fortnightly	33.00	15.00
Monthly	36.00	17.00
Average number of days required for approving loan	8.00	6.00
Average number of loans approved per year	12.00	15.00
Average loan period in months	10.00	12.00
Interest rate per annum	24.00	12.00

Source: Calculations based on Field Survey, 2008.

It is inferred from Table 4.10 that there was a slight change in the periodicity of weekly savings from 72 per cent in the base year to 58.33 per cent in 2007-08 and a corresponding increase in the monthly savings from 11 per cent to 26.67 per cent. Regarding the credit services offered by the SHGs there was a significant shift from weekly to monthly credit services from 31 per cent to 68 per cent, the average number of days required for approving loan has come down marginally from eight to six over the years. The average number of loans approved per annum as well as the average loan period per member has increased over the years and the average rate of interest charged by the SHGs has decreased significantly from 24 per cent to 12 per cent.

Credit Linkage Programme of SHGs

The group places its savings in the group deposit account in the bank. Using its group savings and group guarantee as collateral, the bank starts lending loans to the group. NABARD provides subsidised refinancing support to banks to encourage such lending. In practice, the first credit linkage extended by the banks to the SHGs, is largely based on the satisfactory group performance during the first six months.

NABARD has stipulated certain norms for linking SHGs to bank credit such as:

(i) The group should have been in existence for at least six months.

(ii) The group should have scored 120/150 marks based on its evaluation criteria.

Once the groups are linked to the banks, in the first stage they become eligible for credit equal to their savings. Subsequently, repeated loans may be availed at the savings credit ratio of 1:2 and 1:4 depending on the repayment performance of the groups concerned. These provisions motivate members to exert peer pressure for prompt repayment.

The Bank Linkage Programme of SHGs is discussed under the following sub headings:

- Bank linkage pattern among SHGs.
- Bank loan.

Bank Linkage Pattern among SHGs

The details of bank linkage pattern and availability of revolving fund are given in Table 4.11.

Table 4.11: Distribution of SHGs by Bank Linkage Pattern

S. No.	Bank Linkage Pattern		No. of SHGs	Percentage
1.	Bank linkage period	6-7 months	92	76.67
		8-9 months	28	23.33
		Total	**120**	**100.00**
2.	Revolving fund availed	One time	32	26.67
		Two time	88	73.33
		Total	**120**	**100.00**

Source: Field Survey, 2008

It could be inferred that among the sample SHGs, 76.67 per cent of the groups were credit linked between sixth and seventh month from their formation and 23.33 per cent of SHGs were credit linked between eighth and ninth month. It is to be noted that 73.33 per cent of the groups received revolving fund two times and rest of them received one time.

Bank Loan

Bank loan is mainly given for initiating micro enterprises and the details of bank loan availed are given in Table 4.12.

A look into Table 4.12 indicates that 120 groups had availed a bank loan of ₹ 36.64 lakh and ₹ 138.50 lakh during the years 2003-04 and 2004-05 respectively. In 2005-06, 23 groups had availed repeat loans, in 2006-07, 24 groups availed repeat loans and in 2007-08, 31 groups had availed repeat loans from the banks. Total bank loan availed by SHGs was ₹ 296.19 lakh and the average bank loan per group was ₹ 2.47 lakh indicating a sizable amount borrowed to run the micro enterprises. (*See table 4.12 on next page*)

Table 4.12: Bank Loan Availed

Range \ Year	2003-04	2004-05	2005-06	2006-07	2007-08
Less than ₹ 25,000 (N)	86 (71.67)	–	–	–	–
₹ 25,001 - ₹ 75,000 (N)	28 (23.33)	23 (19.17)	11 (9.16)	–	–
₹ 75,001 - ₹ 1,50,000 (N)	6 (5.00)	97 (80.83)	– (20.00)	24	–
₹ 1,50,001 - ₹ 2,25,000 (N)	0 (0.00)	0 (0.00)	12 (10.00)	–	31 (25.83)
Total (N)	**120 (100.00)**	**120 (100.00)**	**23 (19.16)**	**24 (20.00)**	**31 (25.83)**
Total amount of loan (in ₹ Lakh)	36.64	138.50	229.65	25.60	65.80

Source: Calculations based on Field Survey, 2008.
N: Number of groups.
Figures in parentheses indicate the percentage to the total number of groups.

Total bank loan availed	296.19 (₹ in lakh)
Average bank loan per group	2.47 (₹ in lakh)

Repayment Behaviour of the Groups

Sustainability shows its strengths in repayment performance of SHGs to banks and members to SHGs. SHGs are known for prompt repayment. Repayment behaviour of SHGs is discussed under the following sub-headings:

- Repayment of bank loan by SHGs.
- Opinion of the leaders on the peer group pressure.

Repayment of Bank Loan by SHGs

The repayment behaviour of SHGs is given in Table 4.13 and Figure 4.3.

It could be observed from Table 4.13 that 60 per cent of the groups were excellent and five per cent of the groups were not up to the level of satisfaction in repayment of loan during 2003-04. This trend has gradually increased and 75 per cent of the groups were excellent in repayment in 2004-05 and 96.67

Table 4.13: Repayment Behaviour of Sample SHGs to Banks

Repayment / Year	Excellent (Above 90%)	Good (81-90%)	Satisfied (71-80%)3	Not Satisfied (Below 70%)	Total
2003-04 (N)	72 (60.00)	32 (26.67)	10 (8.33)	6 (5.00)	120 (100.00)
2004-05 (N)	90 (75.00)	20 (16.67)	8 (6.67)	2 (1.66)	120 (100.00)
2005-06 (N)	106 (88.33)	14 (11.67)	0 (0.00)	0 (0.00)	120 (100.00)
2006-07 (N)	108 (90.00)	12 (10.00)	0 (0.00)	0 (0.00)	120 (100.00)
2007-08 (N)	116 (96.67)	4 (3.33)	0 (0.00)	0 (0.00)	120 (100.00)

Source: Field Survey, 2008.
N: Numbers stated.
Figures in parentheses indicate the percentage to the row total.

per cent in 2007-08. This reveals that almost all the SHGs except four groups were reported for cent per cent repayment of bank loan. Overall, the repayment behaviour of the SHGs was excellent.

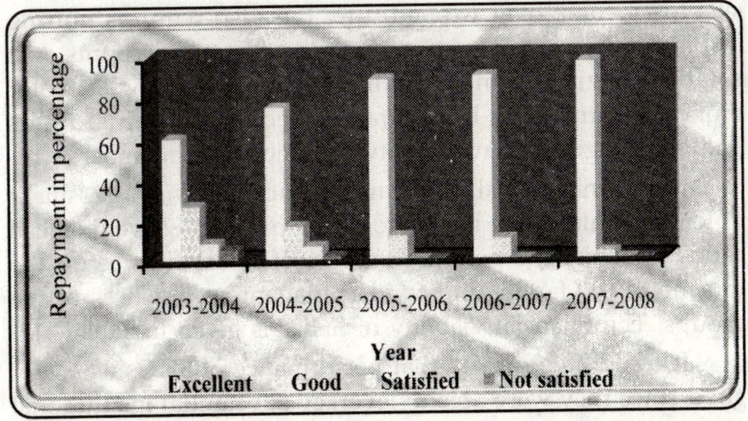

Fig. 4.3: Repayment Behaviour of Sample SHGs to Banks

Opinion of the Leaders on the Peer Group Pressure

The peer group pressure is a strong influencing factor in repayment of loan which is given in Table 4.14.

Table 4.14: Opinion of the Leaders on the Peer Group Pressure

S.No.	Opinion	No. of the SHGs	Percentage
1.	Strongly Agree	60	50.00
2.	Agree	56	46.67
3.	Disagree	2	1.67
4.	Strongly Disagree	2	1.66
	Total	**120**	**100.00**

Source: Field Survey, 2008.

As regards the role played by peer group pressure on loan repayments, Table 4.14 reveals the fact that a large majority (96.67%) of the groups have answered in tune with agreement, which highlights the facts about the harmony, communication and bondage among the various members of the SHGs, which might have nurtured their responsibility for prompt repayment.

Financial Viability of SHGs

Financial viability not only consists of generation of surplus income over expenditure, but also requires putting in place a very good system of audit of group accounts, fast rotation of group funds, mixing 'warm' money with 'cold' money[1], control over loan defaults, access to external funds and ensuring credit availability to majority of members.

Micro finance analysts are more concerned with assessment of loan default rate. It is time to develop few effective financial ratios to assess the potential impact of micro finance on the income of the family and fund management practices of the groups. The financial viability of SHGs is given in Table 4.15.

It could be observed that performance of SHGs was very good since they were able to leverage substantial institutional finance as indicated by average loan saving ratio of 3.18 times.

Table 4.15: Fund Management among SHGs

S. No.	Fund Management Practice	Details
1.	Average savings mobilised	₹ 0.775 lakh
2.	Average internal lending	₹ 1.71 lakh
3.	Credit saving ratio	2.20 times
4.	Average bank loan availed	₹ 2.47 lakh
5.	Loans savings ratio	3.18 times
6.	Internal loan repayment rate	98.50 (%)
7.	Bank loan repayment rate	96.67 (%)
8.	SHGs' audit systems by NGOs (Quarterly)	53.33%

Source: Calculations based on Field Survey, 2008.

The fund management practices of the groups were better since the average credit saving ratio of the group was 2.20 times, internal loan repayment rate was 98.50 per cent and the bank loan repayment rate was 96.67 per cent. Since financial transactions are involved in all SHG programmes, it becomes necessary for them to have proper auditing system. The sample SHGs' records are updated and checked with the help of NGOs and by the system of intergroup checking.

Entrepreneurial Activities of the Groups

The SHGs has to initiate income-generating activities for their long term sustainability. The details of entrepreneurial activities undertaken by the groups are given under the following sub-headings:

- Income-generating activities.
- Members' participation in business activities.

Income-Generating Activities

The basic concept of SHGs is that all the group members should initiate and actively involve in micro enterprises in order to generate income which will help them to alleviate poverty. However, only in a few groups all the members had practically engaged in the group activity and in majority of the groups a few members or a single member had engaged in economic activity and it is shown in the Table 4.16.

Table 4.16: Income-Generating Activities

S.No.	Particulars	No. of SHGs	Percentage
1.	All members of the group	22	18.00
2.	Some members of the group	98	82.00
	Total	**120**	**100.00**

Source: Field Survey, 2008.

It is understood that in 82 per cent of the groups, one or few members have initiated micro enterprises and in 18 per cent of the groups, all the members joined together and started income-generating activities.

SHG Members' Participation in Business Activities

The SHG members are encouraged to initiate income-generating activities mostly in groups, because members in groups will have collective strength and achieve more in the family activities and outside activities. The number of members engaged in income-generating activities is given in the Table 4.17 and Figure 4.4.

Table 4.17: Members' Participation In Business Activities

<table>
<tr><th>S. No.</th><th colspan="2">Particulars</th><th>No. of Members</th><th>Percentage</th></tr>
<tr><td rowspan="2">1.</td><td rowspan="2">Participation in business</td><td>Members engaged in micro enterprises</td><td>1,102</td><td>75.00</td></tr>
<tr><td>Members not engaged</td><td>382</td><td>25.00</td></tr>
<tr><td></td><td></td><td>Total</td><td>1,484</td><td>100.00</td></tr>
<tr><td rowspan="4">2.</td><td rowspan="4">Types of micro enterprises</td><td>Agriculture and allied activities</td><td>330</td><td>29.95</td></tr>
<tr><td>Manufacturing activities</td><td>252</td><td>22.87</td></tr>
<tr><td>Trading activities</td><td>394</td><td>35.75</td></tr>
<tr><td>Service activities</td><td>126</td><td>11.43</td></tr>
<tr><td></td><td></td><td>Total</td><td>1,102</td><td>100.00</td></tr>
</table>

Source: Field Survey, 2008.

It is inferred that of the total number of members, 75 per cent of them initiated micro enterprises and 25 per cent were not engaged in any business. Further it could be noted that among the members who initiated micro enterprises, 35.75

per cent were engaged in trading activities, 29.95 per cent in agriculture and allied activities, 27.87 per cent in manufacturing activities and 11.43 per cent in service activities.

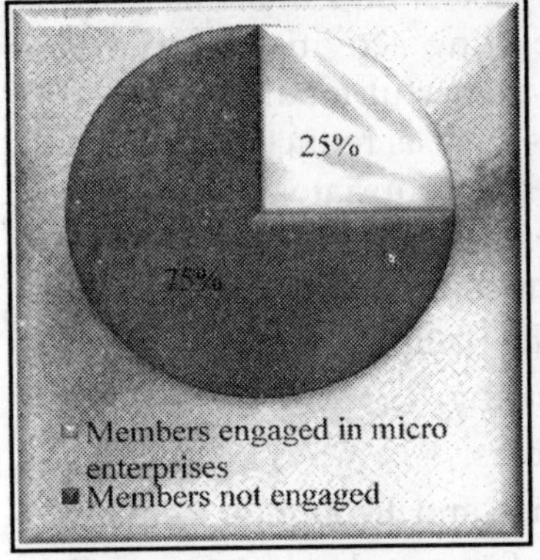

Types of Micro Enterprises

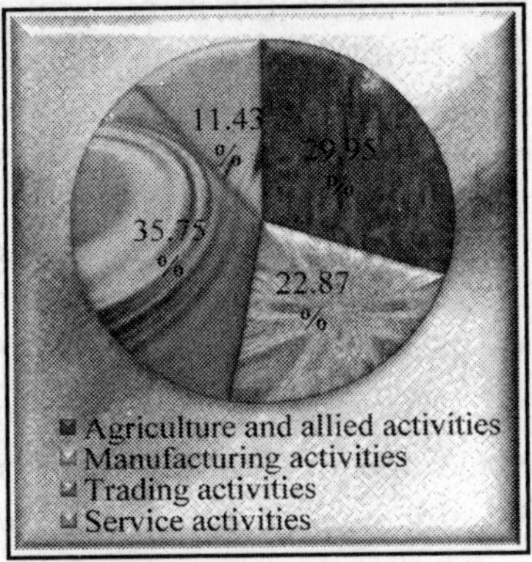

Participation in Business

Fig. 4.4: Members' Participation in Business Activities

The above analysis revealed that the SHGs were able to provide various credit services such as business loan, consumption loan, loan for settlement of old debts and loan for other contingency purposes to their members. The success of SHGs in terms of high repayment is mostly related to the expansion of prevailing social ties and social cohesion found among women members.

SECTION TWO

IMPACT OF MICRO FINANCE THROUGH SHG-BANK LINKAGE PROGRAMME ON RURAL WOMEN

Micro Finance interventions are well recognised world over as an effective tool for poverty alleviation and improving socio-economic conditions of the poor. In India too, micro finance is making head way in its efforts for reducing poverty and empowering women in particular. The impact of micro finance through SHG-Bank Linkage Programme has been effective in making positive social changes to all the members, irrespective of the direct borrowers of the micro credit. Importantly in the rural context, the SHGs have facilitated the poor, especially the women to overcome the existing constraints grappling the formal credit institutions. These groups provide considerable social protection and income opportunities to the members. The SHGs have acquired a prominent status in maximising social and financial returns. The promotion of income-generating activities for the poor rural women is perceived as a powerful medium to resolve several socio-economic problems such as reduction of poverty, provision of goods and services appropriate to local needs, redistribution of income and opportunities in the community etc. This section is discussed under the following headings:

- Socio-economic Profile of the Sample Members.
- Participation in Microfinancing.
- Capacity Building of Members.
- Income-Generating Activities and Economic Returns.
- Impact of Micro Finance on Savings, Income-Generation, Asset Creation, Employment Generation and Overall Empowerment.
- Problems faced by the Members.

Socio-economic Profile of the Sample Members

Today economic independence is considered to be the prime basis for improving the status of women in India. It is generally agreed that the availability of credit to women would result in reducing their dependency, enhancing their social and economic activities, as well as empowering them to assert more in the household decisions. In India, women cannot be viewed as a homogenous group as the society is stratified on the basis of class, caste and religion. It has been observed that the position of women and their demand for bank credit remain tied to class, caste and religious affiliations. In order to grasp the nature of these causal relationships, it is imperative to understand the socio-economic characteristics of women members in the study area.

The socio-economic profile of the members is discussed under the following headings:

- Socio-economic status of the members.
- Family background of the members.
- Living conditions of the members.

Socio-Economic Status of the Members

Table 4.18 draws a detailed description on the socio-economic status of the members.

Table 4.18: Distribution of Sample Members by Socio-economic Status

S. No.	Socio-Economic Factors		Members of GOME		Members of SOME		Total	
1	2		3		4		5	
			No.	%	No.	%	No.	%
1.	Age of the members (in years)	Below 25	14	4.20	25	9.36	39	6.50
		26-35	159	47.74	139	52.06	298	49.67
		36-45	104	31.25	60	22.48	164	27.33
		46-55	48	14.41	43	16.10	91	15.17
		55 and above	8	2.40	0	0.00	8	1.33
		Total	**333**	**100.00**	**267**	**100.00**	**600**	**100.00**
2.	Educational status of the members	Illiterate	125	37.54	44	16.48	169	28.17
		Primary	114	34.24	82	30.71	196	32.67
		Middle	58	17.42	62	23.22	120	20.00
		Secondary	12	3.60	51	19.10	63	10.50
		Higher Secondary	16	4.80	17	6.37	33	5.50
		Graduate	8	2.40	11	4.12	19	3.16
		Total	**333**	**100.00**	**267**	**100.00**	**600**	**100.00**

Contd...

1	2		3		4		5	
3.	Religion of the members	Hindu	211	63.36	167	62.55	378	63.00
		Muslim	50	15.02	43	16.10	93	15.50
		Christian	72	21.62	57	21.35	129	21.50
		Total	**333**	**100.00**	**267**	**100.00**	**600**	**100.00**
4.	Community of the members	Backward	94	28.23	143	53.56	237	39.50
		Most Backward	44	13.21	37	13.86	81	13.50
		Scheduled Caste	169	50.75	68	25.47	237	39.50
		Scheduled Tribe	26	7.81	19	7.11	45	7.50
		Total	**333**	**100.00**	**267**	**100.00**	**600**	**100.00**
5.	Occupation of the members	Agricultural Labourers	188	56.46	112	41.94	300	50.00
		Animal Husbandry	62	18.62	74	27.72	136	22.66
		Small Business	57	17.12	49	18.35	106	17.67
		Others	26	7.80	32	11.99	58	9.67
		Total	**333**	**100.00**	**267**	**100.00**	**600**	**100.00**

Source: Field Survey, 2008.

Age of the Members

The major proportion of the sample SHG members (49.67%) was in the age group of 26-35 years followed by the members in the age group of 36-45 years (27.33%), 46-55 years (15.17%) and below 25 years (6.50% only). A similar distribution pattern was observed across members of GOME and SOME. The proportion of members in the age group between 26-35 years was 47.74 per cent in GOME and 52.06 per cent in SOME, 31.25 per cent of members in the age group of 36-45 years in GOME and 22.48 per cent in SOME; 14.41 per cent of GOME members and 16.10 per cent of SOME members were in the age group of 46-55 years and 4.20 per cent of GOME members and 9.36 per cent of SOME members were below 25 years. The SHG members in the age group of 55 years and above were reported to be only 2.40 per cent and they were in group-owned micro enterprises.

Level of Literacy

The weaker sections of the society are generally characterised by high level of illiteracy without any formal education. An analysis of the educational status of the sample members revealed that 28.17 per cent of them were illiterate. It was found that 32.67 per cent of the sample members studied up to primary level. Members who studied up to middle, secondary and higher secondary levels were reported to be 20 per cent, 10.50 per cent and 5.50 per cent respectively. It is surprising to note that 3.16 per cent of the sample members were graduates.

Illiterate members and members with primary level of education were observed to be relatively more in GOME (37.54% and 34.24%) than in SOME (16.48% and 30.71%) indicating that these members preferred GOME than SOME. It is interesting to know that members with education of middle level, secondary level, higher secondary level and graduate levels are more in SOME (23.22%, 19.10%, 6.37% and 4.12%) than in GOME (17.42%, 3.60%, 4.80% and 2.40%). From this, it is evident that the level of education influences the choice of ownership of business enterprise.

Religion

It is observed that 15.50 per cent of members were Muslims; followed by Christians 21.50 per cent and the major proportions of the members were Hindus (63%). It is inferred that the SHG-Bank Linkage Programme strongly influences the women who are secluded by their religion to come out and take part in the SHG activities. A similar distribution pattern was observed in GOME and SOME.

Community

The programme envisaged the covering of socially and economically weaker sections particularly social groups like: SC/STs and backward classes. The distribution of sample members according to community revealed that a similar proportion of members belonging to backward class and scheduled caste accounted for 39.50 per cent each followed by 13.50 per cent most backward communities and 7.50 per cent scheduled tribes. The highest proportion (53.56%) of backward classes was observed in the case of SOME compared to GOME (28.23%). As against this, the highest proportion of SC members were reported in GOME (50.75%) compared to SOME (25.47%). Hence it is observed that members of weaker sections of the society were interested in group-ownership of business than individual-ownership.

Occupation

The classification of the sample members based on occupational pattern revealed that the agricultural labourers constituted the major share of 50 per cent, 22.66 per cent of members engaged in dairy farming and goat rearing and 17.67 per cent of members as small business dealers while others were 9.67 per cent. The proportion of agricultural labourers were higher in GOME (56.46%) compared to SOME (41.94%), while the proportion of members engaged in dairy farming and goat rearing (27.72%) and members engaged in other occupations (11.99%) were higher in SOME compared to GOME with 18.62 per cent and 7.80 per cent respectively.

To sum up, the majority of the sample members, both among the GOME and SOME were Hindus in the age group of 26-35 years, with primary level of education, having equal representation of backward community and scheduled caste and were agricultural labourers.

Family Background of the Members

Family is a social institution, formed by marriage and it serves for a number of purposes. It is an organized system of relationships and norms. It provides security, love, affection and all kinds of emotional and social support like needs and fulfilment. Hence, family background forms the base for women's work participation and in this section, an attempt has been made to discuss the family background like: marital status, type of family, family size, education of spouse, income of spouse and annual family income.

Marital Status

The distribution of sample members according to the marital status revealed that 90.67 per cent of the members were married followed by divorced/separated 7.17 per cent and widowed 2.16 per cent. The proportion of divorced/separated and widowed members were more in GOME (12.31%) than in SOME (5.62%) indicating that these categories of women members preferred joint-ownership of the business than single-ownership of business.

Type of Family

It was observed that 68.67 per cent of the members were from nuclear families and 31.33 per cent were from joint families. In the case of joint families, 53.18 per cent of members are Single-Owned Micro Entrepreneurs (SOME) and 13.81 per cent are Group Owned Micro Entrepreneurs (GOME) indicating that members from joint family system preferred individual-ownership of business.

Family Size

It was found that the family size was between five and six members in 49.67 per cent of the sample members, below five members in 47 per cent of the sample members and the

Family backgrounds of the members are given in Table 4.19.

Table 4.19: Distribution of Sample Members by Marital and Family Status

S. No.	Factors		Members of GOME		Members of SOME		Total	
1	2		3		4		5	
			No.	%	No.	%	No.	%
1.	Marital status	Married	292	87.69	252	94.38	544	90.67
		Unmarried	0	0.00	0	0.00	0	0.00
		Divorced/Separated	32	9.61	11	4.12	43	7.17
		Widowed	9	2.70	4	1.50	13	2.16
		Total	**333**	**100.00**	**267**	**100.00**	**600**	**100.00**
2.	Type of family	Nuclear	287	86.19	125	46.82	412	68.67
		Joint	46	13.81	142	53.18	188	31.33
		Total	**333**	**100.00**	**267**	**100.00**	**600**	**100.00**
3.	Family size	Below 5 members	223	66.97	59	22.09	282	47.00
		5-6 members	105	31.53	193	72.28	298	49.67
		7-9 members	5	1.50	15	5.63	20	3.33
		Total	**333**	**100.00**	**267**	**100.00**	**600**	**100.00**

Contd...

1	2		3		4		5	
4.	Education of the husband	Illiterate	69	20.72	38	14.23	107	17.83
		Primary	218	65.47	140	52.43	358	59.67
		Secondary	31	9.31	71	26.59	102	17.00
		Higher Secondary	15	4.50	18	6.75	33	5.50
		Total	**333**	**100.00**	**267**	**100.00**	**600**	**100.00**
5	Employment of the husband	Employed	317	95.20	208	77.90	525	87.50
		Unemployed	13	3.90	28	10.49	41	6.83
		Self-Employed	3	0.90	31	11.61	34	5.67
		Total	**333**	**100.00**	**267**	**100.00**	**600**	**100.00**
6.	Annual income (in ₹)	Below 12,000	80	24.02	55	20.60	135	22.50
		12,001 - 18,000	253	75.98	188	70.41	441	73.50
		18,001 - 24,000	0	0.00	24	8.99	24	4.00
		24,000 and above	0	0.00	0	0.00	0	0
		Total	**333**	**100.00**	**267**	**100.00**	**600**	**100.00**

Source: Field Survey, 2008.

family size was between seven and nine members in 30.33 per cent of the sample members. The share of family size of 5-6 members was higher in SOME (72.28%) than in GOME (31.53%) and respondents having family size of 7-9 members were more in SOME (5.63%) than in GOME (1.50%). As against this, members with family size of below five were higher in GOME (66.97%) than in SOME (22.09%). This categorisation indicates that respondents having the family size of less than five members preferred group-ownership business and respondents having family size of 5-6 and 7-9 members preferred individual-ownership business.

Education of the Husband

It was observed that 59.67 per cent of members' spouses have completed primary education and 17.83 per cent of the members' spouses were illiterates. About 17 per cent of the members' spouses studied up to secondary level and 5.50 per cent completed higher secondary education. The spouses of the members having primary education (65.47%) and illiterates (20.72%) were more in the case of GOME than in SOME (52.43% and 14.23%), whereas the spouses of members having secondary education (26.59%) and higher secondary education (6.75%) were more in SOME than in GOME (9.31% and 4.50%).

Employment of the Husband

It is noted that 87.50 per cent of the members' spouses were employed, 5.67 per cent were self-employed and 6.83 per cent were unemployed. The proportion of the members' spouses employed was higher in GOME (95.20%) than in SOME (77.90%). Similarly the proportion of the members' spouses who were unemployed (10.49%) and self-employed (11.61%) was more in SOME than in GOME (3.90% and 0.90%).

Annual Income

The annual income of the members has a great influence on the member's involvement in SHG activities. A look into the table reveals that the majority of the members (73.50%) were earning between ₹ 12,001 and ₹ 18,000 per annum, 22.50

per cent of members who had an annual income of less than ₹ 12,000 and four per cent of the members earned between ₹ 18,001 and ₹ 24,000. The proportion of the member's earnings below ₹ 12,000 and between ₹ 12,001 and ₹ 18,000 per annum was more in GOME (24.02% and 75.98%) than in SOME (20.60% and 70.41%). It is interesting to note that all the 24 members earning between ₹ 18,001 and ₹ 24,000 per annum were in SOME and not in GOME indicating that the annual income of the members influences the choice of ownership of the business.

Thus the majority of the members both among the GOME and SOME were married hailing from nuclear family with the family size ranging between 5 and 6 members. Again the majority of the members' spouses had completed primary level of education and was employed with the annual income ranging between ₹ 12, 001 and ₹ 18,000.

Living Conditions of the Members

The prime objective of the SHG-Bank Linkage concept is to improve the economic and social status of the poor people. So it is essential to analyse the living conditions of the sample members before joining SHGs.

It is observed from Table 4.20 that 53.33 per cent of the members had own houses and 46.67 per cent of the members were living in rented houses. The proportion of the members living in own houses was higher in SOME (67.42%) than in GOME (42.04%). It is inferred that 54.67 per cent of the members were living in tiled houses, 26.83 per cent were living in huts and 18.50 per cent were living in reinforced concrete houses. The proportion of the members living in huts (28.83%) and in tiled houses (57.96%) was higher in GOME than in SOME (24.36% and 50.55%).

Toilet facility was not available in 86.67 per cent of the members' houses. The proportion of the members not having toilet facilities is same both in GOME (86.79%) and in SOME (86.52%). Electricity facility was available for 90 per cent of the members reflecting in GOME (83.48%) and in SOME (90.64%); 12.67 per cent of the members had independent tap connections

Living condition of the members are given in Table 4.20.

Table 4.20: Distribution of Sample Members by Living Conditions

S. No.	Nature of Living Condition		Members of GOME		Members of SOME		Total	
1	2		3		4		5	
			No.	%	No.	%	No.	%
1.	Type of house	Own house	140	42.04	180	67.42	320	53.33
		Rented house	193	57.96	87	32.58	280	46.67
		Total	**333**	**100.00**	**267**	**100.00**	**600**	**100.00**
2.	Nature of house	Huts	96	28.83	65	24.36	161	26.83
		Tiled	193	57.96	135	50.55	328	54.67
		R. C. Roofing	44	13.21	67	25.09	111	18.50
		Total	**333**	**100.00**	**267**	**100.00**	**600**	**100.00**
3.	Toilet facilities	Available	44	13.21	36	13.48	80	13.33
		Not available	289	86.79	231	86.52	520	86.67
		Total	**333**	**100.00**	**267**	**100.00**	**600**	**100.00**
4.	Electricity	Available	278	83.48	242	90.64	540	90.00
		Not available	55	16.52	25	9.36	60	10.00
		Total	**333**	**100.00**	**267**	**100.00**	**600**	**100.00**

Contd...

1	2		3		4		5	
5.	Water facilities	Independent tap Connection	34	10.21	42	15.73	76	12.67
		Common tap	232	69.67	148	55.43	380	63.33
		Hand pump	52	15.62	68	25.47	120	20.00
		Common well	15	4.50	9	3.37	24	4.00
		Total	**333**	**100.00**	**267**	**100.00**	**600**	**100.00**
6.	Medium of cooking	Firewood	210	63.07	98	36.70	308	51.33
		Kerosene stove	111	33.33	160	59.93	271	45.17
		Gas stove	12	3.60	9	3.37	21	3.50
		Total	**333**	**100.00**	**267**	**100.00**	**600**	**100.00**
7.	Land holding	Less than 1 Acre	52	15.62	46	17.23	98	16.33
		1-2 Acres	47	14.11	25	9.36	72	12.00
		2-3 Acres	8	2.40	12	4.49	20	3.33
		Above 3 Acres	0	0.00	0	0.00	0	0.00
		Landless	226	67.87	184	68.92	410	68.34
		Total	**333**	**100.00**	**267**	**100.00**	**600**	**100.00**

Source: Field Survey, 2008.

and the remaining 87.33 per cent had common taps, common wells and hand pumps. The proportion of the members having independent tap connections was more in SOME (15.73%) than in GOME (10.21%). A majority of 51.33 per cent of the members were using fire wood for cooking, 45.17 per cent had kerosene stove and only 3.50 per cent had gas stove. The proportion of the members using fire wood was more in GOME (63.07%) than in SOME (36.70%), as against this, the proportion of the members using kerosene stove was more in SOME 59.93 per cent than in GOME 33.33 per cent.

The classification of the members based on land holding pattern revealed that 3.33 per cent of them are having 2-3 acres of the land, 12 per cent of them having 1-2 acres of land, 16.33 per cent had less than one acre and 68.34 per cent were landless labourers. The proportion of members having less than one acre of land and 2-3 acres land were more in SOME (17.23% and 4.49%) than in GOME (15.62% and 2.40%), whereas the proportion of members having 1-2 acres land was more in GOME (14.11%) than in SOME (9.36%). To conclude, the majority of the members were having own houses with tiled roof and electricity, common tap water, fire wood as medium for cooking, inadequate toilet facilities and were landless.

The detailed discussion gives the fact that SHG set-up is necessary to overcome exploitation and create confidence for economic self-reliance among women especially the rural women who are mostly invisible in the social structure.

Participation in Microfinancing Activities

SHGs would essentially be formed for the purpose of empowering the poor to take charge of critical decisions concerning their life and improve their quality. The process adopted for formation of the group has major influence over the way the group would evolve overtime. Women's participation in SHGs and in its various activities is important for meeting out the broad objectives of micro financing and effective functioning of SHGs.

Members' participation in micro financing activities is discussed under the following sub-headings:

- Motivating factors for joining the SHGs.
- Group dynamics among members.
- Socio-economic factors influencing the choice of ownership of business.
- Awareness about SHG's activities.
- Savings and credit activities of the members.

Motivating Factors for Joining the SHGs

The analysis in the preceding sections reveals that majority of the members in the total sample belonged to landless households, deriving most of their income from non-farm sector followed by agricultural activity. Hence the members of SHGs were asked to prioritise the motivating factors for joining the groups. Therefore, the reasons behind joining SHGs by members were analysed by using Garrett ranking technique. The sample respondents were asked to rank the given factors from 1-8, giving one to the highest motivating factor and eight to the least motivating factor.

The order of the merit as given by sample respondents was changed into per cent position by using the following formula:

$$\text{Percent position} = \frac{100\,(R_{ij} - 0.5)}{N_{ij}}$$

where

R_{ij} - Is rank given for the ith factor by the jth respondent

N_j - Number of factors ranked by the jth respondent

The per cent position of the each rank thus obtained was converted into scores by referring to the table given by Garrett (1969). For each factor the scores of individual sample respondent were added together and divided by the total number of sample respondents. Based on these mean scores, ranks were assigned.

The mean scores of all the factors for the entire study groups were arranged and the ranks were given in the following Table 4.21.

Table 4.21: Motivating Factors for Joining the Group

S. No.	Motivating Factors	Members of GOME			Members of SOME		
		Total Score	Mean	Rank	Total Score	Mean	Rank
1.	To mobilise savings	27568.75	82.78	1	18356.25	68.75	2
2.	To avail internal loan	27218.75	81.73	2	26656.25	99.83	1
3.	To avail bank loan	22031.25	66.15	3	15893.75	59.52	3
4.	To initiate income-generating activities	17318.75	52.00	4	11256.25	42.15	5
5.	To reduce unemployment	10956.25	32.90	5	7718.75	28.90	6
6.	To develop Socio-economic status	9993.75	30.01	6	15831.25	59.29	4
7.	NGOs encouragement	9006.25	27.04	7	5843.75	21.88	7
8.	To set off old debts	6918.75	20.77	8	1975.00	7.39	8

Source: Calculations based on Field Survey, 2008.

From Table 4.21 it could be seen that 'mobilising savings' was the most compelling factor for the GOME members to join SHGs and the mean score for this factor was 82.78. The desire 'to avail internal loan' emerged as second important motivating factor for joining SHGs, with mean score 81.73. As per the ranking by the members of GOME 'availing bank loan' stood in third position with the mean score 66.15 followed by other reason 'to initiate income-generating activities' which ranked fourth (52), 'to reduce unemployment' ranked fifth (32.90), to develop socio-economic status in the sixth position (30.01). NGOs encouragement ranked seventh (27.04) and 'to set off old debts' was the least motivating factor with the mean score 20.77. The range between the highest and the lowest score was 62.01.

It could be noted that 'availing internal loan' was the most compelling motivating factor for SOME members for joining SHGs with the mean score of 99.83. The interest of 'mobilising savings' was second important motivating factor for joining SHGs with the mean score 68.75, 'availing bank loan' was third factor to motivate them to join the SHGs with the mean score 59.52, followed by 'to develop socio-economic status' with the mean score of 59.29, to initiate income-generating activities with the mean score of 42.15, 'to reduce unemployment' with the mean score 28.90, NGOs encouragement with the mean score 21.88 and to 'set off old debts' was the least motivating factor with the mean score of 7.39.

In general the most important reasons for joining SHGs were obtaining loans from the groups and mobilising savings. The result is in consistence with the findings of NABARD (2002).

Group Dynamics Among Members

The participation of the members in various activities of the group is given in Table 4.22. (*See table on next page*)

The women members can be either the head of the group or representative of the group along with being an ordinary member. Holding some administrative positions in the group have the ability to improve managerial skills of the participating women. From the sample size of 600 members, 60 per cent were members and 20 per cent each representing animator of the group and representative of the group. The proportion of members holding the position of animator (28.46%) and representative (32.21%) was higher in SOME compared to GOME (13.21% and 10.21%) as against this the members not holding any position was higher in GOME (76.58%) compared to SOME (39.33%). The preference exercised to be the head; the representative and ordinary member have the scope to influence their activity level in SHGs.

The members acquire strength and power through the process of continued functioning and close interaction by attending meetings. It was found that 70.33 per cent of members were always regular in attending the meetings, while 29.67 per cent of the members were attending the meetings frequently. The proportion of members attending the meetings regularly

Table 4.22: Profile of the SHG Members in Group Activities

S. No.	Activities		Members of GOME		Members of SOME		Total	
1	2		3		4		5	
			No.	%	No.	%	No.	%
1.	Position of the members	Animator	44	13.21	76	28.46	120	20.00
		Member	255	76.58	105	39.33	360	60.00
		Representative	34	10.21	86	32.21	120	20.00
		Total	**333**	**100.00**	**267**	**100.00**	**600**	**100.00**
2.	Regularity in attending the meeting	Always	220	66.07	202	75.66	422	70.33
		Frequently	113	33.93	65	24.34	178	29.67
		Total	**333**	**100.00**	**267**	**100.00**	**600**	**100.00**
3.	Deciding agenda for meeting	Majority of members	200	60.07	133	49.81	333	55.50
		Some members	42	12.61	62	23.22	104	17.33
		Animator	83	24.92	62	23.22	145	24.17
		Representatives	8	2.40	10	3.75	18	3.00
		Total	**333**	**100.00**	**267**	**100.00**	**600**	**100.00**

Contd...

1	2		3		4		5	
4.	Taking decision in meeting	All members	252	75.68	137	51.30	389	64.83
		Animator	54	16.22	70	26.22	124	20.67
		Representatives	22	6.61	50	18.73	72	12.00
		Some members	5	1.50	10	3.75	15	2.50
		Total	**333**	**100.00**	**267**	**100.00**	**600**	**100.00**
5.	Bases of decision-making	Consensus	49	14.71	62	23.23	111	18.50
		Voting	227	68.17	162	60.67	389	64.83
		Group Representatives	57	17.12	43	16.10	100	16.67
		Total	**333**	**100.00**	**267**	**100.00**	**600**	**100.00**

Source: Field Survey, 2008.

was a little higher in the case of SOME (75.66%) compared to GOME members (66.07%). The majority of the members, 55.50 per cent expressed that they actively participated in deciding the agenda for the meetings. The proportion of members' participation in deciding the agenda was higher in GOME (60.07%) compared to the members of SOME (49.81%). Regarding the decision-making aspect, majority of the members, 64.83 per cent expressed that all the members participated in decision-making, 20.67 per cent reported that the animators decided the issue and 12 per cent revealed that the decisions were taken by the representatives. Members' participation in decision-making was higher in the case of GOME members (75.68%) compared to SOME members (51.30%). With regard to the method of decision-making in meetings, 64.83 per cent of members expressed that decisions were taken by means of voting.

To sum up, the majority of sample respondents both among the members of GOME and SOME were regular in attending the meetings, participating actively in decision-making, deciding agenda of meetings and taking decision by means of voting.

Socio-Economic Factors Influencing the Choice of Ownership of Business

To analyse the extent of influence of socio-economic factors in deciding the ownership of activity either as a single or a group, a chi-square analysis was carried out with the following hypothesis and is shown in Table 4.23.

H_o = There is no significant association between the choice of enterprises and a set of socio-economic characteristics of the respondents.

H_a = There is a significant association between the choice of enterprises and a set of socio-economic characteristics of the respondents namely: the age of the members, education of the members, community, annual income, occupation, marital status, type of family, family size, education of the husband, employment of the husband and position of the member in the group.

Table 4.23: Socio-economic Factors and Choice of Ownership of Business Chi-square Test

Socio-Economic Factors	Chi-square Value	Degrees of Freedom	Table Value
Age	17.473*	9	16.919
Education	62.312**	11	24.725
Community	83.993**	7	18.475
Annual income	31.229**	7	18.475
Occupation	14.451*	7	14.067
Marital status	6.888[NS]	7	14.067
Type of family	106.752**	3	11.341
Family size	120.561**	5	15.086
Education of the husband	35.099**	7	18.475
Employment of the husband	44.452**	5	15.086
Position of the member in the group	87.364**	5	15.086

Source: Calculations based on Field Survey, 2008
NS : Non-significant
* Significant at 5 percent level
** Significant at 1 percent level

The chi-square analysis reveals that there has been a significant relationship at five per cent level between the nature of ownership of business and age of members and occupation of members. The results have also revealed that there has been a significant relationship at one per cent level between the nature of ownership of business and the members' education, community, annual income, type of family, family size, education of the husband, employment of the husband and position of the member in the group. Hence the null hypothesis was rejected and it is concluded that the socio-economic factors of the respondents have highly influenced their choice of business enterprise either as group-owned micro enterprise or self-owned micro enterprise.

Awareness About SHG's Activities

SHG is a basic unit for intervention which works for women in a number of ways. It provides guidance, gives support and assistance to its members, gives an identity and promotes livelihood among its members. Groups in link with other institutions help them to mobilise credit from main stream of financial institutions. Therefore, proper awareness about the performance of SHGs by its members helps them to advance to a post of leader, women entrepreneur and gain social upliftment in the society.

It could be observed that the issues like: cash in hand, balance in bank, savings of the group, number of members taken loan, number of members repaid loan, name of the bank and income of the group, meeting calendar, rules and regulations, total capital of the group, total loan of the group and achievements of the group were well known to the group members.

However, awareness regarding information in group records, outstanding loan, objectives of the group and constraints of the group had been low among the group members.

Savings and Credit Activities of the Members

Cultivating the habit of regular savings and the ability to access them when required through credit not only reduces significantly the vulnerability of the livelihood base of the poor and their dependence, it also enhances human development. It enables them to borrow for urgent needs instead of going to money lenders, which increases their dependency since he/she is often the one who provides them labour employment at low wages. This in turn gives them a degree of freedom to bargain for better wages and working conditions and enables them to build a capital base which hitherto had been impossible since the exorbitant interest rates demanded by money lenders siphoned off all surpluses. The 'feel good' factor is evident in a group that has been able to save enough in the group to meet the urgent needs. However, the members of the group need to go further if they are to justify the claim that savings empower people. They need to ensure that savings and credit are managed effectively. Savings and credit activities of the members are discussed under the following sub-headings:

Table 4.24, depicts the members' level of awareness of the SHG's activities.

Table 4.24: Awareness About SHG's Activities

S. No.	Group Activities	Members of GOME (N:333)		Members of SOME (N:267)		Total (N: 600)	
		No.*	%	No.*	%	No.*	%
1.	Meeting calendar	285	85.58	244	91.39	529	88.17
2.	Rules and regulations	262	78.67	240	89.89	502	83.67
3.	Information in group records	236	70.87	208	77.90	444	74.00
4.	Cash in hand	315	94.59	255	95.51	570	95.00
5.	Balance in Bank	315	94.59	258	96.63	573	95.50
6.	Outstanding loan	240	72.00	196	73.40	436	72.67
7.	Total capital of the group	278	83.48	212	79.40	490	81.67
8.	Savings of the group	325	97.60	258	96.63	583	97.17
9.	Total loaning of the group	254	76.27	234	87.64	488	81.33
10.	Number of members taken loan	333	100.00	265	99.25	598	99.67
11.	Number of members repaid loan	333	100.00	258	96.63	591	98.50
12.	Name of the bank	333	100.00	267	100.00	600	100.00
13.	Income of the group	310	93.09	256	95.88	566	94.33
14.	Objectives of the group	244	73.27	201	75.28	445	74.17
15.	Achievements of the group	276	82.88	232	86.89	508	84.67
16.	Constraints of the group	248	74.47	226	84.64	474	79.00

Source: Field Survey, 2008. *Multiple response. N: Number stated.

- Sources of income for savings.
- Savings pattern.
- Enterprise wise savings.
- Internal lending.
- Frequency of internal loaning.
- Purpose of availing internal loan.
- Utilisation of internal loan.
- Bank loan.
- Frequency of bank loan availed.
- Purpose wise share of bank loan.
- Sector wise share of bank loan.

Sources of Income for Savings

Savings is one of the foundations on which SHG edifies. Sources of income for savings mobilised by SHG members are reported in Table 4.25 and Figure 4.5.

Table 4.25: Distribution of Members by Sources of Income for Savings

S. No.	Sources of COME	Members of SOME	Members	Total
1.	Minimising the expenditure (N)	50 (15.00)	28 (10.50)	78 (13.00)
2.	Savings from their own income (N)	226 (67.90)	197 (73.78)	423 (70.50)
3.	Savings from the family income (N)	32 (9.60)	22 (8.23)	54 (9.00)
4.	Other sources (N)	25 (7.50)	20 (7.49)	45 (7.50)
	Total (N)	**333 (100.00)**	**267 (100.00)**	**600 (100.00)**

Source: Field Survey, 2008.

N: Number stated.

Figures in parentheses indicate the percentage to the column total.

It is seen that savings from their own income was the major source (70.50%) towards the mobilisation of savings;

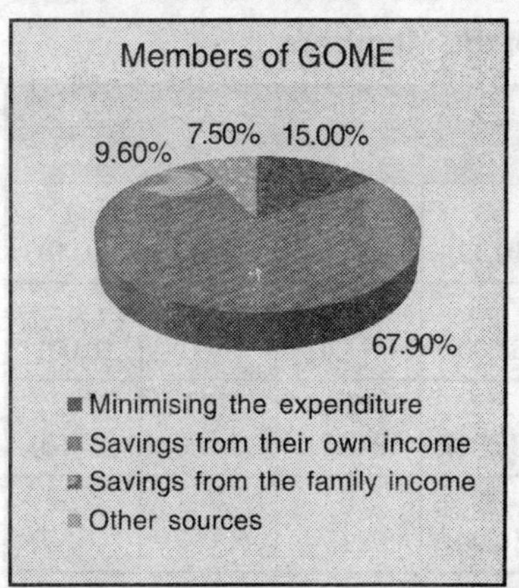

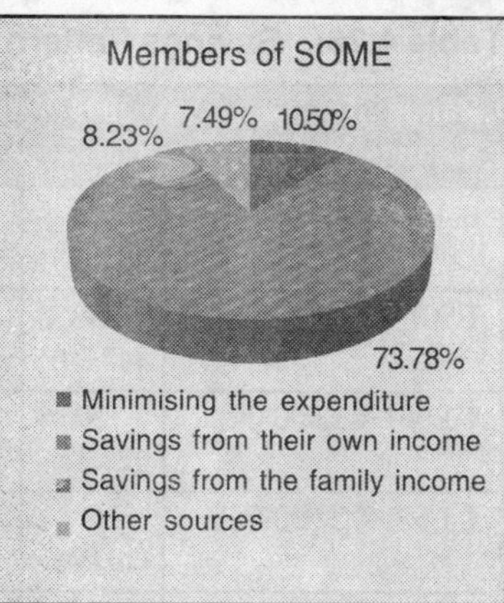

Fig. 4.5: Distribution of Membership by Sources of Income for Savings

followed by minimising the expenditure by 13.00 per cent, savings from the family income (9.00%) and others 7.50 per cent . The proportion of members who find their 'own income' as a source for savings was little higher in SOME (73.78%) compared to GOME (67.90%). Overall for both the types of members savings from their 'own income' was a major source towards thrift contribution.

Savings Pattern

Savings is an essential feature of all SHG members, creating pools of funds for giving loan to members and also as the basis to attract additional loan from financial institutions. The quantum of money saved by the members ranged from ₹ 40 to ₹ 200 per month, per member during the study period. The savings pattern of the members is given in Table 4.26 and Figure 4.6.

Table 4.26 indicates that quantum of money saved by members through the SHGs has significantly increased during the study period from 2003-04 to 2007-08. It is evident from the table that the savings of the members have increased from a meagre amount of ₹ 40 per individual per month to above ₹ 200 per individual per month. The yearly savings increased from ₹ 3.84 lakh in 2003-04 to ₹ 11.47 lakh in 2007-08.

Table 4.26: Savings Pattern of the Members

Range of Savings	2003-04	2004-05	2005-06	2006-07	2007-08
Below ₹ 500 (N)	190 (31.67)	62 (10.33)	0 (0.00)	0 (0.00)	0 (0.00)
₹ 501-₹ 1,000 (N)	258 (43.00)	186 (31.00)	102 (17.00)	54 (9.00)	0 (0.00)
₹ 1,001-₹ 1,500 (N)	152 (25.33)	212 (35.34)	127 (21.17)	120 (20.00)	142 (23.66)
₹ 1,501-₹ 2,000 (N)	0 (0.00)	96 (16.00)	316 (52.67)	262 (43.67)	274 (45.67)
₹ 2,001-₹ 2,500 (N)	0 (0.00)	44 (7.33)	55 (9.16)	164 (27.33)	184 (30.67)
Total (N)	**600 (100.00)**	**600 (100.00)**	**600 (100.00)**	**600 (100.00)**	**600 (100.00)**
Year wise savings (in ₹ Lakh)	3.84	6.13	7.29	8.79	11.47
Growth index (%)	100	159.41	189.57	228.81	298.36
Cumulative savings (in ₹ Lakh)	3.84	9.97	17.26	26.05	37.52
Mean savings (Value in ₹)	640.50	1,021.00	1,214.00	1,465.50	1,911.00
Cumulative savings of individual (Value in ₹)	640.50	1,661.50	2,875.50	4,341.00	6,252.00

Source: Calculations based on Field Survey, 2008

N : Number stated

Figures in parentheses indicate the percentage to the column total

The estimated mean savings was worked out as ₹ 640.50 in 2003-04 and it was increased constantly to ₹ 1,021.00 in 2004-05, ₹ 1,214.00 in 2005-06 and ₹ 1,465.50 in 2006-07 and stood at ₹ 1,911.00 in 2007-08. Similarly it has been observed that the cumulative savings of the individual has increased from ₹ 640.50 in 2003-04 to ₹ 6,252.00 in 2007-08. The growth index indicates that the savings had been increased constantly throughout the study period. In 2004-05 it was increased by

59.41 per cent compared to the base year 2003-04, in 2005-06 by 89.57 per cent, in 2006-07 by 128.81 per cent and in 2007-08 by 198.36 per cent. This increasing trend was also automatically reflected in the mean savings.

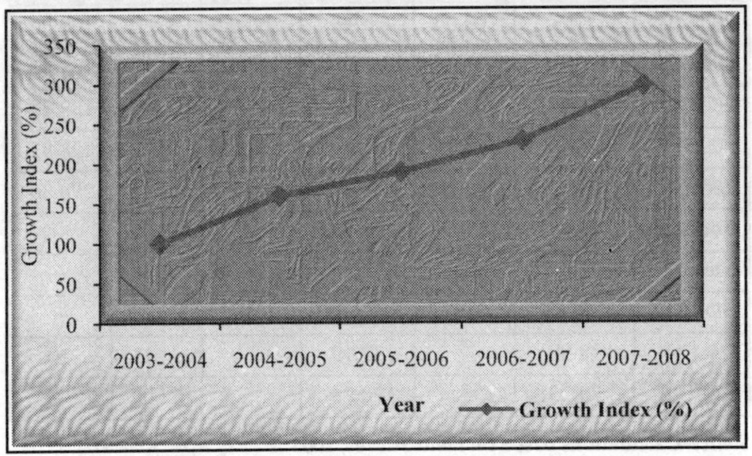

Fig. 4.6: Growth Index of Savings of Members

This increasing trend in savings helps the SHG members to overcome financial dependence and vulnerability. Studies made by MYRADA in 2003 have shown that in remote villages where the SHGs meet about 25 per cent of the credit requirements, the interest rates of private moneylenders fell considerably often by 50 per cent and moneylenders from outside the village stopped coming since the cost of transactions cannot be met with the lower interest rates.

Enterprise wise Savings

Savings of the SHG members based on the ownership of the enterprise are given in Table 4.27 and Figure 4.7.

The quantum of money saved by the members is increased from 100, the base year growth index to 196.28 per cent in the case of GOME members and 200.97 per cent in the case of SOME members during the study period. Annual growth rate of savings in GOME was 29.23 per cent and in SOME was 28.78 per cent and the overall growth rate was 29.00 per cent.

Table 4.27: Savings of the Members by Enterprise Wise

(Amount in ₹ Lakh)

Year	Members of GOME	Growth Index	Members of SOME	Growth Index	Total	Growth Index
2003-04	2.15	100.00	1.69	100.00	3.84	100.00
2004-05	3.25	151.12	2.88	169.89	6.13	159.41
2005-06	3.92	182.32	3.37	198.73	7.29	189.57
2006-07	4.80	223.73	3.99	235.22	8.79	228.81
2007-08	6.37	296.28	5.10	300.97	11.47	298.36
Total	**20.49**	–	**17.03**	–	**37.52**	–
Mean	4.09	–	3.40	–	7.50	–
SD	1.5966	–	1.2669	–	2.8595	–
CV (%)	38.98	–	37.19	–	38.11	–
CGR (%)	29.23	–	28.78		29.00	–

Source: Calculations based on Field Survey, 2008

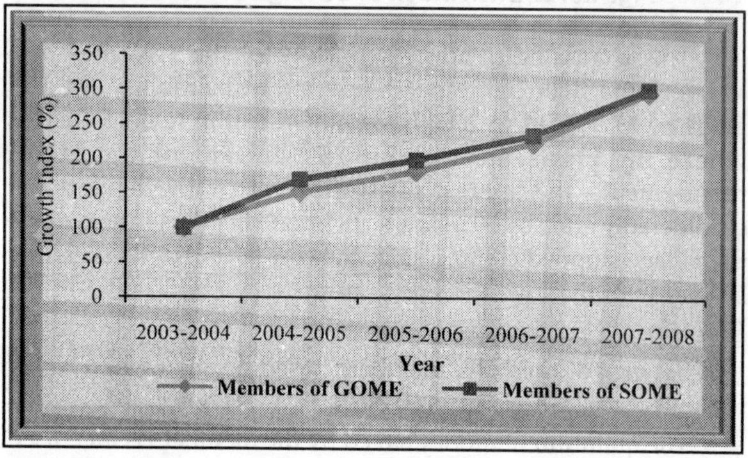

Fig. 4.7: Savings of the Members by Nature of Enterprise Wise

The co-efficient of variation of GOME (38.98%) and SOME (37.19%) indicates consistency in the growth rate of savings and it correlates to overall growth rate.

Internal Lending

The corpus funds accumulated by the SHGs are generally utilised as internal loan to its members for various purposes. The details of quantum of internal loan availed by the members are given in Table 4.28.

Table 4.28: Internal Loan Availed by the Members

Range of Internal Loan	Members of GOME	Members of SOME	Total
Below ₹ 15,000 (N)	79(23.70)	57(21.40)	136(22.67)
₹ 15,001 - ₹ 20,000 (N)	88(26.40)	63(23.60)	151(25.17)
₹ 20,001 - ₹ 25,000 (N)	128(29.50)	121(34.10)	249(41.50)
₹ 25,001 - ₹ 30,000 (N)	38(20.40)	26(20.90)	64(10.66)
Total (N)	**333(100.00)**	**267(100.00)**	**600(100.00)**
Amount in ₹ Lakh	62.91	52.57	115.48
Mean loan ₹	18,892	19,688	19,246

Source: Field Survey, 2008.
N: Number stated.
Figures in parentheses indicate the percentage to the column total.

A look into Table 4.28 reveals that 41.50 per cent of the members had availed internal loan between ₹ 20,001 and ₹ 25,000, and another 25.17 per cent had availed loan between ₹ 15,001 and ₹ 20,000. It is clearly understood that 22.67 per cent of members had availed loan below ₹ 15,000. It is important to note that 10.66 per cent of members had availed internal loan between ₹ 25,001 and ₹ 30,000. The proportion of members availed internal loan of ₹ 20,001- ₹ 25,000 was observed to be a little more in the case of SOME members (34.10%) than the GOME members (29.50%). As against this the proportion of loan availed between ₹ 15,001-₹ 20,000 and below ₹ 15,000 was little higher in the case of GOME members (26.40% and 23.70%), compared to the SOME members (23.60% and 21.40%). Further it is interesting to note that 20 per cent of the members of both the categories availed the maximum internal loan of ₹ 25,001-₹ 30,000. The mean loan amount availed by the SOME members (₹ 19,688) was more than the GOME members (₹ 18,892). It is a very encouraging trend to note that the members had availed internal loan to the extent of ₹ 115.48 lakh during the study period, proving the potentials of the self-help and mutual groups for any developmental agenda.

Frequency of Internal Loan

Table 4.29 depicts the frequency of internal loan availed by the members.

Table 4.29: Frequency of Internal Loan Availed by the Members

Frequency	Members of GOME	Members of SOME	Total
Up to 4 times (N)	14(4.20)	16(5.99)	30(5.00)
5-6 times (N)	92(27.63)	63(23.60)	155(25.83)
7-8 times (N)	164(49.25)	138(51.69)	302(50.34)
9 and above (N)	63(18.92)	50(18.72)	113(18.83)
Total (N)	**333(100.00)**	**267(100.00)**	**600(100.00)**

Source: Field Survey, 2008.
N : Number stated.
Figures in parentheses indicate the percentage to the column total.

It could be noted that the majority, 50.34 per cent of the members had availed the internal loan for 7-8 times, 25.83 per cent had availed loan for 5-6 times and five per cent had availed up to four times. It is remarkable to note that 18.83 per cent of members had availed internal loan more than nine times during the study period. A similar distribution was found between the members of GOME and SOME. An analysis of the data indicates that the SHG members have taken several loans over a period of 3-5 years. This is the only way that they were able to move out of poverty. A single dose or a one time infusion of subsidised credit does not significantly raise them above the poverty line.

Purpose of Availing Internal Loan

Preference of the members in using the internal loan is given in Table 4.30.

Table 4.30: Distribution of Members on the Basis of Purpose of Internal Loan

S. No.	Purposes		Members of GOME (N : 333)		Members of SOME (N : 267)		Total (N : 600)	
			No.*	%	No.*	%	No.*	%
1	Consumption	Food materials	285	85.58	202	75.66	487	81.16
		Children's education	201	60.36	187	70.00	388	64.67
		Health	195	58.56	190	71.16	385	64.16
		Life-Cycle ceremonies	235	70.58	212	79.40	447	74.50
		To repay debts	175	52.55	135	50.56	310	51.66
2	Business	Agriculture	75	22.52	4	1.50	79	13.17
		Animal husbandry	19	5.70	23	8.61	42	7.00
		Manufacturing	65	19.51	62	23.22	127	21.16
		Trading	72	21.62	121	45.30	193	72.28
		Service	28	8.41	11	4.11	39	14.60
3	Asset creation	Personal assets	311	93.39	264	98.88	575	95.83
		Business assets	117	35.13	177	66.29	294	49.00

Source: Calculations based on Field Survey, 2008.

* Multiple response.

N: Number stated.

It is revealed that 81.16 per cent of members had availed the internal loan for food materials followed by 74.50 per cent spent towards life cycle ceremonies, 64.67 per cent availed the loan for children's education, 64.16 per cent availed the loan for health aspects and 51.66 per cent availed the amount to repay debts.

The significant proportion of members had availed the loan amount towards income-generating activities. It is inferred that 72.28 per cent of members had invested in trading sectors 21.16 per cent members in manufacturing sector, 14.60 per cent invested in service sector, 13.17 per cent invested in agriculture sector and seven per cent invested in animal husbandry. It is worthwhile to note that 95.83 per cent of members had availed the amount for purchasing personal assets and again 49 per cent of members invested in business assets. The proportion of members availed the internal loan for the purchase of personal assets in SOME was (98.88%) a little higher compared to GOME (93.39%). Similarly 66.29 per cent SOME members invested the amount for the purchase of business assets where as it was only 35.13 per cent in the case of GOME members.

Seventy per cent of the members availed the amount towards children's education, 71.16 per cent towards health aspect and 79.40 per cent of the members availed the amount for life cycle ceremonies in the case of SOME, where as it was little less for the GOME members (60.36%, 58.56% and 70.58%), as against this 85.58 per cent GOME members spent for food materials which was less in SOME (75.66%).

So what emerges from this evidence is the potential of self-insurance through savings.

Utilisation of Internal Loan

The amount utilised by the members for different purposes is given in Table 4.31.

It is observed that 79.19 percent of internal loan amount was spent for consumption and 20.81 per cent of the amount was spent towards business purposes. In the case of GOME,

Table 4.31: Utilisation of Internal Loan by the Members
(Amount in ₹ Lakh)

S. No.	Purposes	Members of GOME (N : 333)		Members of SOME (N : 267)		Total (N : 600)	
		Amount	%	Amount	%	Amount	%
1.	Consumption	51.34	81.61	40.11	76.30	91.44	79.19
2.	Business	11.57	18.39	12.46	23.70	24.03	20.81
	Total	**62.91**	**100.00**	**52.57**	**100.00**	**115.48**	**100.00**

Source: Calculations based on Field Survey, 2008
N: Number stated

the amount spent towards consumption was (81.61%) a little higher compared to SOME (76.30%) as against this, the amount spent towards business purpose by SOME (23.70%) was little higher compared to GOME (18.39%). The share of internal loan spent for personal assets was added with consumption loan. The share of internal loan spent for business assets was added with business loan.

Therefore, consumption loans fairly outstripped business loans. This is possibly due to poverty and liquidity constraints, faced by the household.

Bank Loan

The Reserve Bank of India advises the commercial banks to participate actively in the linkage programmes. Normally, after six months of existence of SHGs and after collecting a sufficient savings fund, the group approaches the banks with its credit plan.

Bank loan will be given to the SHGs. The groups in turn will disperse the loan to its members for initiating income-generating activities. The details of borrowings from the banks by the SHG members are presented in Table 4.32.

It is observed from Table 4.32 that 37.33 per cent of the members had availed a bank loan between ₹ 30,001 and ₹ 40,000 followed by 25 per cent of members availed bank loan between ₹ 20,001 and ₹ 30,000. Further 23.67 per cent availed bank loan below ₹ 20,000 and 4.17 per cent of the members availed bank loan above ₹ 50,000. Table 432 indicates that 23.12

Table 4.32: Distribution of Members on the Basis of Bank Loan Availed

Range of Bank Loan	Members of GOME	Members of SOME	Total
Below ₹ 20,000 (N)	77(23.12)	65(24.34)	142(23.67)
₹ 20,001- ₹ 30,000 (N)	86(25.83)	64(23.97)	150(25.00)
₹ 30,001- ₹ 40,000 (N)	130(39.04)	94(35.21)	224(37.33)
₹ 40,001- ₹ 50,000 (N)	28(8.41)	31(11.61)	59(9.83)
Above ₹ 50,000 (N)	12(3.60)	13(4.87)	25(4.17)
Amount (₹ in lakh)	87.03	70.88	157.91
Total (N)	**333(100.00)**	**267(100.00)**	**600(100.00)**
Average in ₹	26,135	26,546	26,317

Source: Calculations based on Field Survey, 2008.
N: Number stated.
Figures in parentheses indicate the percentage to the column total.

per cent of the members of GOME and 24.34 per cent of SOME members had availed bank loan below ₹ 20,000, 25.83 per cent of GOME members and 23.97 per cent of SOME members had availed bank loan between ₹ 20,001 and ₹ 30,000, 39.04 per cent of GOME members and 35.21 per cent of SOME members had availed between ₹ 30,001 to ₹ 40,000, 8.41 per cent of GOME members and 11.61 per cent of SOME members had availed the bank loan between ₹ 40,001 and ₹ 50,000 and the rest 3.60 per cent of GOME members and 4.87 per cent of SOME members had availed loan above ₹ 50,000. It is appreciable to note that the bank loans to the extent of ₹ 157.91 lakh was availed by the members. On the whole the average loan per member in both the cases of enterprises remains almost the same, (₹ 26,135 in GOME and ₹ 26,546 in SOME), it had only a meager difference. Hence it is evident that SHGs are proving to be the most effective instrument for financial inclusion. The women SHG movements emerged as an important strategy for achieving financial inclusion, contributing to inclusive growth and generating social capital in order to address larger issues like poverty eradication and women empowerment. SHGs are also proved to be a profitable business for rural and semi-urban bank branches. Banks consider lending to SHGs as a business opportunity.

Frequency of Bank Loan

Frequency of bank loan availed by the members from their groups is given in Table 4.33.

Table 4.33: Frequency of Bank Loan Availed by the Members

Frequency	Members of GOME	Members of SOME	Total
1-2 times (N)	80(24.03)	69(25.84)	149(24.83)
3-4 times (N)	239(71.77)	192(71.91)	431(71.84)
Above 5 times (N)	14(4.20)	6(2.25)	20(3.33)
Total	**333(100.00)**	**267(100.00)**	**600(100.00)**

Source: Field Survey, 2008.

N : Number stated.

Figures in parentheses indicate the percentage to the column total.

It could be observed that the major proportion of sample SHG members (71.84%) had availed bank loan for 3-4 times during the study period. Further it could be noticed that 24.83 per cent of the members had availed bank loan between one and two times and 3.33 per cent of the members had availed the bank loan above five times. It could be noted that 71.77 per cent of GOME members and 71.91 per cent of SOME members had availed the bank loan between 3-4 times followed by it, 24.03 per cent of GOME members and 25.84 per cent of SOME members had availed the loan between one and two times and the rest 4.20 per cent of GOME members and 2.25 per cent of SOME members had availed the bank loan above five times. After joining SHGs, members had gained the confidence of conducting bank transactions on their own and approaching bank officials for the loan.

Utilisation of Bank Loan

The members utilised the bank loans for business purposes and a margin of amount for consumption purposes and the details are shown in Table 4.34.

Table 4.34: Utilisation of Bank Loan – Enterprise Wise

(Amount in ₹ Lakh)

S. No.	Purposes	Members of GOME (N : 333)		Members of SOME (N : 267)		Total (N : 600)	
		Amount	%	Amount	%	Amount	%
1.	Consumption	9.94	11.41	3.19	4.50	13.13	8.30
2.	Business	77.09	88.59	67.69	95.50	144.78	91.70
	Total	**87.03**	**100.00**	**70.88**	**100.00**	**157.91**	**100.00**

Source: Calculations based on Field Survey, 2008.
N : Number stated.

An attempt to analyse the pattern of utilisation of bank loan among the members revealed that 91.70 per cent bank loan had been utilised for business purposes and the rest 8.30 per cent of amount had been utilised for consumption purposes. Members of SOME had utilised 95.50 per cent of the loan amount for business purposes and this was little higher when compared to the members of GOME (88.59%). Similarly the members of GOME had utilised 11.41 per cent of the loan amount for consumption purposes which was a little higher compared to the members of SOME (4.50%). Hence, it is evident that the members used the bank credit mainly for investment in income-generating activities to improve their income and it is concluded that the SHG-Bank Linkage Programme had paved the way to participate in self-employment activities.

Sector Wise Share of Bank Loan

The distribution of bank loan according to the income-generating activities is given in Table 4.35.

The distribution of loan among different income-generating activities revealed that 38.65 per cent of the bank loan was utilised in trading sector. While 26.35 per cent was invested in agriculture and allied sector followed by 24.46 per cent of the amount invested in manufacturing sector and the rest 10.54 per cent of the amount in the service sector. The proportion of loan amount utilised by the members in trading sector was higher in SOME (50.48%) compared to GOME (28.27%).

Table 4.35: Sector Wise Distribution of Bank Loan

(Amount in ₹ Lakh)

Sector	Members of GOME		Members of SOME		Total	
	Amount	%	Amount	%	Amount	%
Agriculture and allied sector	28.59	37.08	9.56	14.12	38.15	26.35
Manufacturing sector	17.42	22.60	18.00	26.58	35.42	24.46
Trading sector	21.79	28.27	34.17	50.48	55.96	38.65
Service sector	9.29	12.05	5.96	8.82	15.25	10.54
Total	**77.09**	**100.00**	**67.69**	**100.00**	**144.78**	**100.00**
Total (N)	333		267		600	
Average (₹)	23,151		22,342		24,130	

Source: Calculations based on Field Survey, 2008.

N : Number stated.

As against this, the proportion of business loan amount utilised in agriculture and allied sector was higher in GOME (37.08%) compared to SOME (14.12%). Further in SOME the proportion of utilisation of bank loan in manufacturing sector (26.58%) was a little higher compared to GOME (22.60%). Hence it is evident that the members used the bank credit mainly for income-generating activities to generate their income and it is concluded that the SHG-Bank Linkage Programme has paved the way to participate in income-generating activities.

Capacity Building of Members

The rural poor who join SHGs are helped to acquire capability and competence to maintain and manage their groups in a productive way. They are encouraged to undertake income-generating activities, to deal with financial, trading and input agencies and to manage their accounts and activities in such a way that they continue growing socially and economically and become progressive and responsible citizens of the nation. For this, they are exposed to various training programmes to provide them with the necessary knowledge, skill, motivation and competence. Hence, the training programmes organized for the SHG members are of great significance in the poverty alleviation programme pursued through SHGs.

Training Programme

Number of members participated in the training programme is given in Table 4.36.

Table 4.36: Participation in the Training Programme

S. No.	Participation	Members of GOME	Members of SOME	Total
1.	Participated (N)	257(77.18)	229(85.77)	486(81.00)
2.	Not Participated (N)	76(22.82)	38(14.23)	114(19.00)
	Total (N)	**333(100.00)**	**267(100.00)**	**600(100.00)**

Source: Field Survey, 2008.

N : Number stated.

Figures in parentheses indicate the percentage to the column total.

By observing Table 4.36 it could be noticed that 81 per cent of the members received one or other training programme. The proportion of the members attended training in SOME (85.77%) was more than the GOME (77.18%).

Nature of Training Attended by the Members

Nature of training programme attended by the members is given in the Table 4.37.

It is inferred from Table 4.37 that 486 members attended SHG orientation training, followed by 90.33 per cent attended personality development training, 90.12 per cent participated in micro enterprises development training, 86.83 per cent attended bank transaction training, 85.18 per cent received marketing linkage training and 79.63 per cent took part in health education training. Further 77 per cent participated in book keeping and fund management, general training and 67.69 per cent received skill development training. The proportion of training attended by the SOME members was higher than the GOME members in respect of book keeping and fund management, bank transactions, skill development, micro enterprises development, health education and general training.

Table 4.37: Nature of Training Attended by the Members

S. No.	Nature of Training Programme	Members of GOME (N : 257)	Members of SOME (N: 229)	Total (N : 486)
1.	SHG awareness (N)*	257(100)	229(100)	486(100.00)
2.	Personality development (N)*	238(92.60)	201(87.77)	439(90.33)
3.	Elements of book keeping and financial management (N)*	196(76.26)	178(82.40)	374(77.00)
4.	Familiarisation with bank transactions (N)*	215(83.65)	207(90.34)	422(86.83)
5.	Skill development (N)*	205(79.76)	197(86.00)	329(67.69)
6.	Entrepreneurial development programme (N)*	226(87.93)	212(92.50)	438(90.12)
7.	Marketing linkage (N)*	228(88.70)	186(81.22)	414(85.18)
8.	Health education (N)*	202(78.60)	185(80.79)	387(79.63)
9.	General training (N)*	195(75.87)	178(79.73)	373(76.75)

Source: Calculations based on Field Survey, 2008.

N: Number stated

* - Multiple response.

Figures in parentheses indicate the percentage to the number stated.

As against this, the proportion of members who participated in personality development training and marketing linkage was higher in GOME than in SOME.

Impact of Training Programme

Factor analysis was carried out to study the impact of training. Factor analysis is a multivariate statistical technique used to condense and simplify the set of large number of variables to smaller number of variables called factors. This technique is helpful to identify the underlying factors that determine the relationship between the observed variables and provides an empirical classification scheme of clustering of statements into groups called factors.

Using all the 11 variables on training and exposure visits namely X_1- confidence building, X_2- skill development, X_3- marketing linkage, X_4- bank linkage, X_5- linkage with government officials, X_6- knowledge on rights, X_7- managerial efficiency, X_8- enhanced income and savings, X_9- active participation in decision-making in the family, X_{10}- active participation in developmental programmes and X_{11}- active participation in decision-making outside the family. Factor analysis was performed in order to condense, simplify, extract groups called factors on priority basis and to cluster these aspects of training into groups. In order to reduce the number of factors and enhance the interpretability, the factors are rotated. The rotation increases the quality of interpretation of the factors. There are several methods of the initial factor matrix to attain simple structure of the data. The varimax rotation is one such method to obtain better result for interpretation and was employed and the results are given in Table 4.38.

Table 4.38: Rotated Factor Loadings

Variables	Factor				Communality (h^2)
	1	2	3	4	
Confidence building (X_1)	0.172	0.054	-0.920	-0.100	0.890
Skill development (X_2)	0.150	0.764	-0.056	0.122	0.625
Marketing linkage (X_3)	0.233	0.234	0.087	0.853	0.844
Bank linkage (X_4)	0.381	0.508	-0.092	-0.53	0.694
Linkage with Government officials (X_5)	0.074	0.823	0.267	0.038	0.755
Knowledge on rights (X_6)	0.794	0.091	-0.051	0.171	0.670
Managerial efficiency (X_7)	0.926	-0.100	-0.075	-0.080	0.879
Enhanced income and savings (X_8)	0.553	0.257	0.108	0.114	0.397
Active participation in decision-making in the family (X_9)	0.635	0.231	0.449	-0.230	0.709
Active participation in developmental programmes (X_{10})	0.332	0.209	0.795	0.058	0.789
Active participation in decision-making outside the family (X_{11})	0.727	0.255	0.130	0.037	0.611
Eigen value	3.092	1.822	1.808	1.142	7.864
% of variation explained	28.110	16.564	16.432	10.378	71.486
Cumulative % of variance	28.110	44.674	61.108	71.486	

Sources: Calculations based on Field Survey, 2008.

Table 4.38 gives the rotated factor loadings, communalities, eigen values and the percentage of variance explained by the factors. Out of the 11 variables on training, four factors have been extracted and these four factors put together explain the total variance of these problems to the extent of 71.48 per cent. Under each factor variables, the factors loading which exceeds 0.50 are included and are given in Table 4.39.

Table 4.39: Clustering of Impacts of Training and Exposure Visits into Factors

Factors	Rotated Factor Loadings	Percentage of Variance Explained
Knowledge on rights (X_6)	0.794	
Managerial efficiency (X_7)	0.926	
Enhanced income and savings (X_8)	0.553	I (28.11%)
Decision-making in the family (X_9)	0.635	
Decision-making outside the family (X_{11})	0.727	
Skill development (X_2)	0.764	
Bank linkage (X_4)	0.764	II (16.56%)
Linkage with Government officials (X_5)	0.823	
Confidence building (X_1)	0.795	
Active participation in developmental programmes (X_{10})	0.795	III (16.43%)
Marketing linkage (X_3)	0.853	IV (10.38%)

Sources: Calculations based on Field Survey, 2008.

Four factors were identified as being maximum percentage variance accounted. The five aspects on training namely: X_6, X_7, X_8, X_9 and X_{11} were grouped together as factor I which accounts 28.11 per cent of the total variance. The three aspects on training namely: X_2, X_4 and X_5 constituted the factor II and accounts 16.56 per cent of the total variance. The two aspects X_1 and X_{10} constituted the factor III and accounts 16.43 per cent of the total variance. The one aspect X_3 constituted the factor IV and accounts 10.38 per cent of the total variance. Thus the factor analysis condensed and simplified the 11 variables on training and grouped into four factors on priority basis, explaining 71.48 per cent of the variability of all the 11 variables of training. It was concluded that the members' participation in training programme has more impact on factor I followed by factor II, factor III and factor IV respectively.

Income-generating Activities and Economic Returns

India's development strategy faces the twin problems of unemployment and poverty. These problems could be handled effectively by activating the latent potentials-human and physical. In recent years, the policy planners have been emphasising to stimulate the dormant entrepreneurial capabilities among wider segments of the society and dispelled the classical thinking, 'entrepreneurs are born and not made'. Development of micro entrepreneurship at the grass root level is perceived as a powerful medium to ameliorate several socio-economic problems such as reduction in poverty, balanced regional development, distribution of goods and services appropriate to the local needs, redistribution of both income and opportunities in the community in general. The redistribution of wealth and opportunity leads to decentralisation of economic power within the community.

In this section the researcher has focused on the women venturing into income-generating activities and their performances in the same.

Income-Generating Activities

Details of incoming-generating activities undertaken by the members are given in Table 4.40.

The positive benefits of micro credit lending are clearly depicted in Table 4.40. The members started income-generating activities either as group activity or individually. It could be noted that a majority of the members (39%) were engaged in trading activities. Further 23.67 per cent of the members were engaged in manufacturing activities followed by it 27.66 per cent engaged in agricultural and allied activities and 9.67 per cent of the members engaged in service sectors.

Table 4.40: Income-generating Activities Undertaken by the SHG Members

Sector	Ownership of Micro Enterprises		
	Members of GOME	Members of SOME	Total
Agriculture and allied sector (N)	130(39.04)	36(13.48)	166(27.66)
Manufacturing sector (N)	72(21.62)	70(26.22)	142(23.67)
Trading sector (N)	91(27.33)	143(53.56)	234(39.00)
Service sector (N)	40(12.01)	18(6.74)	58(9.67)
Total (N)	**333(100) [55.50]**	**267(100) [44.50]**	**600 (100.00)**

Source: Calculations based on Field Survey, 2008
N : Number stated
Figures in parentheses indicate the percentage to column total
Figures in square brackets indicate the percentage to row total

The proportion of the members engaged in agriculture sector was higher (39.04%) in GOME compared to SOME (13.48%) indicating that agricultural operations could be carried out successfully in group than individually. Similarly the proportion of members engaged in service sector in GOME (12.01%) was higher compared to SOME (6.74%). As against this the percentage of members engaged in trading sector in SOME (53.56%) was higher compared to GOME (27.33%).

From Table 4.40 it could be inferred that 44.50 per cent of the women preferred to carry business ventures individually than working as group. The reasons might be to seek assistance from their spouse or family members or to provide job opportunities to their kith and kin.

Sources of Borrowing

Venturing into any new business, needs adequate financial investment that may be borrowed from SHGs, banks, friends and relatives or investment of own capital. The following table depicts the amount of investment made by the aspirant women entrepreneurs.

The extent of borrowed fund and own contribution of micro entrepreneurs of the SHGs according to the sources is given in Table 4.41.

Table 4.41: Sources of Funds for Investment

(Amount in ₹ Lakh)

Sources	Members of GOME (N : 333)	Members of SOME (N : 267)	Total (N : 600)
SHGs	11.57(12.35)	12.46(14.63)	24.03(13.45)
Banks	77.09(82.36)	67.69(79.50)	144.78(80.99)
Friends and relatives	4.52(4.85)	4.48(5.26)	9.00(5.03)
Money lenders	0.42(0.44)	0.52(0.61)	0.94(0.53)
Total borrowed amount	93.60(82.32)	85.15(81.46)	178.75(81.90)
Owned fund	20.10(17.68)	19.38(18.54)	39.48(18.10)
Total	**113.70(100.00)**	**104.53 (100.00)**	**218.23(100.00)**

Source: Calculations based on Field Survey, 2008

Figures in parentheses indicate the percentage to the column total

N : Number stated

An attempt to analyse the pattern of loan amount among different agencies revealed that bank loan accounted for a major source for borrowings (80.99%) followed by SHGs (13.45%), friends and relatives (5.03%) and money lenders (0.53%). Further it could be noted that out of the total funds for investment, borrowed capital constitutes a higher percentage of 81.90 per cent compared to owned capital of 18.10 per cent. The proportion of borrowings from SHGs by SOME members (14.63%) was more compared to GOME members (12.35%). As against this the proportion of borrowings from friends and relatives in SOME (5.26%) was a little higher compared to GOME (4.85%). Similarly own contribution by the SOME members (18.54%) was a little higher compared to GOME members (17.68%).

It could be revealed that the members borrowed a very little amount from money lenders (0.53%) and tried to avail the loan facilities from the banks and SHGs at lesser rate of interest. It is evident that SHG members are active in utilising the opportunities to be self-sufficient.

Investment Pattern

The amount of investments made in micro enterprise projects by the members across the study area are given in Table 4.42.

Table 4.42: Investment Pattern

Range of Investment	Members of GOME	Members of SOME	Total
Below ₹ 10,000 (N)	46(13.82)	38(14.23)	84(14.00)
₹ 10,001- ₹ 20,000 (N)	51(15.32)	33(12.36)	84(14.00)
₹ 20,001- ₹ 30,000 (N)	32(9.61)	34(12.73)	66(11.00)
₹ 30,001- ₹ 40,000 (N)	74(22.22)	52(19.48)	126(21.00)
₹ 40,001-₹ 50,000 (N)	42(12.61)	30(11.24)	72(12.00)
₹ 50,001- ₹ 60,000 (N)	39(11.71)	45(16.85)	84(14.00)
Above ₹ 60,000 (N)	49(14.71)	35(13.11)	84(14.00)
Total (N)	**333(100.00)**	**267(100.00)**	**600(100.00)**
Total Amount in ₹ Lakh	113.70 [56.46]	104.53 [43.54]	218.23 [100.00]
Average in ₹	34,144	39,150	36,372

Source: Calculations based on Field Survey, 2008
N: Number stated
Figures in parentheses indicate the percentage to the column total
Figures in square brackets indicate the percentage to the row total

Table 4.42 reveals that the amount of investment in micro projects made by entrepreneurs ranged from less than ₹ 10,000 to more than ₹ 60,000 during the study period. On the whole, 14 per cent of the entrepreneurs had invested more than ₹ 60,000, followed by another 14 per cent invested between ₹ 50,001 and ₹ 60,000. Twelve per cent of the members invested between ₹ 40,001 and ₹ 50,000, 21 per cent of the members between ₹ 30,001 and ₹ 40,000, 11 per cent of them invested between ₹ 20,001 and ₹ 30,000, while 14 per cent of them invested between ₹ 10,001 and ₹ 20,000 and the rest 14 per cent invested below ₹ 10,000. The proportion of members' investment between ₹ 50,001 and ₹ 60,000 in SOME (16.85%) was more compared to

GOME (11.71%). It was reported that ₹ 113.70 lakh had been invested in GOME and ₹ 104.53 lakh in SOME. The average investment of members was more in SOME (₹ 39,150) compared to GOME (₹ 34,144). It shows that some of the members invested more than their share of loan amount indicating that the additional investment was mobilised from their own funds and by resorting to borrowings.

Enterprise Wise Investments and Returns of the Members

The investments made and returns thereon in group-owned enterprises and single-owned enterprises are given in Tables 4.43 and 4.44.

Table 4.43: Investments and Returns From Micro Enterprises (GOME)

(Amount in ₹ Lakh)

Year	Members of GOME (N : 333)				ROI (%)
	Investments		Net Income		
	Cumulative Value	Growth Index (%)	Cumulative Value	Growth Index (%)	
2003-04	62.50	100.00	7.81	100.00	12.50
2004-05	74.00	118.40	11.99	153.00	6.20
2005-06	92.50	148.90	20.26	259.00	21.19
2006-07	103.71	165.93	20.39	260.00	19.66
2007-08	113.70	181.92	24.83	317.00	21.84

Source: Calculations based on Field Survey, 2008.
N : Number stated.

The amount of investment of the members of GOME had risen from ₹ 62.50 lakh in the beginning of the study period 2003-04 to ₹ 113.70 lakh by the end of the study period 2007-08. It registered 81.92 per cent growth in comparison to the base year 2003-04, assumed to be 100. Similarly it has been noted that the income had increased from ₹ 7.81 lakh to ₹ 24.83 lakh during the same period. The growth of net income had been registered more than that of investment. It stood at 217 per cent in comparison to the base year income assumed to be 100.

Table 4.44: Investments and Returns from Micro Enterprises (SOME)

(Amount in ₹ Lakh)

Year	Members of SOME (N : 267)				
	Investments		Net Income		ROI (%)
	Cumulative Value	Growth Index (%)	Cumulative Value	Growth Index (%)	
2003-04	53.75	100.00	6.98	100.00	13.00
2004-05	61.41	114.25	10.81	154.77	17.61
2005-06	81.43	151.50	20.04	286.81	24.61
2006-07	95.25	177.21	22.56	322.93	23.69
2007-08	104.53	194.47	24.19	346.31	23.15

Source: Calculations based on Field Survey, 2008.

N : Number stated.

In the case of SOME members, the investments increased by 94.47 per cent in 2007-08 compared to the base year 2003-04 assumed to be 100. The net income also increased by 246.31 per cent in 2007-08 compared to the base year 2003-04 which was assumed to be 100. ROI had increased from 13 per cent to 23.15 per cent during the study period. Thus it is inferred that investments, net income and ROI showed an increasing trend in both the categories but compared to that of members of GOME, investments, net income and ROI was a little higher in SOME.

Sector Wise Investments and Net Income Earned

Investments and return on investments from different sectors are given in Table 4.45. (*See table on next page*)

Thus it is inferred that for GOME members, ROI was high in service sector (27.45%) followed by trading sector (22.95%), the agriculture and allied sector (19.80%) and the least was in the case of manufacturing sector with 18.70 per cent. Similarly for SOME members, ROI was higher in service sector (32.83%) followed by trading sector (24.87%), manufacturing sector (19.66%) and agriculture and allied sector (17.50%).

Table 4.45: Sector Wise Investments and Net Income Earned

(Amount in ₹)

Sector	Members of GOME			Members of SOME		
	Average Investment	Average Net Income	ROI (%)	Average Investment	Average Net Income	ROI (%)
Agriculture and allied sector	35,685	7,065.63	19.80	32,205	5,635.88	17.50
Manufacturing sector	33,197	6,207.84	18.70	34,554	6,793.30	19.66
Trading sector	33,297	7,641.67	22.95	37,075	9,220.55	24.87
Service sector	32,789	9,000.58	27.45	37,505	12,312.90	32.83

Source: Calculations based on Field Survey, 2008.

To conclude that the ROI was a little more in manufacturing sector (19.66%), in trading sector (24.87%) and in service sector (32.83%) in SOME compared to GOME (18.70%, 22.95 per cent and 27.45% respectively). But agriculture and allied sector earn more in GOME than in SOME. Overall the ROI was found to be satisfactory for the members.

Impact of Micro Finance on Income, Savings, Asset Creation, Employment Generation and Social Empowerment of the Members

Micro financing in recent times, has come to be recognised and accepted as one of the new development paradigms for alleviating poverty through social and economic empowerment of the poor, with the focus on empowering women. Experiences of different anti-poverty and other welfare programmes within the country and elsewhere have shown that the key to its success lies in the participation of the community based organization at the grass root levels.

An attempt had been made to quantify the impact of micro finance through SHG-Bank Linkage Programme on the rural women with reference to their economic and social status after their being in SHGs for a minimum period of five years.

Economic Impact

Economic empowerment is recognised as an important goal of the SHGs. Economic empowerment may be defined as a state wherein the SHG members are able to fulfill their basic needs through reasonable opportunities for income-generation and to own assets of liquid and immovable properties through individual or group activities. The economic impact is discussed under the following sub-headings:

- Changes in the annual income of the members.
- Shift of members to higher income groups.
- Changes in the annual savings of the members.
- Institutionwise changes in the savings.
- Types of business assets obtained by SHG members.
- Employment generation.
- Changes in the level of indebtedness of members.
- Types of household assets obtained by SHG members.
- Repayment behaviour.

Changes in the Annual Income of the Members

The SHG-Bank Linkage Programme with better access to credit brings in its wake increased income to SHG members. The income of the members after joining SHGs had increased and this is shown in Table 4.46. (*See table on next page*)

The frequency distribution of annual income of members revealed that 22.50 per cent of the members were having income below ₹ 12,000 during the pre SHG situation, 73.50 per cent in the income range between ₹ 12,001 and ₹ 18,000 and four per cent in the income range of ₹ 18,001 to ₹ 24,000. This proportion had declined to 35 per cent in the post SHG situation indicating the shift in the income distribution to higher slabs. It is remarkable to note that 33 per cent of total members' annual earnings increased above ₹ 30,000. The proportion of members whose earnings increased above ₹ 30,000 was higher in SOME (38.58%) compared to GOME (28.53%).

Table 4.46: Changes in the Annual Income of the Members

Range of Annual Income	Members of GOME		Members of SOME		Total	
	Pre-SHG Period	Post-SHG Period	Pre-SHG Period	Post-SHG Period	Pre-SHG Period	Post-SHG Period
Below ₹ 12,000	80 (24.02)	0	55 (20.60)	0	135 (22.50)	0
₹ 12,001-₹ 18,000	253 (75.98)	43 (12.91)	188 (70.41)	26 (9.74)	441 (73.50)	69 (11.50)
₹ 18,001-₹ 24,000	0	97 (29.13)	24 (8.99)	44 (16.48)	24 (4.00)	141 (23.50)
₹ 24,001-₹ 30,000	0	98 (29.43)	0 (35.20)	94 (32.00)	0	192
Above ₹ 30,000	0	95 (28.53)	0	103 (38.58)	0 (33.00)	198
Total (N)	**333**	**333**	**267**	**267**	**600**	**600**
Total amount (₹ in lakh)	52.21	93.12	42.80	83.09	95.00	176.20
Mean amount ₹	15,679	27,986	16,030	31,121	15,835	29,553

Source: Calculations based on Field Survey, 2008
N: Number stated
Figures in parentheses indicate the percentage to the column total

Further it is inferred that the average annual income of GOME members before joining SHGs was ₹ 15,679 (monthly average income ₹ 1,307) and this increased to ₹ 27,986 (monthly average income ₹ 2,330) after their joining SHGs. Similarly in the case of SOME members it increased from ₹ 16,030 (monthly average income ₹ 1,336) to ₹ 31,121 (monthly average income ₹ 2,593).

Thus it could be interpreted that the intervention of SHG-Bank Linkage Programme has resulted in the increase of income among the poor members.

To find the significant change in the average annual income of the members before joining SHG and after joining SHG, the paired 't'-test was computed and it is shown in Table 4.47. The following hypothesis had been framed.

Ho : "There is no significant difference in the average annual income of the members between pre and post SHG period."

Ha : "There is a significant difference in the average annual income of the members between pre and post SHG period."

Table 4.47: Paired 'T' Test - Changes In The Average Annual Income of the Members

S. No.	Groups	Pre-SHG		Post-SHG		Increment		Percentage of Increment	Paired 't' value
		Mean	SD	Mean	SD	Mean	SD		
1.	GOME	15697	2263.44	27986	6880.05	12289	5618.05	78.29	39.976**
2.	SOME	16030	2310.36	31121	7494.21	15091	5987.5	94.14	41.185**

** Significant at 1 percent level.

The null hypothesis was rejected since the calculated 't' value was more than the table value (2.576). Therefore it is inferred that the increase in the average annual income of GOME and SOME members between pre and post SHG period was statistically significant. The percentage increase in the average annual income of members was higher in SOME with 94.14 per cent compared to GOME with 78.29 per cent.

Shift of Members to Higher Income Groups

Change in the average income of the members resulted in shifting to higher income. The income of the members has been categorised into five groups as:

1. Below ₹ 12,000
2. ₹ 12,001 - ₹ 18,000
3. ₹ 18,001 - ₹ 24,000
4. ₹ 24,001 - ₹ 30,000
5. Above ' 30,000

It is not possible to expect that all the groups will reach the level of above ₹ 30,000. One can consider that some progress is achieved if a member moves from a lower income group to a higher income group. An overall upward shift of income of the members is shown in Table 4.48.

Table 4.48: Upward Income Shift of Members

	After Joining SHG						
	Income Range	Below ₹12,000	₹12,001 - ₹18,000	₹18,001 - ₹24,000	₹24,001- ₹30,000	Above ₹30,000	Number of Members
Before Joining SHG	Below ₹ 12,000	– (36.30)	49 (14.81)	20 (23.70)	32 (25.19)	34 [22.50]	135
	₹ 12,001- ₹ 18,000	–	20 (4.53)	121 (27.44)	152 (34.47)	148 (33.56)	441 [73.50]
	₹ 18,001- ₹ 24,000	–	–	–	8 (33.33)	16 (66.67)	24 [4.00]
	₹ 24,001- ₹ 30,000	–	–	–	–	–	–
	Above ₹ 30,000	–	–	–	–	–	–
	Total	–	**69 (11.50)**	**141 (23.50)**	**192 (32.00)**	**198 (33.00)**	**600 (100.00)**

Source: Calculations based on Field Survey, 2008
Figures in parentheses indicate the percentage to the row total
Figures in square brackets indicate the percentage to the column total

The data depicts the frequency distribution of members in different income groups. The two point of times used are before joining SHG and after joining SHG. It is evident from Table 4.48 that the percentage decline of the income group of less than ₹ 12,000 was 100 over the base year. Out of 135 members of below ₹ 12,000 before joining SHG, 36.30 per cent have shifted to the income range of ₹ 12,001 to ₹ 18,000, 14.81 per cent to the income range of ₹ 18,001 to ₹ 24,000, 23.70 per cent to the income group of ₹ 24,001 to ₹ 30,000 and 25.19 per cent to the income range of above ₹ 30,000.

Out of 441 members who were in the income range of ₹ 12,001 to ₹ 18,000, 33.56 per cent have shifted to the income range of above ₹ 30,000, 34.47 per cent have shifted to the income range of ₹ 24,001 to ₹ 30,000, 27.44 per cent have shifted to the income range of ₹ 18,001 to ₹ 24,000 and 4.53 per cent remained in the same group. Out of 24 members who were in the income range of ₹ 18,001 to ₹ 24,000, 66.67 per cent have shifted to the income range of above ₹ 30,000 and 33.33 per cent have shifted to the income range of ₹ 24,001 to ₹ 30,000.

Thus the above analysis shows that the shifting the members in the income ladder from the lower to higher income groups is impressive and substantial and this is in consistence with the findings of Jerinabi (2006).

Changes in the Annual Savings of the Members

The SHG-Bank Linkage Programme distinctly differs from other micro finance programmes across the world mainly in terms of its greater emphasis on savings. The changes in the annual savings of the members after joining SHGs are given in Table 4.49. (*See table on next page*)

In the pre SHG period 5.33 per cent of the sample members were not saving anything because of the poor condition and the meager income. It could be noted that about 22.68 per cent of the members whose annual savings before joining SHGs was below ₹ 500 had been reduced to 6.17 per cent and 45.50 per cent of the members who had savings between ₹ 501 and ₹ 1,000 had been reduced to 17 per cent during the study period. The percentage of members who were saving between ₹ 1,001 and ₹ 1,500 before SHG period increased from 14.83 per cent to 29.67 per cent after joining SHGs. Further the percentage of the members who were saving between ₹ 1,501 and ₹ 2,000 before joining SHGs had increased from 7.83 per cent to 25 per cent and the percentage of members who were saving above ₹ 2,000 before SHG increased from 3.83 per cent to 22.16 per cent.

The proportion of increase in the savings of the members between ₹ 1,001 to ₹ 1,500 was little more in GOME with 17.41 per cent compared to SOME with 11.61 per cent. As against this, in SOME the proportion of increase in the savings of the members between ₹ 1,501 and ₹ 2,000 (by 19.47%), and above ₹ 2,000 (by 22.85%) was slightly higher compared to GOME (by 15.32% and 14.72%). There was an increasing trend in the savings of members before and after SHG. This was expected over the years and the members recognised the need for savings and had the tendency to increase the rate corresponding to the loan amount. The average savings of the members had increased from ₹ 775 to ₹ 1,490 in the case of GOME and from ₹ 674 to ₹ 1,622 in SOME.

Table 4.49: Changes in the Annual Savings of the Members

S. No.	Range of Savings	Members of GOME			Members of SOME			Total		
		Pre-SHG Period	Post-SHG Period	Incremental Percentage	Pre-SHG Period	Post-SHG Period	Incremental Percentage	Pre-SHG Period	Post-SHG Period	Incrmental Percentage
1.	Nil (N)	18 (5.41)	–	–	14 (5.24)	–	–	32 (5.33)	–	–
2.	Less than ₹ 500 (N)	84 (25.23)	21 (6.31)	-18.92	52 (19.49)	16 (5.99)	-13.50	136 (22.68)	37 (6.17)	-16.51
3.	₹ 501- ₹ 1,000 (N)	137 (41.14)	60 (18.02)	-23.12	136 (50.93)	42 (15.74)	-40.19	273 (45.50)	102 (17.00)	-28.5
4.	₹ 1,001 - ₹ 1,500 (N)	55 (16.52)	113 (33.93)	17.41	34 (12.73)	65 (24.34)	11.61	89 (14.83)	178 (29.67)	15.84
5.	₹ 1,501- ₹ 2,000 (N)	28 (8.40)	79 (23.72)	15.32	19 (7.12)	71 (26.59)	19.47	47 (7.83)	150 (25.00)	17.17
6.	Above ₹ 2,000 (N)	11 (3.30)	60 (18.02)	14.72	12 (4.49)	73 (27.34)	22.85	23 (3.83)	133 (22.16)	18.33
	Total (N)	**333 (100.00)**	**333 (100.00)**		**267 (100.00)**	**267 (100.00)**		**600 (100.00)**	**600 (100.00)**	
	Mean amount in ₹	775	1,490		674	1,622		724.5	1,556	

Source: Calculations based on Field Survey, 2008

N: Number stated

Figures in parentheses indicate the percentage to the column total

To find the significant changes in the level of savings of the members before and after joining SHGs, the paired't' test was computed and it is shown in Table 4.50. The hypothesis tested was.

Ho : "There is no significant difference in the average annual savings of the members before and after joining SHGs."

Ha : "There is a significant difference in the average annual savings of the members before and after joining SHGs."

Table 4.50: Paired 'T' Test - Changes in the Average Level of Savings

S. No.	Groups	Pre-SHG		Post-SHG		Increment		Percentage of Increment	Paired 't' value
		Mean	SD	Mean	SD	Mean	SD		
1.	GOME	775	447.98	1490	514.58	715	237.27	92.25	55.007**
2.	SOME	674	412.38	1622	605.33	948	303.33	140.65	48.379**

** Significant at 1 percent level

The calculated 't' value of GOME and SOME was more than table value of 2.576 at one per cent level of significance and hence the null hypothesis was rejected. Therefore it was concluded that the changes in the average annual savings of GOME and SOME members, between pre and post SHG period was statistically significant. The incremental savings was found to be significant at one per cent level in the case of GOME and SOME as indicated by the 't' value in the Table 4.50. The percentage of increment of savings was higher in SOME (140.65%) than in GOME (92.25%).

Institution Wise Changes in the Savings

The institution wise share of savings during pre and post SHG situation are presented in Table 4.51.

It could be observed that during pre SHG situation, 52 per cent of the members were keeping their savings with themselves, 26.17 per cent in insurance and other private savings, 13 per cent in post office savings, 9.67 per cent in bank deposits and 3.17 per cent in co-operative societies. After joining SHGs, all the members started pooling their savings

Table 4.51: Institution Wise Changes in the Savings

S. No.	Institution	Members of GOME (N: 333)			Members of SOME (N: 267)			Total (N: 600)		
		Pre-SHG Period	Post-SHG Period	Incremental Percentage	Pre-SHG Period	Post-SHG Period	Incremental Percentage	Pre-SHG Period	Post-SHG Period	Incremental Percentage
1.	Self/SHGs (N)*	167 (50.15)	333 (100.00)	49.85	145 (54.31)	267 (100.00)	45.69	312 (52.00)	600 (100.00)	48.00
2.	Savings in post office (N)*	37 (11.12)	68 (20.42)	9.30	41 (15.36)	73 (27.34)	11.98	78 (13.00)	141 (23.50)	10.50
3.	Savings in banks (N)*	23 (6.91)	204 (61.26)	54.35	35 (13.13)	223 (83.52)	70.39	58 (9.67)	427 (71.17)	61.50
4.	Co-operative societies (N)*	11 (3.30)	103 (30.93)	27.63	8 (3.00)	116 (43.45)	40.45	19 (3.17)	219 (36.50)	33.33
5.	Insurance and other private savings (N)*	88 (26.43)	126 (37.83)	11.40	69 (25.84)	125 (46.82)	20.98	157 (26.17)	246 (41.00)	14.83

Source: Calculations based on Field Survey, 2008

N : Number stated

* : Multiple response

Figures in parentheses indicate the percentage to the number stated through SHGs, 71.17 per cent of the members in banks, 41 per cent in insurance and other private savings, 36.50 per cent in co-operative societies and 23.50 per cent in post offices. The percentage of members' savings in different institutions significantly increased and the increment was high in banks by 61.50 per cent after their savings in SHGs.

Similarly there was a significant improvement in the percentage of members' savings in different institutions both in GOME and in SOME. Among them the incremental percentage was high for the SOME members in banks (70.39%), co-operative societies (40.45%), insurance and other private savings (20.98%) and post offices (11.98%) than for GOME members which was 54.35 per cent, 27.63 per cent, 11.40 per cent and 9.30 per cent respectively.

Thus the members' awareness and preferences towards bank savings were higher indicating the positive impact and healthy attitude to avail bank credit for business venture. Further higher incremental percentage of members towards bank savings indicates the positive impact of the SHG-Bank Linkage Programme on banks as an avenue of resource mobilisation.

To find the significant changes in the institution wise savings of GOME and SOME members before and after joining SHGs, the 'z' test for proportions was computed and it is shown in Table 4.52. The hypothesis tested was.

Ho : "There is no significant difference in the institution wise savings of the members before and after joining SHGs."

Ha : "There is a significant difference in the institution wise savings of the members before and after joining SHGs."

The calculated 'z' value for GOME and SOME was more than table value of 2.56 at one per cent significant level and hence the null hypothesis was rejected and concluded that there was a significant difference in the institution wise proportion of members' savings in SHGs, banks and insurance companies between pre and post SHG period. There was an increase in the number of members' savings in post offices before and after joining SHGs, but the increase was statistically insignificant.

Table 4.52: 'Z' Test for Institution Wise Changes in the Savings

S. No.	Institution	Members of GOME		Members of SOME		'z' Test	
		Pre-SHG Period	Post-SHG Period	Pre-SHG Period	Post-SHG Period	GOME	SOME
1.	Self/SHGs (N)	167 (50.15)	333 (100.00)	145 (54.31)	267 (100.00)	4.269**	5.279**
2.	Savings in post office (N)	37 (11.12)	68 (20.42)	41 (15.36)	73 (27.34)	1.2NS	1.384NS
3.	Savings in banks (N)	23 (6.91)	204 (61.26)	35 (13.13)	223 (83.52)	7.012**	8.13**
4.	Co-operative societies (N)	11 (3.30)	103 (30.93)	8 (3.00)	116 (43.45)	3.566**	4.672**
5.	Insurance and private savings (N)	88 (26.43)	126 (37.83)	69 (25.84)	125 (46.82)	1.471NS	2.424**

** Significant at 1 percent level.
NS - Non significant.

Further the proportion of members savings in private saving schemes was improved both in GOME and SOME but it was statistically significant only for SOME members.

Types of Business Assets Acquired by SHG Members

The different types of business assets acquired by the members for the income-generating activities are given in Table 4.53.

It is inferred that, during the post SHG period in GOME, 18.62 per cent of members had acquired building, 70.57 per cent machineries, 61.86 per cent furniture and 81.68 per cent other assets like tools and equipments. Similarly in SOME 11.99 per cent had acquired buildings, 81.27 per cent machineries and furniture each, 86.89 per cent other assets after joining SHGs. Thus it is evident that the SHG-Bank Linkage Programme has a positive impact on creation of productive assets among the members and this is in consistence with the results of Puhazhendi and Satyasai (2002) and Nair (2005).

Table 4.53: Types of Business Assets Acquired by SHG Members

S. No.	Types of Business Assets	Members of GOME (N : 333)		Members of SOME (N : 267)		Total (N : 600)	
		Pre-SHG Period	Post-SHG Period	Pre-SHG Period	Post-SHG Period	GOME	SOME
1.	Building(N)*	0	62 (18.62)	6 (2.25)	32 (11.99)	6 (1.00)	94 (15.67)
2.	Machinery(N)*	11 (3.30)	235 (70.57)	13 (4.87)	217 (81.27)	24 (4.00)	452 (75.33)
3.	Furniture(N)*	15 (4.50)	206 (61.86)	18 (6.74)	217 (81.27)	33 (5.50)	423 (70.50)
4.	Other assets(N)*	32 (9.60)	272 (81.68)	42 (15.73)	232 (86.89)	74 (1.30)	504 (84.00)

Source: Calculations based on Field Survey, 2008.
N : Number stated
* : Multiple response.
Figures in parentheses indicate the percentage to the number stated.

Employment Generation

Income-generation is the major thrust of the micro credit programme for the SHG women. This programme is initiated to promote micro enterprises for the benefit of the rural and urban poor women. The micro enterprises initiated by SHG women were providing employment opportunities to the members as well as the non-members.

The impact of micro finance on employment generation is shown in Table 4.54.

Employment Generation

It could be observed from Table 4.54 that 478 male members and 446 female members were given employment opportunities by the SHG members. Further, it could be noted that among the male members 69.45 per cent were the spouse of members, 16.75 per cent were family members and 13.81 per cent were hired labourers. Among the female members, 75.11 per cent were family members and 24.81 per cent were hired labourers.

Table 4.54: Employment Generation

Relationship	Employment Generation					
	Members of GOME (N : 333)		Members of SOME (N : 267)		Total (N : 600)	
	Male	Female	Male	Female	Male	Female
Spouse	87 (51.48)	–	245 (79.30)	–	332 (69.45)	–
Family members	37 (21.89)	164 (78.00)	43 (13.91)	171 (72.46)	80 (16.75)	335 (75.11)
Hired labours	45 (26.63)	46 (22.00)	21 (6.79)	65 (27.54)	66 (13.81)	111 (24.81)
Total	**169 (100.00)**	**210 (100.00)**	**309 (100.00)**	**236 (100.00)**	**478 (100.00)**	**446**
Relationship	Regularity of the Work					
	Members of GOME (N: 333)		Members of SOME (N : 267)		Total (N : 600)	
	All Days	As Per Job Availa-bility	All Days	As Per Job Availa-bility	All Days	As Per Job Availa-bility
Spouse	71 (30.74)	16 (10.82)	189 (47.85)	56 (37.33)	260 (41.54)	72 (24.16)
Family members	128 (55.41)	73 (49.32)	151 (38.23)	63 (42.00)	279 (44.57)	136 (45.64)
Hired labours	32 (13.85)	59 (39.86)	55 (13.92)	31 (20.67)	87 (13.89)	90 (30.20)
Total	**231 (100.00)**	**148 (100.00)**	**395 (100.00)**	**150 (100.00)**	**626 (100.00)**	**298 (100.00)**

Source: Calculations based on Field Survey, 2008

Figures in parentheses indicate the percentage to the column total

In SOME 309 male and 236 female members were given employment opportunities. Among the male members, 79.30 per cent were the spouses of members. Further among the female members, 72.46 per cent were family members and 27.54 per cent were hired labourers. In GOME 169 male members and 210 female members were given employment opportunities of which 51.48 per cent were the spouses of members. Among the female members, 78 per cent were family members. The number of members given employment opportunities was higher in SOME than in GOME.

Regularity of Work

It could be inferred that 41.54 per cent of members' spouses, 44.57 per cent of the family members and 13.89 per cent of the hired labourers were given regular jobs and the remainings were given jobs according to job availability. Among the groups, 47.85 per cent SOME members' spouses were given regular employment, which was a little higher than in GOME members' spouses (30.74%). As against this, the GOME respondents' family members (55.41%) were given regular jobs compared to SOME (38.23%). It was found that 13.92 per cent and 13.89 per cent of the hired labourers of GOME and SOME were given regular jobs.

Hence it could be interpreted that access to formal credit through SHG-Bank Linkage had positive influence on employment among the members and would provide greater scope for achieving more and more economic benefits to the rural poor. The result is in consistence with the findings of Pitt and Khandker (1995) and Rajasekar (2002).

Changes in the Level of Indebtedness of Members

Most of the literature on micro finance revealed that the intervention of micro finance programme in the rural areas contributed for reduction of outside loans among the poor households. Hence, the details on outside loans[2] among the members before and after the group formation are presented in Table 4.55. The members who have old debts from the informal sources were categorised into loans availed from moneylenders in cash, mortgaging their material assets to the pawnbrokers and relatives and friends. The rate of interest charged for the borrowings in case of moneylenders was found to be higher when compared to other sources and it comes to 120 per cent and it is collected in weekly installments whereas in case of pawnbrokers, the rate of interest was 60 per cent and from relatives and friends, it varied from 24 per cent to 60 per cent.

Table 4.55: Changes in the Level of Indebtedness of Members

Sl. No.	Groups	Members of GOME (N : 333)		Members of SOME (N : 267)		Total (N : 600)	
		Pre-SHG Period	Post-SHG Period	Pre-SHG Period	Post-SHG Period	Pre-SHG Period	Post-SHG Period
1.	Money lenders (N)*	251 (75.38)	36 (10.81)	236 (88.38)	23 (8.61)	487 (81.17)	59 (9.83)
2.	Pawn brokers (N)*	82 (24.62)	0	91 (34.08)	0	173 (28.83)	0
3.	Friends and relatives (N)*	97 (29.13)	17 (5.11)	75 (28.08)	13 (4.87)	172 (28.67)	30 (5.00)

Source: Calculations based on Field Survey, 2008.
N : Number stated.
* : Multiple response.
Figures in parentheses indicate the percentage to the number stated.

It could be observed that after joining the SHG, the dependence on outside sources for credit declined sharply from 81.17 per cent to 9.83 per cent for money lenders; repaid the old debts to pawn brokers and the level of indebtedness due to friends and relatives was declined from 28.67 per cent to five per cent. The proportion of decline on outside loans among GOME and SOME members was the same except in the case of money lenders, in which the percentage of decrease was 80 per cent in SOME and 65 per cent in GOME. Hence, it was proved that the SHG-Bank Linkage Programme has resulted in reduction of past loans with a higher rate of interest and this result is in consistence with the findings of Anjugam and Alagumani (2001) and Dasgupta (2000).

Prior to group formation, 81.17 per cent were borrowed from moneylenders; 28.83 per cent were borrowed from pawn brokers and 28.67 per cent from friends and relatives.

To find the significant changes in the reduction of indebtedness of GOME and SOME members before and after joining SHGs, the'z'test for proportions was computed with the following hypothesis and it is shown in Table 4.56.

Ho : "There is no significant difference in the indebtedness of the members engaged in micro enterprises before and after joining SHGs."

Ha : "There is a significant difference in the indebtedness of the members engaged in micro enterprises before and after joining SHGs."

Table 4.56: 'Z' Test for Changes in the Level of Indebtedness

S. No.	Groups	Members of GOME		Members of SOME		'z' Test	
		Pre-SHG Period	Post-SHG Period	Pre-SHG Period	Post-SHG Period	GOME	SOME
1.	Money lenders (N)	251 (75.38)	36 (1081)	236 (88.38)	23 (8.61)	4.1411**	9.2182**
2.	Pawn brokers (N)	82 (24.62)	0	91 (34.08)	0	–	–
3.	Friends and relatives (N)	97 (29.13)	17 (5.11)	75 (28.08)	13 (4.87)	3.0987**	2.6818**

** Significant at 1 percent level.

The calculated 'z' value for GOME and SOME members' level of indebtedness was more than the table value (2.56) at one per cent level of significance and so the null hypothesis was rejected and hence it is concluded that there was a significant difference in the level of indebtedness of members before and after joining SHGs.

Types of Household Assets Acquired by SHG Members

The poor are characterised by their low asset. Therefore, any programme targeting the poor should strengthen their assets holding pattern. The increase in assets strengthens the financial position of the household and also improves its shock absorbing capacity. The SHG-Bank Linkage Programme through micro finance interventions increases the productive assets of households like milch cattle, farm animals and various consumer durables such as transistor, cycle, furniture, electronic items and others. Table 4.57 depicts the types of household assets acquired by the members after joining SHGs.

Table 4.57: Types of Household Assets Acquired by SHG Members

S. No.	Types of Household Assets	GOME (N: 333)			SOME (N: 267)			Total (N: 600)		
		Pre-SHG Period	Post-SHG Period	Incremental %	Pre-SHG Period	Post-SHG Period	Incremental %	Pre-SHG Period	Post-SHG Period	Incremental%
1.	Thatched House (N)*	146(43.84)	136(40.80)	-3.04	165(61.80)	116(43.44)	-18.36	311(51.80)	252(42.00)	-9.80
2.	Tiled House (N)*	143(42.94)	150(45.04)	2.10	35(13.11)	80(29.96)	16.85	178(29.67)	230(38.34)	8.67
3.	Concrete House (N)*	44(13.21)	47(14.11)	0.90	67(25.08)	71(26.59)	1.51	111(18.50)	118(19.67)	1.17
4.	Material assets[$] (N)*	94(13.21)	311(93.39)	80.18	92(34.46)	243(91.00)	56.54	186(31.00)	554(92.33)	61.33
5.	Gold and silver (N)*	80(24.02)	236(70.87)	46.85	72(26.96)	239(89.51)	62.55	152(25.33)	475(79.16)	53.83
6.	Electricity (N)*	278(83.48)	325(97.60)	14.12	242(90.64)	267(100.00)	9.36	520(86.67)	592(98.67)	12.00
7.	Toilets (N)*	44(13.21)	130(39.00)	25.79	36(13.48)	132(49.43)	35.95	80(13.38)	262(43.67)	30.29
8.	Water tap connections (N)*	34(10.20)	207(62.16)	51.96	42(15.73)	222(83.15)	67.42	76(12.67)	429(71.50)	58.83
9.	Gas connections (N)*	12(3.60)	168(50.46)	46.86	11(4.12)	178(66.66)	62.54	23(3.87)	346(57.67)	53.60
10.	Vehicles (N)*	4(1.02)	72(21.62)	20.60	6(2.25)	98(36.73)	34.48	10(1.67)	117(28.33)	26.66
11.	Farm animals (N)*	62(18.60)	129(38.74)	20.14	74(27.76)	114(42.70)	14.94	136(22.67)	243(40.50)	17.83

Source: Estimates based on Field Survey, 2008.

N : Number stated

* : Multiple response.

Figures in parentheses indicate the percentage to the number stated.

The field study revealed that a very high majority, 61.33 per cent of the members had acquired material assets followed by 53.83 per cent gold and 58.83 per cent got individual water tap connections while 53.60 per cent got gas connections. Similarly the toilet facilities were increased by 30.29 per cent, possession of vehicles by 26.66 per cent, farm animals by 17.83 per cent and electricity connection by 12 per cent. The number of members who renovated their houses from thatched to tiled was increased by nine per cent and from tiled to concrete by 1.17 per cent.

The proportion of members who acquired material assets by 80.18 per cent and farm animals by 20.14 per cent was higher in GOME than in SOME 56.54 per cent and 14.94 per cent respectively. As against this, the proportion of members who added to their assets like renovation of houses (16.85%), toilet facilities (35.95%), water tap connections (67.42%), gas connections (62.54%) and vehicles (34.48%) were higher in SOME than in GOME (2.10%, 25.79%, 51.96%, 46.86% and 20.60% respectively).

Hence it is implied that the access to Bank Linkage Programme has positive impact on creation of assets among the members and attempted to improve the quality of life of the rural SHG members.

To find the significant difference in the household assets acquired by the members of GOME and SOME before and after joining SHGs, the 'z' test for proportions was applied with the following hypothesis and it is shown in Table 4.58.

Ho : "There is no significant difference in the household assets acquired by the members engaged in micro enterprises after joining SHGs."

Ha : "There is a significant difference in the household assets acquired by the members engaged in micro enterprises after joining SHGs."

The calculated 'z' value for the GOME and SOME members was more than table value (2.56) at one per cent

Table 4.58: 'z' Test for Changes in the Household Assets

S. No.	Types of Household Assets	Members of GOME (N : 333)		Members of SOME (N : 267)		'z' Test	
		Pre-SHG Period	Post-SHG Period	Pre-SHG Period	Post-SHG Period	GOME	SOME
1.	Thatched (N)*	146(43.84)	136(40.80)	165(61.80)	116(43.44)	0.3924^{NS}	2.1214*
2.	Tiled (N)*	143(42.94)	150(45.04)	35(13.11)	80(29.96)	0.271^{NS}	1.947^{NS}
3.	Concrete (N)*	44(13.21)	47(14.11)	67(25.08)	71(26.59)	0.116^{NS}	0.174^{NS}
4.	Material assets (N)*	94(13.21)	311(93.39)	92(34.46)	243(91.00)	32.403**	6.533**
5.	Gold and silver (N)*	80(24.02)	236(70.87)	72(26.96)	239(89.51)	7.266**	6.048**
6.	Electricity (N)*	278(83.48)	325(97.60)	242(90.64)	267(100.00)	1.822^{NS}	1.081^{NS}
7.	Toilets (N)*	44(13.21)	130(39.00)	36(13.48)	132(49.43)	2.02*	4.154**
8.	Water tap connections (N)*	34(10.20)	207(62.16)	42(15.73)	222(83.15)	6.706**	7.79**
9.	Gas connections (N)*	12(3.60)	168(50.46)	11(4.12)	178(66.66)	6.048**	7.226**
10.	Vehicles (N)*	4 (1.02)	72(21.62)	6 (2.25)	98(36.73)	2.764**	3.982**
11.	Farm animals (N)*	62(18.60)	129(38.74)	74(27.76)	114(42.70)	2.599**	1.725^{NS}

** Significant at 1 percent level
* Significant at 5 percent level
NS : Non Significant

level of significance in acquiring the assets (namely material assets, gold and silver, water tap connections, gas connections and vehicles) and hence the null hypothesis was rejected and concluded that there was a significant increase in the acquisition of above assets. Regarding the renovation of houses from thatched to tiled, there was a significant increase at five per cent level of significance for the members of SOME and non-significant for the members of GOME. Similarly, regarding the electricity connection the increase is not so significant for all the members. In respect of toilet facilities, the increase was significant at one per cent level for SOME members and at five per cent level for GOME members. Similarly, regarding the acquisition of farm animals there was a significant increase at one per cent level for GOME members and non-significant for SOME members.

Repayment Behaviour

The micro entrepreneurs had depended on various sources for credit to finance the micro enterprises. The credit was a contribution of the SHGs, bank loan, private loan and own sources. A part of the incremental income arising out of the operation of the enterprises had to be utilised to repay the loans given by the financial institutions as per the repayment schedule fixed by the authorities. Since the loan had to be repaid, the financial assistance had to be productively used by the members. Prompt repayment of funds would enable the financial institutions to recycle their funds. One of the important criteria for the success of the micro enterprise was the recovery of the loan advanced to the entrepreneurs. It may be understood that the repayment schedule varies between 12 and 36 months. In the case of bank loan, the repayment has to commence after the lapse of a certain period known as gestation period but in the case of the credit lent by SHGs, the repayment commences the very next month. The repayment level of the members is given in Table 4.59.

Table 4.59: Repayment Level of the Members

S. No.	Repayment Level	Internal Loan			Bank Loan		
		Members of GOME	Members of SOME	Total	Members of GOME	Members of SOME	Total
1.	Excellent (above 90%) (N)	231 (69.50)	196 (73.41)	427 (71.17)	226 (67.87)	191 (71.54)	417 (69.50)
2.	Good (81 -90%) (N)	68 (20.42)	52 (19.48)	120 (20.00)	72 (21.62)	61 (22.85)	133 (22.17)
3.	Satisfactory (71-80%) (N)	21 (6.31)	11 (4.12)	32 (5.33)	23 (6.91)	9 (3.37)	32 (5.33)
4.	Not Satis-factory (below 70%) (N)	13 (3.90)	8 (2.99)	21 (3.50)	12 (3.60)	6 (2.24)	18 (3.00)
	Total (N)	**333 (100.00)**	**267 (100.00)**	**600 (100.00)**	**333 (100.00)**	**267 (100.00)**	**600 (100.00)**

Source: Calculations based on Field Survey, 2008.
N : Number stated.
Figures in parentheses indicate the percentage to the column total.

It is observed from Table 4.59 that the repayment of internal loan was excellent by 77.17 per cent of the members, good by 20 per cent of the members, satisfactory by 5.33 per cent and not satisfactory by 3.50 per cent. The repayment of bank loan was excellent by 69.50 per cent of members, good by 22.17 per cent, satisfactory by 5.33 per cent and not satisfactory only by three per cent of the members.

Since, the groups own accumulated savings were part and parcel of the aggregate loans lent to their members, peer pressure ensures timely repayments. Group solidarity, group pressure and sequential lending provide strong repayment motivation and produce extremely low default rates.

Social Empowerment of Women

The impact of the SHG-Bank Linkage Programme on the social empowerment of SHG members is discussed under the following sub-headings:

- Increase in decision-making capacity.
- Impact on literacy and health.
- Impact on community and village.
- Impact on personality development of women.

Increase in Decision-Making Capacity

One important indicator of the empowerment is the ability to make decision within the household. The changes in the decision-making capacity of women after joining SHGs were analysed by assigning scores.

The various decision-making areas were given and the members were asked to opine the alternatives given for, before SHG and after SHG period. The alternatives given and the scores allotted were as follows.

If the decisions are taken by male member	1
If the decisions are taken by both	2
If the decisions are taken by female member	3

Based on the marking by the members, the total scores were calculated and divided by the total number of respondents to find the mean score of members before SHG and after SHG period. From the results, incremental score and the percentage variation were found out for the analysis and it is shown in Table 4.60. (*See table on next page*)

It is to be noted that the mean incremental score of the GOME members for decision regarding 'education of children' was 0.86 with 59.31 per cent variation and for SOME members, it was found to be 0.98 with 75.38 per cent variation. The variation was a little more for the women of SOME when compared with women of GOME which shows that SOME women are more empowered to decide the education of their children. Similarly regarding the marriage of their children the decision-making capacity of women improved for both GOME (73.33%) and SOME (68%) members.

Further it could be noted that the decision-making capacity of the women increased by more than 50 per cent in all aspects namely: loan arrangement, purchasing, savings, expenditure, interaction with outsiders, asset building,

Table 4.60: Increase In Decision-making Capacity (Value in Scores)

S. No.	Aspects	Members of GOME (N : 333)				Members of SOME (N : 267)			
		Mean Score		Incremental Score	% Variation	Mean Score		Incremental Score	% Variation
		Pre-SHG Period	Post-SHG Period			Pre-SHG Period	Post-SHG Period		
1.	Education of children	1.45	2.31	0.86	59.31	1.30	2.28	0.98	75.38
2.	Marriage of Children	1.35	2.34	0.99	73.33	1.25	2.10	0.85	68.00
3.	Loan arrangements	1.28	2.36	1.08	84.38	1.27	2.28	1.01	79.52
4.	Purchasing	1.24	2.31	1.07	86.29	1.22	2.33	1.11	90.98
5.	Savings	1.37	2.35	0.98	71.53	1.32	2.34	1.02	77.27
6.	Expenditure	1.30	2.21	0.91	70.00	1.23	2.28	1.05	85.36
7.	Interaction with outsiders	1.27	2.23	0.96	75.59	1.31	2.26	0.95	72.52
8.	Asset building	1.39	2.30	0.91	65.46	1.24	2.38	1.14	91.94
9.	Income-generating activities (IGAs)	1.25	2.18	0.93	74.40	1.31	2.31	1.00	76.34
10.	Utilisation of Income from SHG initiated IGAs	–	2.36	2.36	–	–	2.28	2.28	–

Source: Calculations based on Field Survey, 2008.

N : Number stated.

income-generating activities and utilisation of income from SHG initiated income-generating activities in both the category of enterprises. The increase in decision-making capacity of GOME members ranged from 59.31 per cent to 86.29 per cent and in the case of SOME members, it ranged from 68 per cent to 91.94 per cent. Regarding the utilisation of income from SHG initiated income-generating activities about 74.40 per cent of GOME members and about 76.34 per cent of SOME members decided jointly with their spouse.

Hence it is concluded that the intervention of SHG-Bank Linkage Programme considerably improved the decision-making capacity of rural SHG members on various aspects after joining SHGs.

To find the significant difference in the decision-making capacity of the members after joining SHGs, the paired 't' test was applied with the following hypothesis and it is shown in Table 4.61.

Ho : "There is no significant difference in the decision-making capacity of the members before and after joining SHGs."

Ha : "There is a significant difference in the decision-making capacity of the members before and after joining SHGs."

Table 4.61: Paired "T" Test- Increase in Decision-making Capacity

S. No.	Groups	Pre-SHG		Post-SHG		Increment		Percentage Variation	Paired 't' value
		Mean	SD	Mean	SD	Mean	SD		
1.	GOME	1.1900	0.424	2.2950	0.066	1.105	0.4464	92.86	7.828**
2.	SOME	1.1450	0.038	2.2844	0.078	1.139	0.0857	99.48	35.434**

** Significant at 1 percent level

The calculated 't' value was more than the table value (2.576) at one per cent level of significance for both GOME and SOME and hence the null hypothesis was rejected and it is concluded that there was a significant difference in the decision-making capacity of the members of both GOME and

SOME before and after joining SHGs. The percentage of increase in decision-making capacity was higher among SOME women (99.48) than GOME women (92.86).

Impact on Literacy and Health

The impact of SHG-Bank Linkage Programme on the literacy and health of the members is given in Table 4.62.

Table 4.62: Impact of Micro Finance on Literacy and Health

S. No.	Aspects	Members of GOME (N : 333)		Members of SOME (N : 267)		Total (N : 600)	
		No.*	%	No.*	%	No.*	%
		Impact on Literacy					
1.	Increase in the ability to sign	125	37.54	44	16.48	169	28.17
2.	Increase in the ability to read and write	256	76.87	202	75.66	458	76.33
3.	Learnt to do simple arithmetic calculations	262	78.68	232	86.89	494	82.33
4.	Increase in the ability in talking to a group	305	91.59	252	94.38	557	92.83
5.	Increase in the ability to discuss various topics in group	298	89.49	227	85.02	525	87.50
6.	Improvement in the quality and quantity of the diet	231	69.37	197	73.78	428	71.33
7.	Increased awareness on cleanliness and hygiene	301	90.39	245	91.76	546	91.00
8.	Increased awareness on healthcare	276	82.88	226	84.64	502	83.67
9.	Increased awareness on sanitation facility	152	45.65	177	66.29	329	54.83
10.	Increase in use of PHC	285	85.99	252	94.38	537	89.50

Source: Calculations based on Field Survey, 2008

* Multiple response

N : Number stated

Impact on Literacy

It could be observed that 92.83 per cent of the members' ability to talk in the group was improved and 87.50 per cent expressed that their ability to discuss various topics in the group improved after joining SHGs. Further, 82.33 per cent of members expressed that they were able to do simple arithmetic calculations, 76.33 per cent reported that their ability to read and write increased and 28.17 per cent who were illiterate were happy that they were able to sign after joining SHGs. The proportion of members who learnt to discuss various topics in the group meetings were little more in GOME (89.49%) than in SOME (85.02%) whereas the number of members who learnt to do simple arithmetic problems were more in SOME (86.89%) than in GOME (78.68%). Similarly, the illiterates who learnt to sign after joining SHGs were more in GOME (37.54%) than in SOME (16.48%). To conclude, there was a significant positive improvement in the literacy level of the members.

Impact on Health

It was also observed that, for 91 per cent of the respondents, the level of awareness on cleanliness and hygiene had improved after joining SHGs. Following it, 89.50 per cent of members reported that their accessibility to Primary Health Centres increased; 83.67 per cent opined that their attention towards health care had increased, 71.33 per cent of members expressed that their quality and quantity of diet increased and 54.83 per cent reported that the usage of sanitation facility had increased. Thus there was a significant positive improvement among the rural women towards literacy and health aspects after joining the SHGs. The percentage of members having positive impact on health aspects was more in SOME than in GOME.

Impact on Community and Village

The impact of SHG-Bank Linkage Programme on the influential role of members in community and village are presented in Table 4.63.

Table 4.63: Impact of Micro Finance on Community and Village

S. No.	Issues	Members of GOME (N : 333)		Members of SOME (N : 267)		Total (N : 600)	
		No.*	%	No.*	%	No.*	%
1.	Getting ration cards	175	52.55	150	56.18	325	54.17
2.	Village roads	261	78.38	225	84.27	486	81.00
3.	Transport facilities	285	85.58	212	79.40	497	82.83
4.	Schools/Balwadis for children	185	55.56	173	64.79	358	59.67
5.	Water supply	192	57.66	201	75.26	393	65.55
6.	Sanitation within the village	285	85.59	192	71.91	477	79.50
7.	Representation in local bodies	64	19.22	32	11.99	96	16.00
8.	Other issues	271	81.38	172	64.42	443	73.83

Source: Calculations based on field survey, 2008

* Multiple response

N : Number stated

The effects of women grouping are clearly replicated in the nature of social amenities enhancement in the surveyed rural areas. It is observed that 82.83 per cent of the members have expressed that they have established and expanded the transport facilities in their villages, 81 per cent of members reported that through group efforts they were able to lay sub roads in their residential areas; 79.50 per cent opined that through the groups, they have taken efforts to establish common sanitation facilities and 73.83 per cent of the members reported that they actively participated in all issues of their villages. Further 65.55 per cent of the members have expressed that they have worked to get water tap connections to their rural areas, 59.67 per cent revealed that with the effort of group activities, balwadies and high schools were started in their villages and 54.17 per cent expressed that they have helped the village people in getting the ration cards. It was quite interesting to note that about 16 per cent of the members were elected to the local body in their respective villages.

The proportion of members addressing the local issues namely: transport facilities (85.58%), sanitation within the village (85.59%) addressing general issues (81.38%) and representation in local bodies (19.22%) were higher in GOME than SOME. As against this, the proportion of SHG members addressing common issues namely getting ration cards (56.18%), establishment of village roads (84.27%), school or balwadies (64.79%) and taking efforts for water tap connections (75.26%) were higher in the case of SOME than in GOME. Hence, the above analysis clearly depicts the positive influential role played by the SHG members in community affairs and this is in consistence with the findings of Tripathy (2004).

The increase in savings and borrowings, the timely repayment of loans, the promptness in attending meetings and the decision-making capacity of the SHG members indicate their enhanced status and empowerment. Puhazhendi and Badatya (2002) found that the SHG programme had a positive social impact. Puhazhendi and Satyasai (2002) further argue that the social impact of these programmes on the household is greater than the economic impact.

Impact on Personality Development of Women

Personality development of women is the process of empowerment by creating awareness and capacity building leading to greater participation to greater decision-making powers and control and for transformative action. The goals of women empowerment are to challenge patriarchal ideology, to transform the structures and institutions that reinforce and perpetrate gender discrimination and social inequality and to enable poor women to gain access to and have control over both material and information resources.

The impact of SHG-Bank Linkage Programme on personality development of women was analysed by following five point scaling technique. The scores were assigned as follows:

Significantly improved	:	5
Improved	:	4
No change	:	3
Not improved	:	2
Significantly not improved	:	1

The respondents were asked to opine their level of empowerment based on which the scores were allotted. The total score and mean score were found out and is given in the Table 4.64.

Table 4.64: Impact on Personality Development of Women

S. No.	Attributes	Members of GOME (N : 333)		Members of SOME (N : 267)		Total (N : 600)	
		Total Score	Mean Score	Total Score	Mean Score	Total Score	Mean Score
1.	Self-confidence	1598	4.80	1316	4.93	2914	4.86
2.	Communicative skills	1431	4.29	1175	4.40	2606	4.34
3.	Co-existence – Ability of the members to mix with others	1647	4.95	1318	4.94	2965	4.94
4.	Leadership quality	1514	4.55	1253	4.69	2767	4.61
5.	Awareness of bank transactions	1514	4.55	1210	4.53	2724	4.54
6.	Participation in official discussion	1405	4.21	1190	4.45	2596	4.33
7.	Commanding respect in the family	1594	4.79	1298	4.86	2892	4.82
8.	Reduction in domestic violence	1624	4.88	1306	4.89	2930	4.88
9.	Family and community living	1506	4.52	1203	4.51	2709	4.52
10.	Self-identity and self-respect	1527	4.58	1198	4.49	2725	4.54
11.	Additional skills gained	1484	4.46	1219	4.56	2703	4.51
12.	Marketing skills	1504	4.52	1269	4.75	2773	4.62
13.	Management skills	1550	4.65	1298	4.86	2845	4.74

Source: Calculations based on Field Survey, 2008.

N : Number stated

The scoring approach reveals that the mean score for the 'ability of the members to mix with others' was the highest (4.94) and it indicates that the majority of members were relieved from sigh and fear to move with others. Awareness generation on different developmental programmes in operation, the possibilities of obtaining better income with the resultant better health and better level of living might have kindled the interest of the women in the smooth running of the family resulting in reduction of domestic violence and obtaining the second position with the mean score of 4.88. Further, there was a great improvement in self-confidence of members (mean score 4.86) which is essential for the development of the members. The improvement in self-confidence might be due to the several opportunities given to the women to interact with the field staff, officials, personnel and the opportunity for independent decision-making.

Again it could be noted that there was a great respect for the members in their family (mean score 4.82) indicating their strength in SHGs followed by their efficiency in managing the enterprises (mean score 4.74) better marketing skills (mean score 4.62) and more assertive roles in domestic sphere (mean score 4.88). The members' awareness of bank transactions and self-respect in the village ranks in the same position with mean score 4.54 indicating their improved knowledge on bank transactions and self-respect in the village. Many members expressed how they were not able to conduct bank transactions, as they used thumb impressions in place of signatures. Only after learning to sign, they were comfortable in visiting the banks. It was after joining the SHGs, that they had gained the confidence to do bank transactions on their own, as well as to approach bank officials for loans.

The members' communicative skills have considerably improved after joining the SHGs (with the mean score 4.34). They agree that they can participate in the meetings, interact effectively in the public sphere and enjoy their mobility. Group meetings and interaction with the officials were the possible facilitating factors for the development of communicative skills.

The members were also empowered to gain better marketing skills (mean score 4.62), better awareness for bank transactions (mean score 4.54) and gained new skills (mean score 4.51). They gained these skills during the study period through the training given by the NGOs and the bank officials.

The members' score with regard to empowerment in self-confidence, communicative skills, assertive role in domestic sphere, ability to meet officials, respect in their family, new skills acquired, improvement in buying and selling skills and management of micro enterprises were higher in SOME than in GOME. Further the GOME members gained more respect and identity in the village (with mean score 4.58) compared to SOME members (mean score 4.49). The overall results revealed that the members were empowered in different traits thereby promoting their personality development. This positive change was made possible because of the intervention of SHG-Bank Linkage Programme and the active involvement of NGOs. This is in consistence with the findings of Sakunthalai and Ganesan (2008) and Kanniammal and Jerinabi (2008).

Problems faced by the Members

The problems of the members were classified into six categories namely: *(i)* manufacturing, marketing problems, *(ii)* financial problems, *(iii)* lack of support from Government, NGOs and others, *(iv)* inner conflicts and non-co-operation of members and *(v)* personal and social problems.

Manufacturing Problems

Most of the SHG members were using low level of technology and were not able to compete with other entrepreneurs.

Marketing Problems

One of the important challenges faced by the SHG members was marketing problems since they were new entrants in the market, and they have to face heavy competition in the market from concerns having fairly long standing and good reputation. A proper potential marketing information is also not available to the SHG.

Financial Problems

Most of the SHGs were having members with limited means and therefore use borrowed capital in their business. Though loan and subsidy were available under different schemes of the government, few of the SHGs were facing financial constraints.

Lack of Support from Government, NGOs and Others

The SHGs were formed by the NGOs and they are providing assistance not only at the time of formation but also at later stages. In some areas, NGOs may not provide timely help for getting loans and training facilities. The benefits and concessions specified under different government schemes also not properly available to the SHGs. In few villages the SHG members were not getting support from the village people, rather they were discouraged.

Inner Conflicts and Non Co-Operation of Members

The sustainability of the SHGs depends upon the co-operation among the members. There must be a mutual understanding and co-ordination among the members. Everyone in the SHG should act in good faith. Some of the SHGs have the problem of inner conflicts and non-co-operation of members.

Personal and Social Problems

The members' participation in group activities is largely inhibited due to their personal problems such as lack of training, education, freedom to take decisions and lack of encouragement from the family members. They also face social problems like lack of mobility due to restrictions in the family and the prevailing communal disparity in the society.

It is inferred from the Table 4.64 that out of the total respondents, 54.33 per cent were having marketing problems, followed by 48.67 per cent were facing manufacturing problems, 34 per cent were having inner conflicts and non co-operation among members, 26.17 per cent were facing personal and social problems, 23 per cent were facing financial problems and lack of support from Government, NGOs and others (23.83%). Further it could be inferred that the

Table 4.65 shows the opinion of the members about the problems in their business.

Table 4.65: Problems faced by the SHG Members

Problems	Members of GOME (N : 333)	Members of SOME (N : 267)	Total (N : 600)
Manufacturing problems (N)*	157(47.15)	135(50.56)	292(48.67)
Marketing problems (N)*	177(53.15)	149(58.80)	326(54.33)
Financial problems (N)*	65(19.50)	72(26.96)	137(22.83)
Lack of support from Government, NGOs and others (N)*	75(22.52)	68(25.47)	143(23.83)
Inner conflicts and non-co-operation of members (N)*	112(33.63)	92(34.46)	204(34.00)
Personal and social problems (N)*	85(25.52)	72(29.20)	157(26.17)

Source: Field Survey, 2008
N : Number stated
* : Multiple response
Figures in parentheses indicate the percentage to the number stated

percentage of members having problems were more in SOME indicating the drawback of doing individual business. The Government, NGOs and SHG Federations have to take the remedial measures to overcome the problems of SHG members.

SHGs have not only produced tangible assets and improved the living conditions of their members, but also helped in changing much of their social outlook and attitudes. The group dynamics have reasonably helped many members to overcome the feeling of low self-esteem and lack of confidence and empowered them psychologically.

The study results concluded that the intervention of micro finance through SHG-Bank Linkage Programme has positive impact on increasing income, savings, employment generation, asset creation of rural women members and their social empowerment.

FOOTNOTES

1. 'Warm', money is defined as the savings and other funds generated directly by the members, whereas 'cold' money is grant or loan funds obtained from the promoting organizations or financial institutions. It has been observed that many SHGs treat both these types of funds differently, leading to lack of adequate concern for the 'cold' money. It is always suggested to mix both so that the members use all funds with sufficient care. Thakur and Tiwari (2005).
2. Outside loans in the present study refer to the borrowings from private or informal sources of credit such as moneylenders, pawnbrokers, relatives and friends etc.

- Material assets include television set, mixie, grinder and steel items.

5

SUMMARY AND CONCLUSION

In the development paradigm, micro finance has evolved as a need policy and programme to cater to the needs of the poor sections especially the rural women. The process of women empowerment is conceptualised in terms of personal assertions, self-esteem and confidence, ability to protect themselves as women attaining socio-political status, economic independence and ownership of productive assets. For the empowerment of women, several programmes and schemes had been launched in the past few years by Government of India in order to fulfill its vision of expanding women's horizons of autonomous decision-making and control over resources, becoming equal partners to their men folk to achieve 'the ultimate goal of complete development'. Several programmes and schemes brought economic and social reforms, though not in a significant manner. This led to search for alternative ways to serve the rural poor in general and rural women in particular. In such a search, the concept of women self-help group is praise worthy and it is a new window for the development of the rural masses.

The present study on the "Microfinancing of Rural Women through SHG and Bank Linkage (A Study in Coimbatore District of Tamil Nadu)" is carried out with the following objectives:

1. To understand the organization, management and financial performance of SHGs in the rural areas of selected blocks in Coimbatore District.
2. To analyse the socio-economic factors influencing the members in the choice of ownership of the micro enterprises.
3. To examine the extent of participation of SHG members in microfinancing.
4. To study the impact of micro finance through SHG-Bank Linkage Programme on income, savings, employment generation, asset creation, decision-making skills and social empowerment of the members.

The following hypotheses were tested:

- There is no association between the choice of enterprises and socio-economic conditions of the members.
- There is no significant difference in the level of income, savings, personal assets, indebtedness and decision-making capacity of the members before and after SHG period.

Using multistage random sampling method 120 groups and 600 members consisting of 120 group leaders, 120 representatives and 360 members belonging to these groups had been selected covering ten blocks in Coimbatore District. Among them, 333 members were engaged in group business and 267 members were engaged in individual business. The analysis was carried out to study the performance of members engaged in group-owned micro enterprises and self-owned micro enterprises. The period of the study was five years from 2003-04 to 2007-08.

The study was mainly based on primary data. The collected data had been analysed with the help of suitable statistical tools namely: summary statistics, fixed index numbers, compound growth rate, ratio analysis, Garrett ranking technique, chi-square test, factor analysis, paired 't' test, 'z' test for proportions and Likert scaling technique.

Findings of the Study

The findings of the current study are given in the following headings:

- Organization and Management of Self-Help Groups.
- Performance of Self-Help Groups.
- Entrepreneurial Activities of the Groups.
- Socio-Economic Profile of the Sample Members.
- Participation in Microfinancing.
- Capacity Building of Members.
- Income-Generating Activities and Economic Returns.
- Impact of Micro Finance on income, savings, asset creation, employment generation and social empowerment of members.
- Problems faced by the Members.

Organization and Management of Self-Help Groups

Profile of the Groups

- It was reported that among the sample SHGs, about 82 per cent of the groups had 12-13 members, 13 per cent had 14-15 members and the rest five per cent had 10-11 members. Majority of the members (75%) were in the age group of 26-45 years and were married (90%). About 46 per cent represented backward communities and nearly 58 per cent were having annual income of less than ₹ 18,000.

Governance of SHGs

- It was reported that in 90 per cent of the groups, the leaders were nominated by the members and in ten per cent of the groups, the leaders were elected. The leadership was changed once in a year in five per cent of the groups, once in two years in 18.33 per cent of the groups, once in three years in 9.17 per cent of the groups and the remaining (67.50% of the groups) without any change.

General Management Practices

- It was noted that 63 per cent of the groups conducted weekly meetings, 15 per cent conducted fortnightly meetings and 22 per cent conducted monthly meetings. It was further noted that only 73 per cent of the groups conducted meetings regularly and the rest were not regular in organizing the meetings.

- The members actively organized meetings in 53 per cent of the groups, the animators in 35 per cent and the representatives in 12 per cent.
- Among the sample SHGs, 51.67 per cent of the groups conducted emergency meetings to discuss the official proceedings, 65.83 per cent urgent loan requirements of the members, 15.83 per cent operational problems of the groups and 62.40 per cent of the groups to discuss the social and surrounding problems of the members of the groups.
- About 72 per cent of the groups reported that their member's attendance in group meetings was above 90 per cent, 18 per cent of the groups reported 81 per cent to 90 per cent attendance, 8 per cent of the groups reported 71 per cent to 80 per cent attendance and only two per cent reported below 70 per cent of attendance.
- About 72 per cent of the groups expressed that they had collected fine from the members who were not attending the meetings and the rest did not impose any fine on the members but strictly advised them to attend the meetings in future.
- Further 60 per cent of the groups expressed that their members were highly interactive and participatory in group meetings, 27 per cent reported that their members participation was medium and 13 per cent expressed that their members participation was low in group meetings.

Financial Management Practices

- Regular records of the SHGs especially bank pass book of the groups and the members, group's minutes books, ledgers, cash books etc., were maintained regularly by 63.33 per cent of the groups and the rest of the groups were irregular in the maintenance of books of accounts and records due to pre occupation with household and business activities of the group members, animators and representatives.
- It was found that the members of 70 per cent of the groups were very particular in verifying the records but the members of 30 per cent of the groups were occasional in verifying the records.

- It was expressed by 53 per cent of the groups that their books of accounts, records and ledgers were audited monthly, 31 per cent of the groups half yearly and 16 per cent of the groups only annually.

Performance of Self-Help Groups

Savings Activities of the Groups

- It was reported by 58 per cent of the groups that the savings money was collected on a weekly basis, 27 per cent of the groups on a monthly basis and 15 per cent of the groups on a fortnightly basis.
- The members of 54 per cent of the groups expressed that their group accounts were operated by leaders, representatives and group members in rotation and 46 per cent of the SHGs stated that their accounts were operated by leaders and representatives only.
- The groups' growth index for savings increased by 311.54 per cent in 2007-08 compared to the base year 2003-04. The total savings of the sample groups during the study period was ₹ 93.10 lakh and the average savings per group was ₹ 77,580. The coefficient of variation of the groups savings was 52.03 per cent showing moderate variance and the compound growth rate was 42.48 per cent indicating the consistency in the increasing trend. The growth in savings led to credit facilities; which in turn reinforces the availability of money for investments in income-generating activities as well as repayment of loans and availing more bank loans.

Lending Activities

- The average internal loan given by the groups to the members had increased from ₹ 0.054 lakh in 2003-04 to 0.54 lakh in 2007-08 during the study period. The average loan given by the group was ₹ 1.71 lakh during the study period and it reflects the several cycles of loan given to members to overcome poverty and to climb up the socio-economic ladder. Mostly, the funds were utilised for consumption purposes rather than for income-generating activities.

- On an average, SHGs are able to approve about 15 loans per year to their members. They offered loans for longer periods in comparison to the base year (12 as against 10 months) and the interest rates per annum were reduced to 12 per cent from 24 per cent.

Bank Loan

- A majority of the SHGs (77%) were credit linked between sixth and seventh month from their formation and 23 per cent of the SHGs were credit linked between eighth and ninth month. The bank loans to the tune of ₹ 296.19 lakh was availed by the SHGs and the average bank loan per group was ₹ 2.47 lakh during the study period indicating a sizeable amount borrowed to run the micro enterprises. About 97 per cent of the groups were excellent in repayment of bank loans and agreed that the peer group pressure played an important role in the repayment of bank loans.

Financial Viability of SHGs

- It was interesting to note that the average loan saving ratio of the groups was 3.18 times, reflecting their ability to leverage substantially the institutional finance. The fund management practices of the groups were better since the average credit saving ratio of the groups was 2.20 times, internal loan repayment rate was 98.50 per cent and the bank loan repayment rate was 96.67 per cent.

Entrepreneurial Activities of the Groups

- It was reported that in 82 per cent of the groups, one (or) few members have initiated income-generating activities and in rest of the groups all the members joined together and started income-generating activities. Of the total number of members 75 per cent of them initiated micro enterprises and 25 per cent were not engaged in any business.

Socio-economic Profile of the Sample Beneficiaries

- The study revealed that the majority of the members were in the age group of 26-35 years and in this age group 47.74 per cent of the members were in Group-Owned

Micro Enterprises (GOME) and 52.06 per cent were in Self-Owned Micro Enterprises (SOME). In the age group of 36-45 years, 31.25 per cent were in GOME and 22.48 per cent in SOME.

- Regarding the educational status, 37.54 per cent of GOME members and 16.48 per cent of SOME members were illiterate.
- Hindus constituted the majority with 63.36 per cent in GOME and 62.55 per cent in SOME.
- Among the respondents majority of the SOME members (53.56%) were from the backward community and in GOME 50.75 per cent were from scheduled castes and this indicates that the members of weaker sections of the society were interested in group ownership of business.
- Regarding the occupation of the members, agricultural labourers constituted the major share with 56.46 per cent in GOME and 41.94 per cent in SOME.
- Only 12.31 per cent of GOME members and 5.62 per cent of SOME members were widowed and divorced.
- The members were mainly from nuclear families in GOME (86.19%) and in SOME 53.18 per cent were from joint families indicating that members from joint family system preferred single-owned micro enterprises.
- It was reported that the family size was below five in 67 per cent of the GOME members and five and six members in 72.28 per cent of SOME members indicating that respondents having family size between five and six preferred single-owned micro enterprises.
- The spouses of 20.72 per cent of the GOME members and 14 per cent of the SOME members were illiterate.
- The annual income of 24.02 per cent of GOME members and 20.60 per cent of SOME members were below ₹ 12,000 and 75.98 per cent of GOME members and 70.41 per cent of SOME members were in the range of ₹ 12,000 - ₹ 18,000. Only 8.99 per cent of SOME member were in the range of ₹ 18,001 - ₹ 24,000.

- Regarding ownership of the house, 57.96 per cent of the GOME members were living in rented houses and 67.42 per cent of SOME members were living in own houses. Only 57.96 per cent of the GOME members and 50.55 per cent of the SOME members were living in tiled houses. Further 83.48 per cent of GOME members and 90.64 per cent of SOME members had electricity. Majority of the members were having common tap water, fire wood as medium for cooking, inadequate toilet facilities and were landless.

Participation in Microfinancing Activities

Motivating Factors for Joining SHGs

- The motivating factors for joining SHGs were analysed by using Garrett ranking technique and was found that for the GOME members, 'mobilising savings' was the most compelling factor followed by the desire to avail internal loan and bank loan, to initiate income-generating activities, to reduce unemployment, to develop socio-economic status, NGO's encouragement and to set off old debts.
- For the SOME members' availing 'internal loan' was the most compelling factor followed by mobilising savings. To avail bank loan, develop socio-economic status, initiate income-generating activities, reduce unemployment, NGO's encouragement and to set off old debts were the main motivating factors to join SHGs.

Group Dynamics

- It was found that 23.42 per cent of the GOME members and 60.67 per cent of the SOME members were leaders or representatives. Regarding the attendance of the meetings 66.07 per cent of GOME members and 75.66 per cent of SOME members were regular. About 68 per cent of GOME members and 61 per cent of SOME members expressed that the decisions in the meetings were taken by voting system.
- To analyse the extent of the influence of socio-economic factors in deciding the ownership of activity, either individually or in a group, a chi-square analysis was carried out. It was found that the age, education,

community, annual income, occupation, type of family, family size, education of the husband, employment of the husband and the position of the member in the group strongly influenced in deciding the ownership of the business.

Awareness about SHG's Activities

- It could be observed that the majority of the members were aware of their group's activities such as: cash in hand, balance in bank, savings of the group, number of members taken loan, number of members repaid the loan, name of the bank and income of the group, meeting calendar, rules and regulations, total capital of the group, total loan of the group, achievements of the group, awareness regarding the information in group records and objectives.

Savings of the Members

- A significant increase in savings had been recorded among all members. The quantum of money saved by the members was increased from 100 (the base year index) to 196.28 per cent for GOME members and 200.97 for SOME members during the study period.
- The GOME members' annual growth rate of savings was 29.23 per cent and that of SOME members was 28.78 per cent and the overall growth rate was 29 per cent. The co-efficient of variation of GOME (38.98%) and SOME (37.19%) indicated the consistency in the growth rate of savings and it correlates to overall growth rate.
- It was seen that savings from their own income was the major source for the GOME members (67.90%) and SOME members (73.78%) towards thrift contributions to the groups. This increasing trend in savings helped the SHGs members to overcome the financial dependence and vulnerability considerably.

Internal Loan and Bank Loan

- Internal loan to the tune of ₹ 115.48 lakh was availed by the members during the study period. The average internal loan availed by the members of GOME was ₹ 18,892 and the purpose of loan was reported to be consumption needs (81.61%) and business needs (18.39%). The average internal loan availed by SOME members was ₹ 19,688 and the purpose of loan was reported to be consumption needs (76.30%) and business needs (23.70%). The consumption loans fairly outstripped the business loans. This is probably due to poverty and liquidity constraints faced by the households.

- Further it was reported that the members have availed bank loans to the tune of ₹ 157.91 lakh during the study period. The members of GOME had availed the average bank loan to the extent of ₹ 26,135 and the utilisation of the loan had been recorded as 88.59 per cent towards business and 11.41 per cent towards consumption. The members of SOME had availed the average bank loans to the tune of ₹ 26,546 and utilised 95.50 per cent towards business and the rest towards consumption during the study period. It is evident that the members used the bank credit mainly for investment in income-generating activities and to improve their income. Thus the SHG-Bank Linkage Programme has paved the way to participate in self-employment activities.

Capacity Building of Members

- It was observed that 77.18 per cent of GOME members and 85.77 per cent of SOME members participated in different types of training programmes and this had an impact on various skills, such as: productivity, efficiency, income-generation and confidence building. The Factor Analysis was applied to analyse the impact of the training programmes on SHG members by taking the variables namely: X_1- confidence building, X_2- skill development, X_3- marketing linkage, X_4- bank linkage, X_5- linkage with government officials, X_6- knowledge on rights, X_7- managerial efficiency, X_8- enhanced income and savings, X_9- active participation in decision-making in the family, X_{10}- active participation in developmental programmes and X_{11}- active participation in decision-making outside the family. The factor analysis condensed and simplified the 11 aspects on training and grouped into four factors on priority basis, explaining 71.48 per cent of the variability of the 11 aspects of training.

- It was concluded that the members participation in training programmes had more impact on factor I namely knowledge on rights (X_6), managerial efficiency (X_7), enhanced income and savings (X_8), decision-making in the family (X_9) and outside the family (X_{11}) accounting 28.11 per cent of total variance. This was followed by factor II consisting of the variables namely: skill development (X_2), bank linkage (X_4) and linkage with government officials linkage (X_5) accounting 16.56 per cent of the total variance.
- The degree of impact was lower in factor – III with variables confidence building (X_1) and active participation in developmental programmes (X_{10}) accounting 16.43 per cent followed by the factor – IV with a variable marketing linkage (X_3) being the lowest of all, accounting 10.38 per cent.

Income-generating Activities and Economic Returns

- The members started income-generating activities either as group activity or individually. It could be noted that a majority of the members (39%) were engaged in trading activities, 27.66 per cent in agricultural and allied activities, 23.67 per cent in manufacturing activities and 9.67 per cent in service sector.
- The proportion of the members engaged in agriculture sector was higher (39.04%) in GOME compared to SOME (13.48%) indicating that the agricultural operations could be carried out successfully in groups than individually. Similarly the GOME members engaged in service sector (12.01%) was higher compared to SOME members (6.74%).
- The proportion of members engaged in trading sector (53.56%) was higher in SOME than in GOME (27.33%) indicating that the majority of members had preference to carry out trading activities individually than in groups.
- The proportion of members engaged in manufacturing sector (26.22%) was little higher in SOME than in GOME (21.62%).

- It was found that 44.50 per cent of the women started business ventures individually than working as groups. The reasons might be to seek assistance from their spouse or family members or to provide job opportunities to their kith and kin.
- The average investment was ₹ 34,144 for GOME members and ₹ 39,150 for SOME members. The majority of the members (81%) borrowed from banks to start income-generating activities. It was found that the investment of GOME members registered a growth rate of 81.92 per cent and SOME members 94.47 per cent compared to the base year 2003-04 which was assumed to be 100.
- Again the ROI was registered a growth rate of 217 per cent for GOME members and 246 per cent for SOME members compared to the base year 2003-04 which was assumed to be 100. It was reported that the investment, net income and ROI showed an increasing trend for the members irrespective of their form of business.
- The GOME members reported that their average investment was high in agriculture and allied sector but the ROI was higher only in service sector. In comparison the SOME members reported that their average investment as well as ROI were higher in service sector.

Impact of Micro Finance on Income, Savings, Asset Creation, Employment Generation and Social Empowerment of the Members

Economic Impact

The impact of SHG-Bank Linkage Programme on the economic status of the members was analysed and the findings are given under the following headings:

- Changes in the annual income of the members.
- Changes in the annual savings of the members.
- Institution wise changes in the savings.
- Changes in the business assets.
- Employment generation.
- Changes in the level of indebtedness.

- Changes in the household asset creation.
- Repayment behaviour.

Changes in the Annual Income of the Members

- The frequency distribution of annual income of the members revealed that 22.50 per cent of the members were having annual income below ₹ 12,000 during the pre SHG period, 73.50 per cent in the annual income range of ₹ 12,001 - ₹ 18,000 and four per cent in the annual income range of ₹ 18,001 - ₹ 24,000. This proportion had declined to 35 per cent in the post SHG period indicating the shift in the income distribution to higher slabs.
- It was remarkable to note that 33 per cent of total members' annual earnings increased above ₹ 30,000. The proportion of members whose annual earnings increased above ₹ 30,000 was higher in SOME (38.58%) than in GOME (28.53%).
- Further it was inferred that the average annual income of GOME members before joining SHGs was ₹ 15,679 (monthly average income ₹ 1,307) and this increased to ₹ 27,986 (monthly average income ₹ 2,330) after their joining SHGs. Similarly for the SOME members, it increased from ₹ 16,030, (monthly average income ₹ 1,336) to ₹ 31,121 (monthly average income ₹ 2,593).
- The paired 't' test also proved that there was a significant increase in the average annual income of the members between pre and post SHG period. The percentage of increase in the average income of members was higher in SOME with 94.14 per cent compared to GOME with 78.29 per cent. The shifting of members in the income ladder from the lower to higher income groups was impressive and sub-stantial.

Changes in the Annual Savings of the Members

- It was found that 5.33 per cent of the members had no savings during pre-SHG period and after joining SHGs they have started savings.
- It was reported that 22.68 per cent of the members whose annual savings before joining SHGs was below ₹ 500 has

been reduced to 6.17 per cent and 45.50 per cent who were saving between ₹ 501 and ₹ 1,000 reduced to 17 per cent.

- The percentage of members who were saving between ₹ 1,001 and ₹ 1,500 before SHG period had increased from 14.83 per cent to 29.67 per cent after joining SHGs.
- Further the percentage of the members who were saving between ₹ 1,501 and ₹ 2,000 before joining SHGs had increased from 7.83 per cent to 25 per cent and the percentage of members who were saving above ₹ 2,000 before SHG had increased from 3.83 per cent to 22.16 per cent.
- The average savings of GOME members was increased from ₹ 775 to ₹ 1,490 and for SOME members from ₹ 674 to ₹ 1,622 during the study period.
- The paired 't' test also proved that the incremental savings was found to be significant and the percentage of increment of savings was higher for SOME members with 140.65 per cent compared to GOME members with 92.25 per cent. Correspondingly the percentage of savings of members in different institutions had significantly increased.

Institution Wise Changes in the Savings

- It was found that during pre-SHG situation, 52 per cent of the members were keeping their savings with themselves, 26.17 per cent in insurance and other private savings, 13 per cent in post offices, 9.67 per cent in banks and 3.17 per cent in co-operative societies.
- After joining SHGs there was a significant increase in the institution wise savings and all the members started pooling their savings through SHGs, 71.17 per cent of the members in banks, 41 per cent in insurance and other private savings, 36.50 per cent in co-operatives and 23.50 per cent in post offices.
- Similarly there was a marked improvement in the savings in different institutions both for the members of GOME and SOME. But the percentage of members having savings in different institutions was higher in SOME than GOME.

- The 'z' test also proved that there was a significant difference in the institution wise proportion of members' savings in SHGs, banks and insurance companies between pre and post SHG period. There was an increase in the number of members' savings in post offices before and after joining SHGs, but the increase was statistically insignificant. Further the proportion of members' savings in private saving schemes increased both in GOME and in SOME but it was statistically significant only for SOME members.
- Thus the members' awareness and preferences towards bank savings were higher indicating the positive impact and healthy attitude to avail bank credit for business ventures.

Changes in the Business Assets

- It was reported that during the post SHG period, 18.62 per cent of GOME members acquired buildings, 70.57 per cent acquired machineries, 61.86 per cent acquired furniture and 81.68 per cent acquired other assets like tools and equipments. Similarly 11.99 per cent of SOME members acquired buildings, 81.27 per cent acquired machineries, as well as furniture and 86.89 per cent acquired other assets. Hence it is implied that the programme has positive impact on creation of productive assets among the members.

Employment Generation

- It was surprising to find that 478 male members and 446 female members were provided employment by the SHG members. Among the male members 69.45 per cent were the spouse of members, 16.75 per cent were family members and 13.81 per cent were hired labourers. Among the female members, 75.11 per cent were family members and the rest were hired labourers.
- Further it was noted that in Group-Owned Micro Enterprises (GOME) 30.74 per cent of the spouses of the members, 55.41 per cent of family members and 13.85 per cent of hired labourers were given employment for all the days.

- It was also reported that in Single-Owned Micro Enterprises (SOME) 47.85 per cent of the spouses of the members, 38.23 per cent of the family members and the rest of hired labourers were given employment for all days.

Changes in the Level of Indebtedness

- The members who had old debts from the informal sources were categorised into loans availed from moneylenders in cash, mortgaging their material assets to the pawnbrokers and relatives and friends. After joining SHGs, the dependence on outside sources for credit declined sharply from 81.17 per cent to 9.83 per cent for moneylenders, repaid the old debts to pawn brokers and in the case of friends and relatives it declined from 28.67 per cent to five per cent. The proportion of decline on outside loans among GOME and SOME members was the same except in the case of money lenders, in which case the percentage of decrease was 80 per cent for SOME members and 65 per cent for GOME members.
- The 'z' test for proportions also proved that there was a significant decrease in the indebtedness of members. Hence it is evident that the micro finance programme has resulted in reduction of past loans among the SHG members.

Changes in the Household Assets Creation

- The percentage of members who acquired household assets and housing facilities had significantly increased after joining SHGs. The majority of the members improved their economic status by acquiring the material assets for utility purposes, followed by gold and silver, vehicles and farm animals.
- It was found that a majority, 61.33 per cent of the members acquired assets such as: television sets, mixie, grinder and steel items, 58.83 per cent water tap connections and 53.60 per cent got gas connections after joining SHGs.
- Similarly 30.29 per cent members had toilet facilities, 26.66 per cent acquired vehicles, 17.83 per cent possessed farm animals and 12 per cent had electricity connections.
- It is remarkable to note that 53.83 per cent acquired gold and silver ornaments after joining SHGs.

- It is noteworthy to find that a marginal number of members had renovated their houses from thatched to tiled (9%) and tiled to concrete (1.17%).
- The proportion of members who acquired material assets by 80.18 per cent and farm animals by 20.14 per cent was higher in GOME than in SOME (56.54% and 14.94% respectively).
- As against this, the proportion of members who added to the assets like renovation of houses (16.85%) and toilet facilities (35.95%) had been higher in SOME than in GOME (2.10% and 25.79% respectively).
- Similarly, the proportion of members who facilitated their house by getting water tap connections (67.42%), gas connections (62.54%) and vehicles (34.48%) were higher in SOME than in GOME (51.96%, 46.86% and 20.60% respectively).
- It was further noted that the proportion of members who had acquired gold and silver (62.55%) was also higher in SOME than in GOME (46.85%).
- The 'z' test for proportions also proved that there was a significant increase in the possession of personal assets namely material assets, gold and silver, toilet facilities, water tap connections, gas connections and vehicles. Overall it shows that SHGs attempted to improve the quality of life of rural poor through micro finance programme.

Repayment Behaviour

- It is pleasing to note that, 97 per cent of the members were able to repay the internal loan and bank loan without any default. Group solidarity, peer pressure and sequential lending ensures timely repayments. This repayment behaviour of the members had gained credibility among the banks which in turn helped them to avail more bank loans. Thus the concept of SHG-Bank Linkage Programme had proved that the conventional banks are not only for the rich, but also for the absolutely poor.

Social Empowerment

The impact of the SHG-Bank Linkage Programme on the social empowerment of the members was analysed and the findings are given under the following headings:

- Increase in decision-making capacity.
- Impact on literacy and health.
- Impact on community and village.
- Impact on personality development of women.

Increase in Decision-Making Capacity

The changes in the decision-making capacity of women after joining SHGs were analysed by assigning scores. The various decision-making areas were given and the members were asked to opine the alternatives given for before SHG and after SHG period. The alternatives given and the scores allotted are as follows:

If the decisions are taken by male members	1
If the decisions are taken by both	2
If the decisions are taken by female members	3

The decision-making capacity of the women on various aspects had improved by more than 60 per cent in all aspects namely: education of children, marriage of children, loan arrangement, purchasing, savings, expenditure, interaction with outsiders, asset building, income-generating activities and income from SHG initiated income-generating activities in both the categories of enterprises. The increase in decision-making capacity of GOME members ranged from 59.31 per cent to 86.29 per cent and for SOME members it ranged from 68 per cent to 91.94 per cent.

The paired 't' test also proved that there was a significant improvement in the decision-making capacity of the members after joining SHGs. The percentage of increase in decision-making capacity was higher among SOME women (99.48) than GOME women (92.86).

Impact on Literacy and Health

- There was a significant positive impact on literacy, health and participation of members in community affairs.

Members ability to sign, read and write, maintenance of documents, discussions in the groups, awareness on quality and quantity of diet, cleanliness and hygiene, health care and usage of primary health centres had significantly improved.

- It was reported that about 77 per cent of the GOME and SOME members had improved their ability to read and write, to do simple arithmetic problems and to participate in group discussions.
- It was found that more than 83 per cent of GOME and SOME members were aware of the importance of health care and were making use of primary health centres.

Impact on Community and Village

- Members' involvement in community issues namely: getting ration cards, village roads, transport facilities, schools and balwadies for children, water supply, sanitation within the village and other community issues had significantly improved and the involvement of GOME and SOME members were ranged from 54.17 per cent to 82.83 per cent. It was quite interesting to find out that about 16 per cent of the members were elected to the local body in their respective villages.

Impact on Personality Development of Women

- The impact of SHG-Bank Linkage Programme on total personality development of women was analysed by following five point scaling technique and the scoring approach revealed that the mean score for the ability of the members to mix with others was the highest (4.94), followed by reduction in domestic violence (4.88), improvement in self-confidence (4.86), commanding respect in the family (4.82), acquiring management skills (4.74), marketing skills (4.62) and leadership quality (4.61), awareness of bank transactions, self-identity and self-respect (4.54), acquiring new skills (4.51) and participation in official discussions (4.33). SHGs have not only acquired tangible assets and improved the living conditions of the members but also helped in changing much of their social outlook and attitude.

Problems of SHG Members

The problems of members were classified into six categories namely: *(i)* manufacturing, *(ii)* marketing, *(iii)* financial, *(iv)* lack of support from Government, NGOs and others, *(v)* inner conflicts and non-co-operation of members and *(vi)* personal and social problems. It was found that 54.33 per cent were having marketing problems, 48.67 per cent were facing manufacturing problems, 34 per cent were having inner conflicts and non-co-operation among members and 26.17 per cent were facing personal and social problems. About 23 per cent were facing financial problems and lack of support from Government, NGOs and others. The percentage of members having these problems were more in SOME indicating the drawback of doing individual business.

Suggestions

On the basis of the findings of the study, the following suggestions have been made to improve the SHG-Bank Linkage Programme.

1. The SHG members are running their micro enterprises with low level of technology and capital. So, steps should be taken to enable the SHG members to expand their business by giving them proper technology oriented training and financial support.
2. The main focus of SHGs is to promote group activities but 45 per cent of the sample respondents are doing individual business. Hence the micro finance institutions should be very lenient in advancing loans. Priority should be given for group-oriented activities to promote cent per cent group business among rural women.
3. Periodic training programmes should be conducted not only for group leaders but also for the group members. To enhance the participation of all the members, exclusive education programmes need to be conducted.
4. In many cases, co-ordination is missing between the banks and the NGOs. It will affect the sustainable development of the SHGs. It is suggested that the bank managers should periodically review the functioning of the concerned

NGOs, to sort out the routine problems and to create good rapport among the banks, NGOs and SHGs.

5. Bank officials should help the SHG members in the identification of suitable micro enterprises.
6. Banks may sanction additional loans to SHGs if needed, even when the previous loans were not repaid, provided they are satisfied with the SHGs performance and potential to repay.
7. It was found that 36.67 per cent of the SHGs do not maintain their accounts properly and get them audited. Books of accounts and records maintained by the SHGs should be audited periodically and the periodical auditing of records should be made mandatory.
8. Every block should concentrate on specialised key activities based on the local resources, occupational skill of the people and the supporting market conditions in order to draw suitable livelihood from the investments for the micro entrepreneurs.
9. It was found that in 28.33 per cent of the groups, the members were not regular in attending the meetings of the groups. Members should be motivated by giving rewards like interest free loan, reduction in interest rate, additional loan, compliments and gifts.
10. The leadership position had not changed in 67.50 per cent of the groups. This might result in domination by the leaders in their group activities (or) they might lose their interest gradually. It is suggested that all the members should be trained to assume the leadership role in rotation for better functioning of SHGs. It is also suggested that some incentives and awards should be given for those who have been selected as leaders.
11. The NGOs are more interested in the newer groups only. The old groups get disintegrated if they do not get the guidance continuously. So it is suggested that the NGOs should guide the federations more effectively and in turn the federations should work as SHG guiding institutions independently.

12. The Government should popularise the products of SHGs by fixing standards and should develop a brand image of the SHG products in the minds of the people.
13. The Government should also take steps to sell the products of the SHGs through regulated markets and co-operative societies.
14. More emphasis should be given in networking and federation of SHGs, continuous monitoring of group activities and capacity building programmes especially in the preparation of business plans, marketing skills and latest development programmes for the long stability and sustainability of SHGs.

Policy Recommendations

The following are the recommendations which may be considered in future policy-making.

To the Government

1. Women's empowerment should be reflected through a direct budgetary commitment rather than a core component of all developmental agenda. The micro credit as a component should reflect in the policies and plans oriented towards women's empowerment to enhance women's agency on social, political and economic activities. Women's agency must be given priority. Women's rights over property rights need to be enhanced and women's access, control and decision-making need to be ensured in all programme components.
2. All programmes need to evolve common set of indicators for measuring progress on women's empowerment in order to assess the contribution of distinct strategies towards women's empowerment.
3. There is a need to streamline government programmes and to ensure convergence of schemes, so that officials' support for skill training, extension support, credit and other enterprises related services may be accessed easily.
4. Government should promote micro credit systems only when they are linked to social mobilsation and community empowerment. The government agencies should not be

involved in mobilising communities themselves. This task should be left to NGOs and CBOs. Financial institutions should concentrate on training and capacity building only on financial matters.

5. Micro credit should be made available not only for income-generation but also for consumption needs arising out of emergencies, crisis, as also for housing, sanitation and provision of basic amenities. Micro credit should be provided in the form of revolving funds so that local communities can identify priorities and not be restricted by any predetermined activities.
6. Government support is required to start income-generating activities. More training in income-generating activities is required. Training programmes should be organized according to market demand and the feasibility studies should be undertaken. Marketing facilities need to be provided to the SHGs.
7. Manpower is a prerequisite to implement social programmes at the grass root level. There is a need for providing project-implementing agencies with specifically designated separate staff, who are supposed to be an umbrella programme of women's empowerment.
8. The agencies of State and Central government should ensure proper monitoring of SHGs, SHG promoters and other development functionaries. The ad-hoc arrangement of supervision, monitoring and regulation of projects should be discouraged.
9. There should be creation of permanent cell at the state level to oversee the functioning, monitoring and evaluation of the projects frequently with fully equipped infrastructure like computers, internet, mobility facility and minimum experienced and qualified staff.
10. Marketing centres may be provided within the village to ensure better selling of products. Quality control of products is needed. There should be more budgetary allocation on market development in order to provide an effective platform for marketing of SHG products.

11. A proper mechanism should be evolved to prepare database on SHGs, SHPIs, MFIs, etc. A census of SHGs may also be undertaken for ensuring effective regulation of micro financing activities and examining their problems. MIS with good management backing needs to be developed to achieve sustainability of micro financing institutions.
12. There is considerable scope for development of micro finance in India since there is enormous unmet demand for financial services in this sector. Therefore, enacting fresh legislation or appropriate amendments in the existing legislation related to micro financial institutions is needed.

To the Banks/Micro Finance Institutions

1. Designing wide range of financial products and services is the need of the hour. SHGs have different kinds of credit needs and thus, the credit needs should be classified into different categories such as: livelihood, income-generating activities, investment in education, health, consumption, household needs, marriages, death ceremonies and products for social security.
2. There is an urgent need to streamline the procedure for applying, seeking and releasing of credit from the banks. The procedural difficulties are one of the major impediments which have denied women, the financial benefits of the banks. Therefore, the procedure for credit access to women should be made easy and simple.
3. Microfinancing institutions need proper regulation and operation of business transactions. Thus RBI, SIDBI, NABARD and other organizations should evolve proper mechanism for monitoring, supervising, directing, appraising and evaluating the micro financial institutions as well as self-help promoting institutions.
4. Transformation in the repayment culture is required. Any expansion of microfinancing services will need not only appropriate and efficient micro products on a very large scale, but also customers, who care willingly to pay the full cost of those services. Bankers must change their attitude towards small loans to poor people, including

women, as a social obligation of treating them as potential business entrepreneurs.

5. Branch managers of financial institutions should in any case be close to the communities they serve and should be aware of distribution channel through which they can profitably reach new customers. They should be ensured of the existing level and types of group activities and informal intermediation and be ready to offer savings and lending products, appropriate for local communities.
6. There should be timely release of funds and its channelisation to the concerned departments and agencies. The delays in allotment of funds and their release should be discouraged and taken seriously by the high level authorities when it happens in any state. There is also a need for timely and quick approval of activities proposed.
7. The banks should open their exclusive branches/counters in rural areas to promote micro finance among the SHGs.
8. Rigorous and more transparent exercise should be undertaken to select only competent NGOs to lend their supporting hands to SHGs, to avoid loopholes in their selection.

To the NGOs

1. Monitoring of SHGs should be made more rigorous to ensure regular and timely savings and contributions. Holding SHG meetings and members' attendance in it should be indispensable. The NGOs should provide necessary guidance to the groups to make every meeting meaningful and to take objective decisions regarding internal loan, interest rate and loan recovery with bank linkage.
2. The NGOs should actively help the SHGs in both backward and forward linkages and provide them market support in particular. The officials of SHG promoting organizations should also be exposed to SHGs sensitisation programmes to avoid being skeptical towards SHGs and to have faith in the SHGs' ability to alleviate rural poverty.

3. The factors responsible for poor performance and functioning of SHGs should be investigated, examined and analysed scientifically and systematically to resolve the emerging problems, difficulties and challenges being faced.
4. Resources should be allocated and spent on creating market support to the SHG's products and also providing some sort of reward to successful SHGs as an incentive for good work.

To the SHGs

1. It is desirable to have a system of office-bearers' rotation of SHGs at regular intervals. If possible, it may be made mandatory.
2. All record keeping has to be done manually and that is very time consuming. So a computer and necessary training to operate the system should be made available to maintain records, accounts, correspondence and to update the same periodically.
3. The key elements in the survival and sustainability of the SHGs should naturally be built on those elements that have brought the groups together. SHGs have to evolve as sustainable village level institutions for taking active role in development and governance.
4. A fully matured group is the one that achieves competence to independently handle issues of its internal practices both financial and non-financial. The group should be able to manage its leadership, to handle problems and conflicts successfully with minimal help. It should also be in a position to maintain its records and other books of accounts independently.
5. In addition to the institutional sustainability, the group should also become financially viable. Financial sustainability of the group is achieved when the group is able to cover its operational costs from its income.
6. The SHG members should be inculcated with a feeling of collective development, social harmony, mutual trust and active role in development process and governance. The members should be mentally prepared for starting income-generating activities and their sustainability.

7. The SHGs should concentrate in building up Memorandum of Understanding (MOU) with different institutions to enhance the value addition and for continued business activities.

To the Educational Institutions

1. Short-term and diploma courses on micro finance should be introduced to create a cadre of professionals in micro finance; to provide a thorough knowledge of the concept of micro finance and insight into the working of micro finance institutions and to build capacity of those who are working in the micro finance sector on the perspectives on micro finance and its operational aspects.
2. A topic on micro finance should be compulsorily introduced in all courses to create awareness among the students.
3. Persons who have completed a course in micro finance should be given preference in bank jobs, who in turn manage the SHG-banking programme.

The suggestions and recommendations will definitely ensure desirable improvement and will make the performance of SHGs better and practically more viable.

Scope for Further Research

The following areas are suggested for further research in micro finance.

- A study may be conducted on the Impact of Micro Finance Schemes on Priority Communities (SCs/STs/Minorities).
- A study on Financial Performance of micro finance institutions may be carried out.
- A study on financial inclusion through SHG-Bank Linkage Programme can be undertaken.
- A study on Health Micro Insurance among SHG women may be conducted.

Conclusion

The study results proved that the intervention of micro finance through SHG-Bank Linkage Programme, has positive impact on the economic and social status of the members, in terms of increase in income, savings, employment generation, asset creation, decrease in the dependency on money lenders, improvement in decision-making skills, participation in community affairs and the empowerment of women. The SHGs had contributed in developing the personalities of women, in moulding the community in the right perspective and in exploring the initiatives of women in taking up entrepreneurial ventures. SHGs had emerged as the providers of social capital for transforming today's rural India into a powerful society through micro finance.

BIBLIOGRAPHY

Books

Bhatia, N., and Bhatia, A., (2000), *Women and Micro Credit*, New Delhi: Sonali Publications.

Choudhury, R. C., Mohanan, N., Purushotham, P., Kumaran, K. P., Mohiuddin, A., Reddy, D. P. R., and Ramanarao D. V., (2001), *Micro Credit for Micro Enterprises*, Hyderabad: National Institute of Rural Development.

Desai, B. M., and Namboodiri N. V., (2001), *Organization and Management of Rural Financial Sector: Text, Cases and Exercises*, New Delhi: Oxford and IBH Publishing Company Private Limited.

Devadas, R., (1998), *Economical Development of Indian Women*, New Delhi: Rathan Publications.

Garrett, H. E., (1969), *Statistics in Psychology and Education*, Bombay: Vakils Feffer and Simons Private Limited.

Gupta, R. C., (1993), *Guidelines for Field Workers on Management of Self-Help Savings and Credit Groups*, New Delhi: Friedrich Ebert Stiffung.

Jain, S., (2000), "Empowerment of Women through NGOs – The SEWA Bank Experience", in Kamta Prasad (eds.), *NGOs and Socio-Economic Development Opportunities*, New Delhi: Deep and Deep Publications Pvt. Ltd.

Jerinabi, U., (2006), *Micro Credit Management by Women's Self-Help Groups*, New Delhi: Discovery Publishing House.

Jerinabi, U., (2008), "Poverty Alleviation through Micro Credit", in Jerinabi (ed.), *Micro Enterprises for Women – Competitiveness, Challenges and Prospects for New Global Environment*, New Delhi: Discovery Publishing House Pvt. Ltd.

Kallur, M. S. and Biradar, A. A., (2000), "The New Paradigm of Micro Finance and the Role of Non-Governmental Voluntary Agencies in its Promotion: A Few Reflections" in Kamta Prasad (ed.), *NGO's and Socio-Economic Development Opportunities*, New Delhi: Deep and Deep Publications Pvt. Ltd.

Kanniammal, K., and Jerinabi, U., (2008), "Role of SHGs in Empowerment of Women", in Jerinabi (ed.), *Micro Enterprises for Women – Competitiveness, Challenges and Prospects for New Global Environment*, New Delhi: Discovery Publishing House Pvt. Ltd.

Karmakar, K. G., (1999), *Rural Credit and SHGs: Micro Finance Needs and Concepts in India*, New Delhi: Sage Publications.

Khandker, R. S., (1998), *Fighting Poverty with Micro Credit: Experience in Bangladesh*, Oxford University Press, New York: World Bank.

Kohili, S., (1998), *Women Entrepreneurs in India*, New Delhi: Mittal Publications.

Kundu, K., (2003), *Sustainable Micro Finance through Self-Help Group: A Case Study of Gurugon District*, New Delhi: Discovery Publishing House.

Lalitha, N., and Nagarajan, B. S., (2002), "Functioning of the SHGs in Selected District of Tamil Nadu", in *Self-Help Groups in Rural Development*, New Delhi: Dominant Publishers and Distributors.

Malhotra, R., (2000), *Women and Empowerment – Approaches and Strategies*, New Delhi: Discovery Publishing House.

Manimekalai, N., (2000), "NGO's Intervention through Micro Credit for Self-Help Women Groups in Rural Tamil Nadu", in Kamta Prasad (eds.), *NGOs and Socio-Economic Development Opportunities*, New Delhi: Deep and Deep Publications Pvt. Ltd.

Prasad, H., (1997), "International Fund for Agricultural Development (IFAD's)", *Women's Development Programme for Economic Empowerment,* in Sushama Sahay (eds.), *Women and Empowerment – Approaches and Strategies,* New Delhi: Discovery Publishing House.

Puhazhendi, V., (1995), *Transaction Costs of Lending to the Rural Poor,* Melbourne, Australia: The Foundation for Development Co-operation Limited.

Puhazhendi, V., (1999), *Transaction Costs of Lending to the Rural Poor – NGOs and SHGs of the Poor as Intermediaries for Banks in India,* Australia: The Foundation for Development Co-operation, Brisbane.

Rajeswari, M. and Sumangala, P., (1999), *Women Entrepreneurs a Scan on their Problems and Prospects in Women Entrepreneurship, Issues and Strategies,* New Delhi: Kanishka Publishers.

Rao, V. M., (1991), *Promotion of Entrepreneurship in Andhra Pradesh,* New Delhi: Deep and Deep Publications Pvt. Ltd.

Rasure, K. A., (2002), *Empowerment of Women through SHGs,* Delhi: Isha Books.

Ray, N. and Vasundhara, D. P., (1996), "Like My Mother's House: Women's Thrift and Credit Co-operatives in South India" in Marilyn Carr, Martha Chen and Renana Jhabvala (eds.), *Speaking out – Women's Economic Empowerment in South Asia,* New Delhi: Vistaar Publications.

Sakunthalai, A., and Ganesan, R., (2008), "Women Empowerment – An Empirical Study", in Jerinabi (ed.), *Micro Enterprises for Women – Competitiveness, Challenges and Prospects for New Global Environment",* New Delhi: Discovery Publishing House Pvt. Ltd.

Sahay, S., (1998), *Women and Empowerment: Approaches and Strategies,* New Delhi: Discovery Publishing House Pvt. Ltd.

Satish, P., (2001), *Empowering the Indian Women,* Publications Division, Ministry of Information and Broadcasting, Government of India.

Sharma, K. C., (2001), *Women Self-Help Groups and Empowerment,* New Delhi: Anmol Publications Pvt. Ltd.

Singh, G., and Singh, A. M. S., (2003), "Economic Participation of Rural Women in Informal Sector through Self-Help Group", *Economic Empowerment of Rural Women in India*, Jaipur: RBSA, Publishers.

Somanath, V. S., (2009), "Micro Finance Redefining the Future", New Delhi: Bycel Books.

Soundarapandian, M., (2006), *Role of Micro Finance in the Growth of SHGs*, New Delhi: Sarup and Sons.

Sreelakshanamma, K., (2000), "Empowerment of Rural Women in Rural Non-Farm Activities through the DWCRA Programme", in M. Koteswara Rao (ed.), *Rural Employment: The Non-Farm Sector*, New Delhi: Deep and Deep Publications Pvt. Ltd.

Srinivasan, S., Varadharaj, S., and Chandrakumar M., (2004), *Financial Performance of Rural and Urban Self-Help Groups*, Hyderabad: National Institute of Rural Development.

Uphoff, N., (1992), *Local Institutions and Participation for Sustainable Development*, IIED, London: Gatekeeper Series No. 31.

Varma, N. B., and Nath, M., (2004), *Women in Development Programme*, New Delhi: Deep and Deep Publications Pvt. Ltd.

Journals

Ahmad, M. A., (1999), "Women Empowerment: Self-Help Groups", *Kurukshetra*, 47: 69-72.

Agarwal, B., (1985), "Impact of Rural Development in Economic Status of Women", *Indian Journal of Agricultural Economics*, 11 (3): 482-487.

Alosyus, G., (1991), "DWCRA – Working Wonders for Kashmiri Women", *Yojana*, 35 (22): 17 24.

Anjugam, M., and Alagumani, T., (2001), "Impact of Micro Finance through Self-Help Groups – A Case Study", *Indian Journal of Agricultural Economics*, 56 (3): 458.

Apparao, G., (1999), "Rural Women and Poverty Alleviation", *Kurukshetra*, 47 (12): 28-34.

Bankers Institute for Rural Development, (1996), "The Bank Performance Improvement under Maharashtra Rural Credit Project (MRCP)", *Rural Banker, Issue,* 21: 22.

Bansal, H., (2003), "SHG-Bank Linkage Programme in India: An Overview", *Journal of Micro Finance,* 5 (1) : 21-50.

Barbara, S. and Mahanta, R., (2001), "Micro-enterprises for Income-Generation", *Indian Journal of Agricultural Economics*, 56 (3): 406-409.

Basu, P., and Srivastava P., (2005), "Exploring Possibilities: Micro Finance and Rural Credit Access for the Poor in India", *Economic and Political Weekly*, 40 (17): 1747-1756.

Besley, T., (1994), "How Do Market Failures Justify Interventions in Rural Credit Market", *The World Bank Research Observer*, 9 (1): 27-47.

Bouman, F. J. A., and Houtman, R., (1988), "Pawn Broking as an Instrument of Rural Banking in the Third World Countries", *Economic Development and Cultural Change*, 37 (1): 69-90.

Braverman, A., and Guash J. L., (1984), "Capital Requirements, Screening and Interlinked Share Cropping and Credit Contracts", *Journal of Development Economics,* 14 (3): 113-117.

Braverman, A., and Guash J. L., (1989), "Rural Credit in LDC's: Issues and Evidence", *Journal of Development Economics*, 14 (6): 7-34.

Chandrakavate, M. S., (2006), "The SHG Model of Micro Finance: A Silent Movement Towards Empowering Women", *Southern Economist,* 44 (17): 29-32.

Chavan, P., and Ram Kumar, R., (2002), "Micro credit and Rural Poverty – An Analysis of Empirical Evidence", *National Bank News Review,* 18 (1) : 17-34.

Chikara, O. P., (1993), "Study on the Impact of Institutional Credit on Weaker Section", *Kurukshetra,* 26 (5): 29.

Dadhich, C. L., (2001), "Micro Finance – A Panacea for Poverty Alleviation: A Case Study of Oriental Grameen Project in India", *Indian Journal of Agricultural Economics,* 56 (3): 420-426.

Dahiya, P. S., Pandey N. K., and Karol, A., (1999), "Socio-Economic Upliftment through Self-Help Groups in Solan District of Himachal Pradesh", *Journal of Agricultural Development and Policy,* 14 (1): 10-18.

Damayanthi, U. T., (1999), "Development of Women and Children in Rural Area: An Impact Study", *The Asian Economic Review,* 41 (2): 349-357.

Dasgupta, R., (2000), "Micro Finance in India: Empirical Evidence, Alternative Models and Policy Imperatives", *Economic and Political Weekly,* 3 (19): 111-114.

Desai, B. M., (1987), "Rapporteurs Report on Credit", *Indian Journal of Agricultural Economics* 42 (1): 29-31.

Desai, B. M., and Namboodiri, N. V., (1996), "Whither Rural Financial Institutions", *Economic and Political Weekly,* 31 (31) : 407-411.

Dwarakanath, H. D., (2002), "Rural Credit and Women Self-Help Groups – A Profile of Rangareddy District in Andhra Pradesh", *Kurukshetra,* 48 (2): 9-15.

Gangaiah, C., Nagaraja, B., and Naidu, V. C., (2006), "Impact of Self-Help Groups on Income and Employment a Case Study", *Kurukshetra,* 54 (5) : 18-23.

Girija, S. and Satish, P., (1999), "Impact of SHG Lending on the Profitability of Branches", *Rural Banker Issue,* 21: 22.

Gupta M. L., and Gupta, N., (2006), "Economic Empowerment of Women through Self-Help Groups", *Kurukshetra,* 54 (4): 23-26.

Gupta, M. S., (2008), "Micro Finance through Self-Help Groups: An Emerging Horizon for Rural Development", *The Indian Journal of Commerce,* 61 (3): 36-47.

Hill, E., (2001), "Women in the Indian Informal Economy: Collective Strategies for Work Life Improvement and Development", *Work, Employment and Society,* 15 (3): 17-24.

Hoff, K., and Stiglitz, J. E., (1990), "Introduction: Imperfect Information and Rural Credit Markets-Puzzles and Policy Perspectives", *The World Bank Economic Review,* 4 (3): 235-250.

Huppi, M., and Feder, G., (1990), "The Role of Groups and Credit Co-operatives in Rural Lending", *The World Bank Research Observer,* 5 (2): 187-204.

Indian Bank, (1995), "Performance of Indian Bank Branches in SHG Lending", *Rural Banker Issue,* 21: 2.

Jha, T. N., (2002) "Micro Credit Finance Models in Bangladesh – A Visitor's Perspective", *The Asian Economic Review,* 44 (1): 58-68.

Kabber, N., (2001), "Conflicts Over Credit: Re-evaluating the Empowerment Potential of Loans to Women in Rural Bangladesh", *World Development,* 29 (1): 63-84.

Kaladhar, K., (1997), "Micro Finance in India – Design, Structure and Governance", *Economic and Political Weekly,* 32 (42): 21.

Kumaran, K. P., (2001), "Self-Help Groups of the Rural Poor in India: An Analysis", *National Bank News Review,* 17(2): 31-37.

Kumar, V., and Sharma, H. R., (2007), "Micro Finance on Mountainous States (Disparities in Outreach)", *Man and Development,* 56 (3): 81-95.

Kunjukunju, B., (2005), "Role of Institutional Finance in Rural Development of Kerala", *Finance India,* 19 (1): 189-194.

Lal, M., (2005), "Information Technology Initiatives: Impact on Self-Help Groups in India", *The Indian Journal of Labour Economics,* 48 (4): 883.

Madheswaran, S., and Dharmadhikary, A., (2001), "Empowering Rural Women through SHGs: Lessons from Maharashtra Rural Credit Project", *Indian Journal of Agricultural Economics,* 56 (3): 398-400.

Manimekalai, M., and Rajeshwari, G., (2001), "Nature and Performance of Informal Self-Help Groups – A Case from Tamil Nadu", *Indian Journal of Agricultural Economics,* 56 (3): 453-454.

Misra, J. P., Verma, P. R., and Singh, S., (2001), "Socio-Economic Analysis on Rural SHG's Scheme in Block Amaniganj District Faizabad (U.P.)", *Indian Journal of Agricultural Economics,* 56 (3): 480-482.

Modekey, M. D., (1999), "SHGs and Micro Credit : Sustaining Rural Women", *Social Welfare*, 3: 19.

Morduch, J., (1999), "The Micro Finance Promise", *Journal of Economic Literature*, 37 (4): 1569-1614.

Mujumadar, N. A., (2004), "Resurrection of Rural Credit", *The Journal of Indian Institute of Banking and Finance*, 8-10.

Mukherjee, N., (1993), "Women's Participation and Jawahar Rozgar Yojana", *Yojana*, 37 (16): 11-15.

Nagayya, D., (2000), "An Informal Arrangement for Credit Supply to the Poor through SHGs", *Kurukshetra*, 17 (8): 24-28.

Naidu, P., (1985), "Impact of Rural Development Programme on Economic Status of Women: A Case Study", *Indian Journal of Agricultural Economics*, 70 (3): 269-270.

Nair, T. S., (2001), "Rural Financial Intermediation and Commercial Bank – Review of Recent Trends", *Economic and Political Weekly*, 36 (4): 399-404.

Nair, T. S., (2005), "The Transforming World of Indian Micro Finance", *Economic and Political Weekly*, 40 (17): 1695-1698.

Namboodiri. N. V., and Shiyani R. L., (2001), "Potential Role of SHGs in Rural Financial Deepening", *Indian Journal of Agricultural Economics*, 56 (3): 401-405.

Nanda, Y. C., (1994), "Significance of Establishing Linkages of SHGs with Banks", *National Bank News Review*, 10 (4): 22-26.

Nanda, Y. C., (1999), "Linking Banks and Self-Help Groups in India and the Role of NGOs: Lessons Learned and Future Perspective", *National Bank News Review*, 15 (3): 1-9.

National Institute of Bank Management (NIBM), (2001), "Maharashtra Rural Credit Project (MRCP)", *Indian Journal of Agricultural Economics*, 56 (3): 400-402.

Nedumaran, S., Palanisamy, K., and Swaminathan, L. P., (2001), "Performance and Impact of Self-Help Groups in Tamil Nadu", *Indian Journal of Agricultural Economics*, 56 (3): 471-472.

Pandey, M., (2008), "Micro Financing: A Blessing for the Poor (A Case Study of Eastern Uttar Pradesh)", *The Indian Journal of Commerce*, 61 (3): 48-52.

Patel, A. R., (2002), "Micro Finance and Micro Finance Institutions – Need for Banks Initiative and Commitment", *National Bank News Review*, 18 (2): 32-37.

Patel, A. R., (2002), "Rural Credit Delivery System", *Kurukshetra*, 11 (2) : 4-8.

Pitt, M. M., and Khandker, S. T., (1998), "The Impact of Group – Based Credit Programmes on Poor Households in Bangladesh: Does the Gender of Participants Matter?", *Journal of Political Economy*, 106 (5): 958-996.

Puhazhendi, V., and Jayaraman, B., (1999), "Increasing Women's Participation and Employment Generation among Rural Poor: An Approach through Informal Groups", *Indian Journal of Agricultural Economics*, 54 (3): 287-295.

Puhazhendi, V., and Satyasai, K. J. S., (2001), "Economic and Social Empowerment of Rural Poor through SHGs", *Indian Journal of Agricultural Economics*, 56 (3): 450.

Puhazhendi, V., and Satyasai, K. J. S., (2002), "Empowerment of Rural Women through SHGs – An Indian Experience", *National Bank News Review*, 18 (2): 39-47.

Rani, L., (1998), "Towards Empowerment of Women: Organizational and Managerial Perspectives of Women Co-operatives, *Journal of Ex Research*, 11 (1): 112-117.

Rani, S., Umadevi, K. D., and Surendra, G., (2002), "SHGs Micro Credit and Empowerment", *Social Welfare*, 20-22.

Rajasekar, D., (2002), "Economic Programmer and Poverty Reduction – NGO Experiences from Tamil Nadu", *Economic and Political Weekly*, 37 (29): 3063-3068.

Rao, V. M., (2002), "Women Self-Help Groups – Profiles from Andhra Pradesh and Karnataka", *National Bank News Review*, 18 (2): 62-68.

Rao, G. G., (1995), "Dimensions of Rural Non-Farm Employment of Women", A Case Study in Andhra Pradesh, *Journal of Rural Development*, 14 (6): 67-74.

Rath, N., (1985), "Garibi Hatao: Can IRDP do it?", *Economic and Political Weekly,* 20 (6): 238 246.

Ravallion, M., (1991), "Reaching the Rural Poor through Public Employment, Arguments, Evidences and Lessons from South Asia", *The world Bank Research Observer,* 6 (2): 153-175.

Revathi, K., and Sumathi, I., (2006), "Self-Help Groups Promote Growth", *Kisan World,* 33 (8): 11-12.

Satish, P., (2001), "Some Issues in the Formation of Self-Help Groups", Working Paper Published in *Indian Journal of Agricultural Economics,* 56 (3): 410-416.

Singh, S. K., and Singh, R. I., (1987), "Impact of Rural Development Programme on Economic Status of Women in Uttar Pradesh," *Kurukshetra,* 35 (8): 43-45.

Singh, S., (1995), "Self-Help Groups in Indian Agri-Business: Reflections from Case Studies", *Artha Vijnana,* 37 (4): 380-388.

Singh, D. K., (2001), "Bank Performance Improvement in Uttar Pradesh Rural Credit Project", *Rural Banker Issue,* 23: 24.

Singh, V. K., Khakkar, R. K., and Kharinta, S. K., (2004), "Working and Impact of Rural SHGs in Hisar District of Hariyana", *Rural Banker Issue,* 21: 22.

Sithalakshmi, S., and Jothimani, G., (1994), "Organizational Behaviour as a Means of Empowerment", *Kurukshetra,* 42 (12): 31-35.

Stiglitz, J. E., (1990), "Peer Monitoring and Credit Markets", *The World Bank Economic Review,* 4 (3) : 351-366.

Swarup, V., (2001), "Micro Finance Could Become a Macro Mess?", *The Economic Times,* 26: 7.

Tripathy, B. L., (1984), "Rural Development Programme at Grass-roots", *Indian Journal of Agricultural Economics,* 39 (3): 288-289.

Tripathy, K. K., (2004), "Self-Help Groups A Catalyst of Rural Development", *Kurukshetra,* 52 (8): 41-43.

Udry, C., (1990), "Credit Markets in Northern Nigeria – Credit as Insurance in Rural Economy", *The World Bank Economic Review,* 4 (3): 251-269.

Venkatesh, H. R., and Rao, B. R. S., (2007), "Micro Finance Institutions and Credit Accessibility to the Poor in Karnataka Professional Bankers", *The ICFAI University Press*, 53-57.

Wydick, B., (1999a), "Group Lending: The Significance of Micro Credit as a Tool of the Third World Development", *Economic Journal*, 93: 75-81.

Wydick, B., (1999b), "Can Social Cohesion be Harnessed to Repair Market Failures? Evidence from Group Lending in Guatemala", *The Economics Journal*, 109 (63): 475.

Yaron, J., (1994), "What Makes Rural Financial Institutions Successful?", *World Bank Research Observer*, 9 (1): 49-70.

Reports

Anand J. S., (2002), "*Self-Help Groups in Empowering Women: Case Study of Selected SHGs and NHGs*", Discussion paper, Kerala Research Programme on Local Level Development, Centre for Development Studies, Thiruvananthapuram.

Banerjee, G. D., (2002), "*Self-Help Groups – A Novel Approach for Reaching and Empowering the Unreached and Underserved Poor in India*", December.

Binswanger, H. P., and Rosenzweig, M. R., (1986), "*Credit Markets, Wealth and Endowments in Rural South India*", Discussion paper, Agriculture and Rural Development Department, World Bank, Washington, D. C.

Chakrabarti, R., (2003), "*The Indian Micro Finance Experience – Accomplishments and Challenges*".

Chowdhry, J. A., (2003), "*Evaluating the Impact of Micro Credit on Poverty in Bangladesh: A Panel Data Approach*", Research Proposal, Department of Finance and Banking, University of Dhaka, Bangladesh.

Feder, G., Huppi, M., and Yaron, J., (1989), "*Agricultural Credit: Experience and Implications for Future Projects*", World Bank, Agricultural and Rural Development Department, Washington, D.C.

Foundation for Development Co-operation, (1992), *'Micro Credit' or 'Micro Finance' or 'Simply Access to Financial Services'*.

Government of India, (1985), *"Evaluation Report on Integrated Rural Development Programme"*, Programme Evaluation Organization, Planning Commission, New Delhi.

Harper, M., (2002), *"Promotion of Self-Help Groups under the SHG-Bank Linkage Programme in India"*, Paper presented at the Seminar on 'SHG-Bank Linkage Programme', November 25th and 26th New Delhi.

House, P. W., (1995), *"Report on Financial Services for the Rural Poor and Women in India: Access and Sustainability"*, New Delhi, India.

Kalpagam, U., (1986), *"Gender in Economics – The Indian Experience"*, MIDS off print – 7 papers presented at the Eleventh World Congress of Sociology, August, New Delhi.

Karduck, S., and Seibel, H. D., (2004), *"Transaction Costs of Self-Help Groups – A Study of NABARD's SHG Banking Programme in India"*, University of Cologne Department Research Centre.

Khandker, S., (2003), *"Micro Finance and Poverty: Evidence Using Panel Data from Bangladesh"*, World Bank Report.

Kroop, E., and Suran, B. S., (2002), *"Linking Banks and Financing Self-Help Groups in India – An Assessment Paper"*, Paper Presented at the Seminar on SHG-Bank Linkage Programme on November 25th and 26th New Delhi.

Meyer, R., (2001), *"Micro Finance, Poverty Alleviation and Improving Food Security: Implications for India"*, Rural Finance Programme, the Ohio University, December.

Micro Credit Summit Report, (1997), Washington, D.C.

Mohiuddin, A., (1987), *"Integrated Rural Development Programme (IRDP) and Development of Women and Children in Rural Areas (DWCRA)"*, National Institute of Rural Development, Hyderabad.

Monica, S. F., and Perrett, H., (1991), *'Women and Credit'*, Money and Finance in Developing Economics, Italy.

MYRADA, (2003), *"Impact of SHGs on the Existing Moneylenders"*, Servicing the Areas Covering Selected Villages in Chamarajnagar, Mysore, Chitradurga and Erode District.

NABARD, (2000), *"Impact of Micro Finance on the Living Standards of SHG Members"*, 1999 2000 Mumbai.

NABARD, (2002), *Annual Report* 2001-02.

NABARD, (2004), *Annual Report* 2003-04.

NABARD, (2008), *Annual Report* 2007-08.

Nelson, M., and Gupta, A., (2003), *"The Role of Micro Finance in Reducing Poverty"*, Paper presented in the Special Seminar in International Management, India, April 23.

Pitt, M. M., and Khandker, R. S., (1995), *"Household and Intra-Household Impacts of the Grameen Bank and Similar Targeted Credit Programmes in Bangladesh"*, Discussion Paper No. 320, World Bank.

Rangarajan, C., (1995), *"Inaugural Address at the NABARD: APRACA International Seminar on Development of Rural Poor through Self-Help Groups"*, Bangalore.

Rao, D. S. K and Zeller, M., (1998), *"Cost of Promoting Micro Finance Self-Help Groups in India – A Comparison of Bank and NGO Promoted Groups"*.

Reddy, P., and Reddy, M. S. N., (2003), *Women in Agriculture*: A Sociological Study in Southern India, Paper presented at *"Women Working to make a Difference"*, IWPR's Seventh International Women's Policy Research Conference, June.

Rengarajan, V., (2001), *"Micro Finance Technology for Poverty Alleviation"*, July.

Seibel, H. D., and Dave, R. H., (2002), *"Commercial Aspects of SHG Banking in India"*, Paper presented at the Seminar on SHG-Bank Linkage Programme, November 25th -26th, New Delhi.

Shylendra, H. S., (1999), *"Micro Finance and Self-Help Groups"*, A Study of the Experience of Two Leading NGOs, SEWA and AKRSP in Gujarat", Institute of Rural Management Anand (IRMA) Research Report.

Tiwari, P., and Fahad, S. M., (2000), *"Concept Paper: Micro Finance Institutions in India"*, Housing Development Finance Corporation, Mumbai.

Yunus, M., (1997), *"Speech Delivered at the Micro Credit Summit"*, February 2-4, Washington D.C.

Zeller, M., and Sharma, M., (1998), *"Rural Finance and Poverty Alleviation"*, Food Policy Report, International Food Policy Research Institute, Washington D.C.

Zeller, M., Schrieder, G., Braun, J. V., and Heidhues, F., (1997), *"Rural Finance for Food Security for the Poor"*, Food Policy Review, No. 4, International Food Policy Research Institute, Washington D.C.

Theses

Anjugam, M., (2005), *"Socio-Economic Impact of SHG Led Micro Finance on Rural Welfare – A Household Model Approach"*, Unpublished Ph.D. Thesis submitted to the Department of Agricultural Economics, Tamil Nadu Agricultural University, Coimbatore.

Manthri, A. A., (2004), *"Study of Women Self-Help Group in Madurai District"*, Unpublished Ph.D. Thesis Submitted to the Department of Commerce, Madurai Kamaraj University, Madurai.

News Papers

Rajan, S. M. S., (2009), *"Indian Bank Registers Rise in Loan Given to SHGs"*, The Hindu, March 26, p. 5.

Tripathy, K. K., (2003), *"Poverty Alleviation: Making Micro Finance Sustainable"*, The Hindu, November 1, p. 3.

Websites

Caroline, F., (2002), *"Assessing the Household – Impact of Micro Finance on Rural Nigerians Women"*, Unpublished Ph.D. Dissertations, The University of Guelph. http://www.lib.umi.com/dissertations.

Census of India, (2001), *"Population Report"*, http: //censusindia.gove.in.

Gaiha, R., and Nandhi, M. A., (2007), *"Micro Finance, Self-Help Group and Empowerment"* in Maharastra, ASARC Working paper, http: www.microfinancegateway.com

Mayoux, L., (2000), *"Micro Finance and the Empowerment of Women – A Review of the Key Issues"*, ILO (International Labour Organization) – Social Finance Unit, http://www.ilo.org/public/english/employment/finance/papers/mayoux.htm.

Panda, D. K., (2005), *"Women's Empowerment through SHG Revolution in Orissa"*. An analysis through Case Studies, http: // www.microfinancegateway.com

Puhazhendi, V., and Badatya, K. C., (2002), *"SHG-Bank Linkage Programme for Rural Poor – An Impact Assessment"*, NABARD Publications, http: // www.microfinance gateway.com

Thakur, S. G., and Tiwari, M., (2005), *"Whether SHG-Based Micro Credit Programmes can Remove Poverty? A Case Study on SHG-Based Programmes in Patan District of Gujarat"*, Report submitted at the International Conference on Membership Based Organizations of the Poor: Theory, Experience and Policy, Ahmedabad, India, January 17-21. http://www.wiego.org/ahmedabad/can-pap.

Vyas, H., (2003), *"SWEA Bank's Savings and Credit Groups and their Influence on Women's Financial Decision-Making Capacity within the Household"*, Unpublished Ph.D. Dissertations, The University of Guelph, http: // www.lib.umi.com/dissertations.

World Bank, World Development Report, (2001), http://web worldbank.org.

INDEX